THE
CHIEF
WITNESS

escape from China's modern-day
concentration camps

SAYRAGUL SAUYTBAY
ALEXANDRA CAVELIUS

translated by Caroline Waight

SCRIBE
Melbourne • London

Scribe Publications
2 John St, Clerkenwell, London, WC1N 2ES, United Kingdom
18–20 Edward St, Brunswick, Victoria 3056, Australia
3754 Pleasant Ave, Suite 100, Minneapolis, Minnesota 55409, USA

First published in German in 2020 by Europa Verlag as *Die Kronzeugin*
First published in English by Scribe 2021

Typeset in Adobe Caslon Pro by the publishers

Printed and bound in the UK by CPI Group (UK) Ltd, Croydon CR0 4YY

Scribe Publications is committed to the sustainable use of natural resources and the use of paper products made responsibly from those resources.

9781913348601 (UK edition)
9781950354528 (US edition)
9781922310538 (Australian edition)
9781925938777 (ebook)

Catalogue records for this book are available from the British Library and the National Library of Australia.

scribepublications.co.uk
scribepublications.com
scribepublications.com.au

Acknowledgements

My heartfelt thanks are due to the human-rights organisations of the United Nations; the Swedish government and its citizens; the people in Kazakhstan; the government of the Federal Republic of Germany; the Kazakh organisation Atajurt; all the international print media that followed my case; television and radio broadcasters in various countries; all journalists across a diverse array of media; and the Kazakh broadcaster Free Asia Television.

Sayragul Sauytbay

CONTENTS

CHAPTER ONE

Ghosts
of the Past

Women begging in the night

Every night, the crying girls crowd around my bed. Their dark eyes are wide, their heads shaved bald. "Save us!" they beg me. "Please save us!" Wherever despots rule, we women are always hardest hit. It's so easy to stifle us with the demons of helplessness, shame, and guilt. Yet it's not women who should be ashamed of the wounds men have inflicted on us. Now all I've got to do is internalise this truth. I try to struggle to my feet, but I'm frozen, lifeless as a corpse.

Ever since the camp, I sometimes can't get out of bed. It's because I spent so long sleeping on a cold concrete floor. My limbs and joints ache with rheumatism. Before all this I was perfectly healthy: today, at forty-three, I'm a sick woman. The minute I do drift off for a few seconds into uneasy sleep, my nightmares wake me.

None of the women, children, men, and elderly people behind those high barbed-wire fences have committed any crime, besides that of being born Kazakh, Uighur, or some other Muslim nationality in the north-west province of China. Of having Muslim names like Fatima or Hussein.

My name is Sayragul Sauytbay. I'm married, once ran five kindergartens before my internment, and I love my family above all else. We come from China's north-west province, which is larger than Germany, France, and Spain combined, and situated roughly 3,000 kilometres as the crow flies from Beijing. Encircled by mountains up to 7,000 metres high, our province borders more foreign nations than anywhere else in China, including Mongolia, Russia, Kazakhstan, Kyrgyzstan, and Tajikistan, as well as Afghanistan, India, and Pakistan. It's here that China is closest to faraway Europe.

Since ancient times, the area has been home to a predominantly Uighur population, but there are also numerous other ethnicities represented, including Mongolians, Kyrgyzstanis, Tartars, and the second-largest group, the Kazakhs, to which I belong. Our province was called East Turkestan until, in 1949, China — the vast empire next door — violently annexed the whole region, a strategically advantageous area known informally as the "Gateway to the West". Mao Zedong renamed it the Autonomous Region of Xinjiang (New Frontier), but to us it remains East Turkestan, our ancestral homeland. Officially, Beijing guarantees the indigenous people here autonomy, independence, and free will. Unofficially, however, the government treats us like a colony of slaves.

Since 2016, our province has been transformed into the largest surveillance state in the world. A network of more than 1,200 internment camps exists above ground, according to estimates by international experts, but there are increasing reports of subterranean camps as well. We estimate that approximately three million people are currently being detained. They have never stood trial. They have never committed a crime. This is the biggest systematic internment of a single ethnic group since the Third Reich.

Party officials forced me to stay silent about everything I witnessed as a senior public-sector worker in the nightmarish camps of East Turkestan — "or else you're dead". I literally had to sign my own death warrant. Despite all these obstacles, however, I ultimately managed to escape the largest open-air prison in the world and reach Sweden.

My situation is unusual, because I was put to work as a teacher in one of these camps. This position offered me an insight into the innermost workings of the system: and what I saw was a meticulously detailed, carefully considered piece of bureaucratic machinery that operated according to explicit instructions from Beijing. This wasn't just about systematic torture, humiliation, and brainwashing. This was the deliberate extermination of an entire ethnic group.

As we sit here, major corporations in the West are making a killing from their business dealings in north-west China. Yet a stone's throw away from their buildings, children, women, men, boys, and the elderly are penned in like animals and tortured in unspeakable ways.

One in ten Muslims in my home province, according to human-rights agencies, is currently interned. This figure tallies with my own experience. I was in a camp myself, alongside 2,500 other prisoners. In the regional centre of Mongolküre — called Zhaosu by the Chinese, home to 180,000 people — there are two large prisons and three camps, set up in a converted former Party school and abandoned buildings. Assuming these house the same number of prisoners, then even in a tiny area like my home county there are roughly 20,000 being detained. By now, every Muslim family has been affected by these arrests. There is no longer anyone in Xinjiang who hasn't lost several relatives.

The evidence for these camps is overwhelming — we have satellite images, documented witness statements, and, most recently, the release of the "China Cables" by a Chinese whistleblower — so Beijing has finally admitted their existence, after long denying it. Yet senior Chinese politicians continue to talk euphemistically about "vocational training centres"; they churn out propaganda films that show students in nice make-up and pretty clothes dancing and laughing, taking classes in bright, beautifully appointed rooms, and being "re-educated into better people". The official Party line is that the foreign media are "spreading malicious lies", that all the "students" are there of their own free will, and that most have already been released anyway.

When I hear this sort of thing, I wonder where all my friends, neighbours, and acquaintances could possibly have gone, then. If they've been set free, why can't anyone get them on the phone? And if these camps really are "vocational training centres", as the government in Beijing so doggedly maintains, then why are small children being torn from their families and classrooms, and sent there? Why should these "boarding schools take the place of parents", as the Communist Party of China (CCP) demands? What is this "re-education" supposed to accomplish for an eighty-four-year-old woman? Why do writers, professors, successful business people, and artists — all of whom are already highly educated — need to take "continuing education courses" behind barbed wire?

Anyone who tells the truth about these camps in East Turkestan is branded a foreign spy, a liar, or a terrorist. Chinese censors immediately erase all the information available online, and anyone who passes on this information within China vanishes without a trace the very next day. As soon as a Western delegation announces it is bringing journalists on a visit to East Turkestan, as happened in autumn 2019, Party officials rapidly transform a re-education camp into a normal school.

The barbed wire disappears from the fences, and the heavily armed guards are whisked away from the gates. Teachers who were previously dismissed — now street sweepers or factory workers — are press-ganged back into service for the duration of the visit. New classes full of Kazakh and Uighur students are quickly set up, and bright, colourful footage is shot for television.

A friend who had been granted a visitor's permit to attend

his mother's funeral in the area told me that all the teachers and students had to memorise Party texts for the benefit of the Western visitors. Anyone who missed out a word or a comma was banished to the camps. The official instructions were as follows: "Students, you are not allowed to say what's really been going on over the past few years. You will tell them how good the Party is and how nice your lives here are ..." We're used to the CCP's theatrical performances and illusions by now. We've been living with them since we were children.

Thinking back to my past, it makes me retch. I can't stop vomiting, as though there were parasites in my body. I have to wrap a scarf around my head, because it feels like it's about to explode. Maybe it's the memories; maybe it's the after-effects of the torture. But no matter how agonising it is to talk about my experiences, I believe it is my duty to warn the world. That said, I do want to emphasise that I don't blame the Chinese people for these appalling crimes: the responsibility lies solely and squarely at the door of the government in Beijing and the Communist Party of China.

As a chief witness, I've shared my knowledge of the inner workings of this fascist system. I speak not just for myself, but in the name of all the people held in these concentration camps, and for those who are in fear of their lives under this dictatorship. We cannot take freedom for granted. If we don't act to protect it in good time, then we've already lost it, because in its final throes it vanishes too fast for us to keep up. The Middle Kingdom — as China calls itself — lays plans many decades in advance. It exploits the opportunities afforded by an open society to undermine democracy piece by piece. I have first-hand experience of what it means to live in an environment controlled by Beijing, in a hypermodern surveillance state the likes of which the world has never seen.

And a world without freedom leaves you running for your life in hell.

Leaving Sweden for Germany

It was a strange situation, saying goodbye to my family in Sweden and travelling with my ten-year-old son, Ulagat, to Germany to be interviewed. Journalist Alexandra Cavelius was planning to use our conversations to write a book about my experiences.

The ferry wasn't setting off till 10.55pm, but we'd left the house four hours early, although the port was only fifteen minutes away. Uali and my fourteen-year-old daughter, Ukilay, had come with us. After a while, both of them suddenly turned very quiet and hung back a little.

My son and I were at the bus stop, waiting for the bus to take us to the boat. "Why aren't they talking to us anymore?" Ulagat wanted to know, tugging at my jacket. "Maybe they're upset because we're going without them?" He ran up to his father. "Do you guys want us to stay here?" Uali shook his head and stroked the boy's thick black hair. "No, no, this is a wonderful opportunity! Just think — you're only ten years old, and soon you'll have visited four very different countries. It's the stuff all little children dream of. You're a man now, and you'll take good care of your mother. When she needs a cup of tea, you'll make one for her. When she needs her medication, you'll give it to her."

My children know I've been sick since the camp. Nobody comes out of a place like that in good health. Often their relatives, too, fall ill, waiting months or years, consumed with anxiety, vainly hoping for a sign of life or of their loved one. My children had to grow up too fast.

When the bus pulled up, my daughter turned around and

started crying bitterly. There was no real cause to be sad, but suddenly all those dark memories came rising up again like bubbles. The children were remembering how they'd fled to Kazakhstan with their father, while they had to leave their mother at the border. Two and a half years. No contact whatsoever.

Since then, our family hadn't gone a single day without worrying. We were always on the run, from one place to the next. Before that evening at the port, we had never been at peace, and could never live in freedom like a normal family. Suddenly, the doors hissed shut, separating me and my son from my daughter and her father. The bus had barely gone five yards before my phone rang. "How are you doing?" asked my husband. "Is everything alright? Take care of yourselves!"

Germany

Today, when I'm on a bus or a train and the ticket inspector comes over, I always have to remind myself that *No, this official doesn't want to lock you up* ... In fact, I can travel through the world like any other free citizen. One of my first destinations was the Foreign Office in Stockholm, then the European Parliament in Brussels, where I gave evidence as a chief witness about my experiences in the camps.

Maybe it's a good thing this book was first published in German. Germany has a tragic history when it comes to fascism, but unlike China it has bravely faced up to its dark past, exploring why those things happened and learning from them. China, on the other hand, simply rewrites its history, because otherwise it could be dangerous to the Party and the government. Germany is a strong country with a highly effective political system. It's thanks to the support of countless international politicians as well as various human-rights organisations that I and my family have found a new home in a free country.

As human beings, we all live on the same planet and in the same twenty-first century, but where I come from a large segment of the population is cut off from the rest of the world and denied basic rights. For someone who takes democracy and human rights for granted, it will be difficult to understand what we deal with every day in East Turkestan.

There's a very popular Chinese television program called *Journey to the West* that illustrates our situation perfectly. The Communist Party uses the main characters to demonstrate its own superiority, since no one is cleverer or stronger than the Party. On the show, a sorcerer travels to as many Western countries as possible at the behest of a monarch, researching their customs and way of life. The West is depicted in a terrible light: backward, factious, and weak. Lost in chaos and bloodshed.

When the magician waves a circle around the people with his wand, everyone inside it falls under his spell. Nobody dares to venture beyond the edge of the circle. These prisoners are no longer free to come and go, no longer free to think; they've forgotten they are human beings with normal human rights. They simply accept everything, like sacrificial lambs, no matter what is done to them. They have no choice. They are trying to survive — just like the people in China's north-west province.

I still have to get used to the feeling that I can go outside or move around my own house unobserved. For the first time in my life, I have witnessed and experienced how a person may be allowed to live with dignity. In East Turkestan, every scrap of information is controlled. Uncensored books and magazines, and social media platforms such as Facebook and WhatsApp, are forbidden. Even though I've been living in Sweden for months, I still feel the pressure we were living under every single day. The constant fear for my relatives, my husband, my children, and myself. Sometimes I find myself glancing over my shoulder on the street, wondering suspiciously, "Who's that Asian-looking person behind me? Is he with the Chinese secret police? Is he watching me?" The Communist Party has serious reach. It can get to dissidents anywhere, even in Germany.

In East Turkestan, it feels like indigenous people are living in a madhouse where nothing makes sense anymore. But if you're always busy not putting a foot wrong for fear of being punished, then you've got no time to ask questions. The fact that I'm free today and able to ask these important questions is a gift from God: why are hundreds of thousands of innocent people being tortured and murdered without any repercussions? How can anybody do such appalling things to other human beings? It can only be because they consider themselves a vastly superior and more valuable race, which is precisely what the CCP and its general secretary, Xi Jinping, are preaching with such ardent nationalism. Countries across the globe are so closely interconnected these days, so why do they allow these human-rights violations to go on unchecked? I wish nothing more than that some external, more just, power would intervene to prevent this in the future.

When people in other countries think of China, they usually picture a highly civilised, advanced, and economically highly successful nation. This is no surprise, given the enormous sums invested by one of the world's most powerful propaganda machines into making it look from the outside like a relatively normal, shiny high-tech society. The state-run media keeps quiet about all the wickedness and uncomfortable truths behind this perception, yet the poison festers underneath like pus. The people of China are aware that their own government frequently lies to them, but do people in the West realise that, too? Or are they allowing themselves to be dazzled by the glittering façade?

My hope is that people will come away with a better understanding of the true essence and intentions of the regime. That they will protect themselves from the threat of tyranny and strengthen their democracies. My own worldview has been thoroughly overhauled since the camp. Previously, I was mainly concerned with fitting in and not breaking any rules, so I wouldn't be punished.

The goal of China's campaign is to achieve political control of the entire world. This is why my advice to all other countries is this: "Don't avert your gaze from East Turkestan! This is how your children and grandchildren will be living in the future if you don't defend your freedoms!" China, currently the largest trading nation on the planet, promotes neither friendly relationships nor open exchange. In the opaque political world of the CCP, nothing happens without an ulterior motive.

And wherever Beijing's influence is on the rise, lies begin to grow like weeds, suffocating the truth.

Threats and hope

At first, my family felt very lonely in Sweden, our new home, far away from all our friends and relatives. In recent weeks, however, we've had no time to feel like that. Reporters from about forty countries so far have come to our apartment to speak to me about my experiences in the camp. But I have never before told my story in as much detail as I did for this book.

Often, the journalists had barely left before our phone would ring and I'd be threatened. "Just stop talking! Think of your children!" Sometimes these men spoke Swedish, sometimes Kazakh, and other times Chinese. Each time, the Swedish police would reassure us afterwards: "Don't worry, this isn't China!" They keep trying to encourage us. "Just try to lead a normal life. You have the same rights as any other Swede. We're protecting you even if you can't see a patrol car outside. It's just that we can't tell you what we're doing."

Over time, I've become more confident about dealing with the strangers on the other end of the line. "You can keep bothering us with these calls," I tell them, "but you can't do anything to us!" Still, they keep trying to break our spirits. Recently, I heard about a message one of these secret-police operatives left on the Facebook wall of a Uighur woman: "Stop or they'll find your body cut up into little pieces in the black bin outside your house." This was the woman who had released the China Cables after a Chinese official leaked them to her in secret. Thanks to the courage of this Uighur woman, there is now fresh and incontrovertible evidence of the systematic oppression of Muslim minorities in these camps. Not even Beijing has disputed the authenticity of these secret documents.

Often, the threatening calls come from China. One time, the number on our display showed that the call originated from the security services in Beijing. "Why are you calling me?" I asked. "I just want to know how you're getting on," replied a male voice. "I know exactly where you live. Have you settled in nicely? And what are your children up to?" I tried to stay calm. "Everything's great here, we're happy."

"If everything's so great, then why don't you stop talking to journalists? Be glad you're still alive, and stop talking about what's in the past."

"I'll never stop," I replied, "and since you're working in Beijing, why don't you go see your Party leader and tell him to stop torturing people in those camps once and for all." At this, his voice turned cold and hard. "Stop having these conversations with journalists immediately! Think of your children!" They always finish with these words. I live in constant fear for my children, who are the most important thing to me in the entire world.

Unsurprisingly, these threats often make me feel very small, and I think, *What chance do we have against such an overwhelmingly powerful opponent?* But I owe it not just to the prisoners in the camps but to my countless supporters in Kazakhstan to tell the truth. So many people there are desperate: their children, parents, and grandparents have vanished without a trace into camps in neighbouring China. It doesn't matter how powerful our opponent is. We can never stop speaking out. Maybe one day we will start a movement that can put an end to China's hideous abuses of power.

How long has it been since I last felt free? As a child, I grew up surrounded by Kazakhs. We had our own school, our own traditions, and we spoke only Kazakh, because the north-east of East Turkestan is the land of my ancestors, which the Chinese call the "Kazakh Autonomous Prefecture in Xinjiang".

We never thought anyone could rob us of our homeland.

CHAPTER TWO

Despite Chinese Invasion and Destruction: dreaming of a golden future and financial security

Lucky

"The baby's here already?" My father, thirty-nine years old and with a short black beard, pushed the flap of felt covering the door of our yurt aside, and stared in astonishment as my mother cradled me in her arms on the sheep's-wool mattress. Her long black hair framed her pale face. She was twenty-seven years old, quick to laugh, and you could hardly tell she'd just had her fourth child. That's how easy it was to give birth to me.

On 16 September 1976, they hung the feathers of an eagle owl on my crib, which protect against dark magic and bring luck. As I opened my eyes — dark brown, like chestnuts, in a round face — smoke from the fire rose through the opening in the roof of our tent. At night, the light of the stars fell through the gap onto our sleeping, fur-swaddled bodies.

East Turkestan has everything from snow-topped peaks to the second-biggest sandy desert in the world. But I was born in the breadbasket of Ili Autonomous Prefecture, in Mongolküre County. We're known for being a lively bunch who love to dance, sing, and tell jokes, but also for our scientists, poets, and the veterans who rebelled against the occupying Chinese forces during the revolution.

"She'll bring luck," my mother and father were convinced. "Not just to us, but to our whole village." For months, they'd been living through a terrible drought, and hunger had burrowed like a monster into many people's stomachs. Just one week before my birth, the co-founder of the CCP and the "Great Helmsman",

Mao Zedong, had died. Mao's cruelty and disdain for humanity had brought the Middle Kingdom to the brink of collapse. On the day I drew my first breath, it started to rain, and the countryside turned green once more.

All my relatives shook their head in wonder. "What a funny little child. The girl never makes a fuss, never screams." When my mother fastened me securely into my cot with twine, I slept soundly for up to nine hours. Now and again, my parents would shake me awake because I'd not made a peep and they were worried I might not still be alive. At five months, I'd already learned to sit up independently and keep myself amused at the edge of the pen while my mother looked after the goats, sheep, and cattle.

Later, my father always used to say, "You're like a cat with nine lives." Looking back, I have to admit he's right. There were so many times I cheated death on the flat, wondrously beautiful grasslands where the wolves howled in the forest. Meadows blooming with herbs, and wide green valleys dotted with — from the perspective of the snowy mountaintops — tiny moving splashes of colour. These were Kazakh herders, kicking up dust on their small, hardy ponies among grazing sheep, cows, and yaks. Above it all was the azure sky, where eagles wheeled on broad wings.

My village was at the foot of the Tian Shan mountains, a vast mountain range that in places reaches more than 7,000 metres above sea level. For a long time it shielded the Kazakhs from China and opened the fertile Ili Valley to the west. It was approximately 450 kilometres from the Kazakh city of Almaty, near the border, and 750 kilometres from Ürümqi, the regional capital.

At the age of six months, I faced death for the first time.

Cheating death

During this period, my parents were half-nomadic, moving from field to field with the changing seasons, accompanied by other families and the baa-ing, maa-ing, and moo-ing herds. In summer, we followed the water and the food for the animals up into the mountains, and before the icy winter descended, we came back down to our permanent homes on the pastureland. My father was a teacher, and gave lessons to the children wherever we set up our tents, but he also raised animals, wrote, sang, and made music; he loved composing new pieces for us on the two-stringed *dombra*.

Next to him, our mother almost seemed small, pale, and slender, although she was actually plump and full of zest for life. But at six foot three, her husband — tall, powerful, and dark-skinned — towered above almost everyone else. My mother was promised to my father when she was still in the cradle. A friend was so enchanted by the sight of her that she exclaimed, "This girl is going to be my daughter-in-law one day!" At that time, my father was twelve years old. Luckily, this decision ended up forging a wonderful bond between the two families, because my parents loved each other very much, even though they'd never been given a choice.

It was a cold and windy day in a stony wilderness when we moved. Ahead of us lay an arduous journey into the valley, bringing all our animals and every possession we owned. But while Kazakhs like us were roaming the broad landscapes, just as we had done for three thousand years, Muslim Uighurs in other areas had settled permanently in cities or villages, including on the many branches of the caravan routes along the Silk Road. Although we spoke different languages, we could understand each other, since our Turkic languages are related.

Towering sky-high, my parents lashed their possessions, along with their tent poles and bundles, to our camels. Using twine, they fastened small children and infants like me into baskets between the humps, so that the weight would be distributed as evenly as possible on either side. Then the caravan set off. It wended down stony, narrow paths, often flanked by yawning chasms.

Animals and humans were sweating, breathing heavily, and putting one foot carefully in front of another when suddenly my camel slipped on the rock-strewn slope, stumbled to its knees, and pitched sideways, bellowing loudly. The bundles came loose and hurtled down into the gorge. The group watched in horror from above as the little basket — with me still tightly fastened inside it — went tumbling down, somersaulting and rolling until it finally came to a stop. For a moment, everybody held their breath and strained to listen: no crying baby. Only deathly silence. Then the cry went up: "No!" My mother's was the loudest scream of all.

"She's dead," realised my father, shattered. Life was hard; most families had many children. When one died, the common sober response would be: "It was God's will!" What else could they do? The others still had to be taken care of. Life went on. It was impossible to cry, mourn, or linger for very long in so inhospitable a place.

Together, they all climbed down to salvage our possessions and bury my body somewhere among the stones. Approaching the basket cautiously, my father peered inside and saw my round face, with my little eyes placidly shut. "It can't be!" he cried, his voice breaking. "She's still alive!" My mother dropped to her knees beside me, sobbing. "What sort of child *are* you? You just almost died and you were fast asleep!" Luckily our camel, too, had only sustained a few minor injuries to its legs.

The caravan moved on.

The snakepit

The second time I cheated death, I was two. My mother had finished milking the last cow of the evening, and my father mounted his horse and drove the animals out onto the pastureland higher up the mountain. Normally, he'd haul me up onto the saddle in front of him. This time, however, he had a few extra jobs to squeeze in, so he told me, "You stay here today!"

He trotted off surrounded by the herd, and didn't notice me tottering after him. I made it pretty far, but obviously the horse was faster than me, and he was soon out of my sight. When he came home later that night, he stared at his five children enquiringly. "Where's my little sweetheart? Isn't she home?" My mother had assumed he'd taken me, as usual. She ran straight outside with my older siblings and started calling for me. "Sayragul, where are you?"

When she asked our relatives, friends and everyone else we knew if they had any idea where I was, they simply shrugged and joined the search. Before long, they'd left no stone unturned and no cranny unsearched — but it was like the earth had swallowed me up. Then, all at once, everyone was struck by the same awful thought: "The snakes killed her!"

We were used to dealing with them, of course, but we preferred to stay out of their way. Occasionally, we'd find one hanging from the ceiling in our yurt, and my mother would coax it out by pouring a bit of milk from a cup in front of the snake and then drawing a trail along the floor with it, leading it outside. The snake would drink the milk and follow the trail.

But the older people had scared us kids to death about the snakepit. "Don't ever go there! There are poisonous snakes!" Since no one had found me in the dark, starry night, they were sure I must have fallen in. Yet my father refused to give up. He rode back up onto one of the broad meadows and asked a herder, "Have you seen a little girl with eagle-owl feathers in her hat?" The herder lifted the curved brim of his tall, bright felt hat, wrapped his long-sleeved leather coat more tightly around his chest, and considered the question. "I saw a dark shadow a little while ago, back over there. Maybe it was your daughter?"

Immediately, my father dug his heels into his horse's flanks, clicked his tongue, and went galloping off to the spot the herder had pointed out. He saw me lying on the ground in the milky light of the moon, my head resting on my hat and my black braid swaddled around me like a shawl. Around me, however, the grass was crawling with snakes. It was impossible to get to me.

My father didn't dare to get off his horse, so he fetched the others, who gingerly removed the snakes one by one with long sticks. Because I was lying there stock-still throughout the entire operation, everybody assumed I must be dead. The snakes had bitten me, they thought.

By this time, some of the more elderly people had arrived on horseback. "Stand aside!" instructed my grandfather, once the snakes were out of the way. He was a tall man, like his son, with a long white beard: you could tell from his athletic build that he had once been a well-known wrestler. Furrowing his brow, he lowered his face to mine and announced, "The girl is breathing."

Back home, my grandfather sent for a shaman. "We should pray and let him examine the child." Our religion blends nature-worship and pagan traditions with elements of Islam. Minutes later, a grey-haired man in a fox-skin cap and a long velvet coat embroidered with animal motifs appeared in the doorway of our yurt, where we had hung animal bones to ward off evil spirits. He looked into my sparkling eyes, felt the pale skin of my cheek, and reassured all the anxious onlookers, "The snakes haven't touched her." Still, to protect against any impending danger, my parents and siblings had to purify the room by burning wild rue. My father said, "This is the second time we've thought she was dead, but each time she's only been sleeping."

After that, my parents were more convinced than ever that I was lucky. With every year that passed after I was born, living conditions in such grindingly poor farming communities improved. Mao's campaign to eradicate the "Four Old Things" — "old ideas", "old culture", "old habits" and "old customs" — seemed to be over. Forced collectivisation, mismanagement and dispossession were behind us. People were allowed to work and till their land independently once more. Wages improved, freedoms flourished, and change was in the air.

I was three years old when the Communist Party, under Deng Xiaoping, began to liberalise the economy, introducing what they termed the "program of reform and opening-up" — although they remained firmly autocratic at heart. "You've got to open the windows even if you let in a few flies," Mao's successor told his critics.

Turning nomads into villagers

In 1981, we and roughly 150 other families settled down at the foot of the Tian Shan mountains and created a village, Aheyazi, which was part of the County of Mongolküre (Zhaosu in Chinese). Gorgeously situated between two emerald-green rivers, the village had a gurgling spring that supplied crystal-clear water straight from the mountains. This was where we fetched our drinking water, lugging the buckets home. Women did the laundry behind the bridge across the river, animals grazed on the broad steppes, and we stored our crops and animal feed in barns.

My father had scarcely fitted the last piece of roof sheeting, black and glittering as the roads, onto our wooden house when he called all the villagers together to build a school. He was a respected figure in the community, because he was a deeply upright, reserved, and patient person who did his best to support not just his family but everyone in the village. As a prominent man and deputy headmaster, he was soon invited to educational events in the surrounding areas and towns. When my father was travelling, my mother was left to cope by herself, dealing with the household, stables, animals, and any other jobs that happened to crop up. Skilful and organised, she handled everything with aplomb, even with young children scurrying around her feet.

Although they had a growing gaggle of children, my parents' three-room house was very small. My father and mother slept in their own room, as did my widowed grandfather and us children. The three boys slept in the first row, then there were two further rows with us six girls. The first thing we did when we got up in the morning was to roll up our woollen mats and put them away beside the chests and boxes in a corner. It was taken for granted that the younger children would wear hand-me-downs from the older ones, so my mother was constantly busy shortening or taking out our trousers or dresses.

Late into the night, you could hear the merry hum of singing and laughter drifting out of all the doors and windows in the village. We always had a lot going on. Aunts, uncles, other relatives, and friends would be popping in and out of every house, re-emerging generously laden with provisions. There was always good food, plenty of reasons to celebrate, and a strong sense of solidarity that was increasingly becoming a thorn in Beijing's side.

On one of these days, we were in our yurt, waiting in feverish excitement for guests to arrive from the city. I and my brother Sawulet, one year younger, were jumping for joy because they usually brought small gifts for us children. Elated, we were handed sweet drinks in glass bottles.

When they were empty, Sawulet and I — now four and five years old — scampered over the hill behind our yurt in our cotton trousers and shirts towards the river Ahesu. We wanted to play on the banks. As we filled our bottles with water, mine abruptly slipped out of my hand. I tried to fish it back out, taking a few hurried steps into the water, but tripped and was swept away by the powerful current.

Floundering, I tried to get back to the riverbank, but the current kept getting stronger, because not far away there was a waterfall — and a steep, thunderous drop. *If I fall down there, I'll drown!* I thought. I kept grabbing the plants on the bank in a panic, but they tore every time, so I'd have to scramble to catch the next one. My little brother ran screaming along the bank beside me, both hands clapped to his mouth: "Please come out of there, Sari May!"

My family used to affectionately call me "Sari May" (meaning butter), because my skin was the pale colour of butter. The further the river tugged me towards the drop, the more desperate my brother became. "Sari May, come back out! I'll never annoy you ever again!" But I couldn't do it. My sopping-wet clothes were pulling me under. I was swallowing water and coughing. "Sari May, come out, I'll share everything with you!"

Unlike my five sisters, my little brother was a naughty little scamp, and picking fights with me was one of his favourite activities. "Sari May!" he cried, "you can play with my toy!" After a while, he realised his offers weren't helping, so he ran as fast as he could on his short legs over the hill and back to the yurt to fetch help. By now, I had managed to cling onto a large mint plant at the edge of the river, and this time the roots were strong enough to hold my weight. Panting heavily, I managed to belly-crawl back onto the gravel bank.

At that moment, I saw my family and our visitors rushing

towards me, gesturing wildly. Leading the way were my father and mother, my mother's hair as black and shiny as her daughter's, but tucked underneath a loose headscarf. "Sayragul!" Screaming, they both hugged me at once, despite me being dripping wet.

Back at the yurt, my mother gave me dry clothes and put me in front of the woodstove. My siblings gazed at me with dark, accusing eyes while my father scolded me. "How many times have we warned you not to go down to the river? You're not supposed to play there! Why did you try to get the bottle out? That's crazy!"

But even on the rare occasions when he was angry, he never lost his cool or raised his voice much. As soon as he'd calmed down again, he put his big, warm hand on my shoulder. "Take better care of yourself, my daughter! You're only five years old, and today's the third time you've had a brush with death." My mother clasped her hands, glanced briefly skyward, and said, "Thanks be to God!"

Our parents were strict, but loving. They never laid a hand on us. Nor did they have to: fathers and mothers are held in the highest esteem in our society. When parents speak, children keep quiet and listen. My mother barely had to signal with her hand and we'd snap to attention …

I've never heard my parents arguing loudly. If my brothers got into a fistfight, all my mother would have to say was *Be good, or I'll tell your father*, and instantly there'd be silence in the room. She was always exhorting us to be considerate of our father and keep the noise down when he was trying to relax after a tough day.

The highest authority in a Kazakh family, however, is the *aksakal*: the white-beard. Whenever an important decision had to be made, my parents turned to my grandfather for advice. He held the place of honour at family parties, and always got the choicest piece of meat.

You must not lie!

Whenever my grandfather came riding back from a visit to a neighbouring village on his horse, he'd bring tiny pieces of sugar wrapped in a cloth in his bag. As soon as we children saw him — a dot on the broad pastureland — we made a beeline straight for him.

My grandfather, a devout man, taught my sisters, brothers, and me the rules of Islam. Fundamentally they're no different from the Ten Commandments in the Bible. "You must not steal, you must not kill, and you should do unto your neighbour as you would have them do unto you." While my eldest sister poured him tea and I passed him the flatbread, a smile would cross the old man's tanned, weather-beaten face, and a thousand tiny crinkles would appear around his eyes like sunbeams. "Children, I want you to always treat people decently! A devoted Muslim never harms another human being."

Kazakhs do not keep men and women separated in different rooms. We eat and celebrate together, just like people in the West. Our form of Islam is a very moderate one. The older women have been wearing a traditional white headscarf for centuries, which they embroider by hand with elaborate, painstaking designs. You never see any long black veils, and certainly no burkas of the type commonly worn by Muslim women in Arab countries and some other places in the Middle East. In 2020, under the "warm-hearted patriarch" Xi Jinping, as the Party likes to call its general secretary, even this embroidered headscarf is forbidden.

Although my grandfather prayed five times a day and went to the mosque, he never insisted his grandchildren do the same. Nor did I ever see my parents pray like that. After we ate, we'd all join hands and wish blessings and good luck to our family, our guests or humanity in general. Sometimes we would simply say, "Thanks be to God."

From a very young age I was eager to live up to the hopes my parents and my grandfather had placed in me. I tried to treat other people with consideration and respect. My father was often pleased with me. He'd laugh and say proudly, "She's my daughter, she's just like me!"

I used to run around all the time dressed like a boy, in trousers and leather boots. My braid hung down to my knees. A long dress would only have got in the way of running and riding. I was constantly busy helping out my father, gathering wood or herding sheep. When I was older, I was even allowed to steer our recently acquired tractor.

My parents used to praise me to my equally hardworking sisters. "Look how independent Sayragul is!" And every bit of praise spurred me on to be even more of a role model. Of course, it didn't always work like that. When I was seven, I was the class representative for Year Two, and one day the teacher asked me to look after the classroom for a whole day because he was going to his son's wedding. "Make sure your fellow students keep quiet and don't get up to any mischief."

But sitting still was a form of punishment for my little classmates, and they soon started to speak up. "We can't sit around here all day long," protested a small boy with a mop of black curls. "So what should we do?" I asked. They decided they wanted to make a ball out of fabric, fill it with grain, and play with it in the classroom. The suggestion seemed reasonable to me — and I didn't have much choice anyway — so I agreed.

Within minutes, the ball was flying from hand to hand, eventually landing in front of me on the teacher's desk. Winding up for a big throw — I was trying to reach a girl at the back — I chucked it as hard as I could. Unfortunately, I missed and hit the window behind her, which immediately shattered into tiny fragments. I stood there rooted to the spot. It was winter, minus fifteen degrees, and the cold instantly started creeping into our bones.

When the other children saw me slowly crumbling into a miserable little heap on the floor, they tried to make me feel better. "It was our fault really. After all, it was our idea." To keep me from being punished, they decided to pin the blame on the usual suspect: a boy who was always getting into trouble anyway. Then we patched up the hole as best we could with bits of our clothing.

Normally, the other children turned to their mothers when they had problems, grievances, or things they wanted. I was the only one in our family who ran to my father first. "I did a bad thing today," I confessed to him, hiding my tear-stained face behind my hands. Stroking his frizzy beard thoughtfully, he declared that only the truth would get me out of my predicament.

I spent all night fitfully tossing and turning. The next morning, the teacher quizzed one child after another: "Who was it?" They all shook their heads. "It wasn't me, it was him ..." They pointed at the class clown, who dutifully accepted all the blame. I was next up. "It's all my fault!" I blurted tearfully.

Because I was so obviously contrite, the teacher was mollified. "I'm not going to punish you, but only because you were so honest. The rest of you, however, all lied, so you deserve to be punished." All the other students had to bring a small sum of money the following day so that the window could be replaced.

After class, the other children crowded around me outside. They were furious about what I'd done, and felt betrayed because I'd left them high and dry. "Why did you do that? We were trying to help you. Traitor!" But what else could I have done? My parents had drummed into my head that lying was a terrible sin.

And God was always watching.

The situation was very unpleasant for me. At home, however, my father nodded kindly. "You did well. You'll see, your friends will understand eventually, so don't worry." Even so, I cried for ages until I finally calmed down.

A harsh environment

We were only able to survive in this harsh environment because the community stuck together. The young and the elderly lived at close quarters, helping and relying on each other. Grandparents offered decades of experience on climate, keeping animals, and growing crops. Unlike in most Kazakh families, under our roof the boys weren't given preferential treatment over the girls. We felt equal and deeply valued.

I got on well with my sisters. The oldest one, especially, was a huge role model. She was prudent, like my father. She was also a good student, very clever, and, like my mother, never complained. I and all my brothers and sisters envied the way she drew Arabic script onto paper in her meticulous handwriting.

I wanted to be as neat and beautiful as she was, too, so I spent as much time around her as possible, helping her with the housework. There was so much to do. Cooking, darning the holes in our clothes, cleaning, caring for the animals, washing clothes in the river …

We heard the same old speech over and over when guests came to eat and drink at our hearth. "Keep the boys in school and have the girls work around the house. Why do they need to learn anything anyway? They're just going to get married and look after the housework." For the sake of politeness, my father and mother bit their tongues.

But once the visitors had left, they hurried to reassure me and my five sisters. "They can say whatever they want, but we see things differently." My father gazed earnestly into our round faces and narrow eyes. "You need just as good an education as your brothers."

And indeed, when the time came, all my siblings earned a university degree.

Party time

Ever since I was a child, I've loved to dance, write, and sing. I used to especially look forward to when the meadows turned purple and pink, the crocuses bloomed, and we celebrated the New Year and the arrival of spring (a festival known as Nauryz) from 21 to 22 March. All the villagers would start preparing ages in advance.

In the forest and the meadows, the children would hunt for splendid, eye-catching feathers and animal teeth to decorate our hats. If you couldn't find any, someone else would give you some, or you could buy them from a trader.

The women decorated their houses with flowers and garlands. They cleaned until everything was sparkling, prepared a special soup with seven different ingredients, and offered congratulations to their guests on the arrival of spring. The next day, we would all celebrate together, old and young, rich and poor, on the big meadow at the edge of the village. There was music, dancing, and bonfires.

Men and women demonstrated their skill with a bow and on horseback. My three brothers, along with the other boys, showed how good they were at wrestling. And us girls had already been rehearsing dances at school, forming groups and singing. Our knee-length black braids were piled on top of our heads and pinned into place.

All the villagers were prettily dressed up in colourful traditional garb. I twirled and twirled in my expensive, flower-embroidered traditional dress, which my mother had sewed for me, until I was dizzy with laughter and joy, fluffy eagle-owl feathers bobbing on my head. Along with the Feast of the Sacrifice and the Festival of Breaking the Fast at the end of Ramadan, these three events represent the high point of the Islamic calendar.

Since 2017, the Chinese government has banned all our traditional and religious celebrations. Instead, they force us to celebrate Chinese festivals, including their New Year. We have to decorate our houses Chinese-style, even though their imagery often looks offensive and frightening to us, incorporating devils and ugly, grimacing faces. Anyone who refuses is branded an extremist and locked up.

The Cultural Revolution: casting a shadow on the soul

At the end of a day's work, the other elderly people liked to gather round my grandfather on our colourfully decorated sheep's wool rug while my siblings and I sat cross-legged near the door and listened in. If they were talking about the uprising against the Chinese, they sent us away, because those stories weren't meant for children.

Like the other "white-beards", my grandfather had once been a fighter in the resistance. In the 1930s and 1940s, our countrymen had briefly driven out the Chinese invaders. My grandfather was there when an independent government was formed in East Turkestan, a place where Kazakhs had lived for centuries in the north-east. Today we're not even allowed to mention the former rebels' names, let alone discuss the uprising.

The native people of East Turkestan had always rebelled under the yoke of the Chinese, trying violently to shake it off. The occupying Chinese forces had quashed these protests every single time with brute force, executing prisoners, gouging out their eyes, or tearing their hair from their heads, which my grandparents and parents witnessed with their own eyes. To pacify the situation, Mao had no choice — given how weakened China then was by starvation and hardship — but to grant Muslims autonomy in 1955.

For centuries, the men of my family had belonged to the upper echelons of our clan. Luckily, however, we had never been rich, so my grandparents managed to survive the Cultural Revolution that began here long before 1966 — even if it says otherwise in the history books — and lasted until 1976. The Red Guard forced local people to hand over their sheep, cattle, and horses to the government, promising to set up one huge farm for everyone in return. After the animals were seized, the CCP simply annexed all their remaining property and possessions, and never fulfilled their promise. By this point, my relatives had, in the truest sense of the word, nothing left to lose — apart from their lives.

By 1962, the greatest mass famine in the history of China had cost the lives of roughly 40 million people. But Mao blamed the Soviet Union, which had supposedly pushed the whole country to the brink by forcing it to pay back its debts too quickly. The ploy worked, and the people directed their anger elsewhere.

"Every household had to put up a huge portrait of Mao," recalled my grandfather, his expression darkening. "Three times a day you had to stand in front of it and pray to Mao like a god." Even at mealtimes, families had to gaze at him adoringly. The words of the Red Guard, preached endlessly, popped into my father's head: "We're going to exterminate the capitalist system." It was then that the great levelling began. There could no longer be any differences between people: no one could own more than anybody else. Though for a millionaire like Mao, of course, other rules applied.

"Yes," agreed my grandfather reflectively, rocking his upper body back and forth. "Then they started playing people off against each other: we were all supposed to denounce as many friends or neighbours as possible as capitalists."

"It was a bad time," added my father. "Lots of people joined in, because it gave them an advantage." You could recognise them by their red armbands and all the talk about enemy spies "bought by the West". And by their victory parades, in which they dragged the violated corpses through the streets.

The reign of terror cast a shadow across the souls of all who survived, leaving them in constant fear. My family rarely spoke about our own past for fear of reawakening those old ghosts, although we were lucky that the period immediately after my birth was the freest in the history of the People's Republic of China. *If we speak up, the Party will punish the whole family for its hostile ideas*, they thought anxiously. That's how ingrained their mistrust had become.

Despite their reticence, as children we understood that the Chinese were dangerous people. And the Chinese themselves would soon start reminding us of that every day. Our village wasn't just home to Kazakhs but to a few Uighurs, Kyrgyzstanis, and Muslim Dungan-Chinese as well, who spoke a form of Mandarin. Still, everybody in the village was fluent in Kazakh, and there was no prejudice: we were a community. I had still never even seen a Chinese person face to face.

"This land is where we've got roots." That's what we learned. You had to be able to rattle off seven generations of your family by heart, including names and places of birth; otherwise you were an orphan or not a real Kazakh. My siblings and I were proud that we could recite the names of our grandfather, great-grandfather, and four more generations back, one after another.

A living ghost from the age of terror

Every time I used our sewing machine, I glanced uneasily at the old labels on it, which were printed with a quote from Mao: "If the Communist Party did not exist, nor would this new China."

There were occasional whispers in every family about the crimes perpetrated under Mao, as well as Russia's crimes under Stalin. Both had trampled bloody footprints through our landscape, the effects of which were still palpable. The village was haunted by a living ghost from this age of terror. At least, she seemed like a ghost to me, with her crazy puff of white hair: a seventy-year-old woman who had lost her mind during the Cultural Revolution.

At one time she had been part of a rich family. Not satisfied with simply seizing all their property, the Red Guard had tortured her husband and their children in prison. One day, her husband had been found hanging in his cell. Chinese officials informed her bluntly, "He admitted he was guilty, and took his own life." But everybody knew they'd killed him. Not long after that, her children's bluish feet were dangling from calving ropes in the open air. The death squads had exterminated her entire family, one by one. She was the last to survive.

Ever since then, she'd been rushing around the village like a madwoman, bursting into houses and crying for help. To calm her down, people would give her something to eat. It was hard to watch a mother in such despair. It made my chest tighten with sadness, but it also set my heart thudding with rage at the people who had done this to her.

Just as it is today, it was forbidden to complain about the killings or disappearances, because "for Mao, no sacrifice is too great". If the great leader decreed it, my grandparents and parents were supposed "to let their bodies be ground to dust and their bones smashed into a thousand pieces".

My early years coincided with China's breathtaking rise towards becoming the second-biggest economy in the world, although in East Turkestan everything remained, as always, under the absolute control of the Communist Party: jobs were distributed, and prices and production quotas were set as before.

The Chinese are coming!

"The Chinese are coming!" A choking cry went from mouth to mouth through the village. It was the early 1980s, and several military convoys came rolling through our settlement, stopping at the bridge over the river. They were not from the Bingtuan, the Xinjiang Production and Construction Corps, a semi-military organisation that set up large corporations in East Turkestan and would soon control entire branches of industry in the area, as well as large swathes of our cotton fields and vineyards. These troops were part of a different, special unit.

The soldiers immediately set about building a large barracks, surrounded by high walls and barbed wire. Behind it, on the hill, they erected a radar station. Construction had barely finished before a thousand Chinese soldiers streamed into the camp on their trucks and shut the gates behind them, vanishing as quickly as they had arrived. None of us was allowed inside. "What are they doing in there?" we wondered.

The profoundly anxious villagers put their heads together. The bridge over the river was important to us — we needed it to herd our animals onto the pastureland — but from day one, the strangers caused nothing but trouble. "Find somewhere else," they snapped, shooing us away.

The arrival of the military convoys marked the end of peace in our village. The soldiers stole our animals and drove them into the barracks before their owners' very eyes. Herders sat on horseback near the walls, watching from above as their sheep were slaughtered, but furious soldiers swarmed out of the barracks like hornets and bawled at them, "What are you doing up there? Get out of here!"

After that, anybody who dared to ask where our animals were — let alone to protest against the theft — was threatened or simply beaten to a pulp. This was my first close encounter with the Chinese. Instantly, everyone in the village was petrified. At that time, I was in Year Three.

From then on, whenever my siblings and I drove our sheep to pasture, we ducked down and watched the soldiers from a distance, their fierce watchdogs tugging on short leads. We were always too scared to stare openly, and as we walked past we'd go as fast as our legs could carry us.

"These men hit us, they don't talk to us, and they never give us any answers," muttered my grandfather bitterly one mealtime. "They don't feel responsible or guilty for anything," added my mother. "It's tyranny," declared my father resignedly. "But what can we do?"

The first settlers: Don't be scared of the Chinese!

After a while, the first few Chinese began settling in our village, opening a greengrocer's, a photography shop, and a car mechanic's.

We got to see the foreigners close-up for the first time, but the other children and I were still afraid and kept our distance. Gradually, their Chinese families and relatives joined them.

The new arrivals soon twigged to what everyday items the villagers urgently needed, and they supplied them to us. We couldn't quite figure them out. Were they friendly or hostile? They spoke only Chinese and exploited the naivety of the local people, who didn't know much about business. They bought our goods and products such as milk, cheese, or meat at rock-bottom prices, and then sold them on to their compatriots with a massive mark-up.

The soldiers started digging huge holes around their camp. Sometimes our animals would fall in and suffer an agonising death. They used what they'd excavated as building material, summarily requisitioning areas of pastureland. "Why do the Chinese keep coming here?" my little brother Sawulet asked me uneasily one day, but I didn't know the answer myself.

While the Chinese shop-owners rapidly became the richest people in the village, the original population sank into poverty. We had no more pastureland, far fewer animals, and less income. Soon every family was struggling financially. Every morning, my parents sent us off with a warning: "Give the barracks a wide berth with the animals. It's too dangerous there."

Meanwhile Beijing was pushing a campaign to promote China and the Chinese people. "Don't be scared of the Chinese! They will transform Xinjiang into a thriving economic wonderland! You will have jobs and prosperity!" Sitting in front of our new cathode-ray tube TV, we wondered whether this was true. Recent events seemed to indicate the opposite. We had gained nothing and lost everything.

In those days, it was very popular to have your photograph taken. Families, men and women, old and young: everyone wanted one. But we never ventured into the only photography shop in the village, because it was Chinese-owned.

The photographer, however, had no such qualms. He was brazen enough to simply barge into our homes without asking for permission. Suddenly, there was a Chinese man standing in our room, taking snaps of everything from the shocked-looking children to the polished chests and pots. After a day or two, he pressed the photos into my mother's hand and demanded a huge sum of money. My mother stared awkwardly down at the floor. My father was too polite to refuse.

From the very beginning, the foreigners treated us with tremendous arrogance and self-importance. The next wave to show up were Chinese beekeepers, putting up fences wherever they pleased, and taking any remaining land for themselves. "Who gave them permission to do that?" croaked my grandfather indignantly. We didn't even know which authority to ask.

Illusions

Although it was clear from the outset that there were different rules for the Chinese and the locals, and despite some painful incidents, most of the teens and children in the village remained confident and optimistic. Our hearts were young, and could not be so easily kept under lock and key. My father avoided any comment on the newcomers' shameless behaviour, focusing instead on the future. "You've got to study hard so you'll get a good job one day."

Unbeknownst to us, he was already preparing us to face even greater injustices. Having experienced this humiliation himself, he did his best to steel us for it with self-confidence, pride in our culture, and an academic education.

My father had barely retired, but he and my mother were concentrating all their energies on our small farm and adding an extension to our house. Things seemed to be looking up. As I turned twelve and slowly entered puberty, my body started to develop, so he built two and then three new bedrooms for my grown-up sisters and brothers. In the summer, an open-air cinema opened opposite a disco. We could buy a ticket from a Chinese Dungan-Muslim for a small fee, and we watched foreign films like *Spartacus* or *Escape from Alcatraz* open-mouthed.

In our village, we lived in a bubble. We heard nothing about what was happening in the world around us. We had no idea that students were demonstrating for more freedoms and protesting against the corrupt regime and the families greedily enriching themselves. We had no idea that on the night of 3 June 1989, tanks rolled onto Tiananmen Square, crushing the students beneath them. That soldiers shot innocent bystanders and stabbed them with bayonets.

It was only later, at university, that I once heard my fellow students whispering to each other. "Did you hear about a Uighur called Urkesh? He fought for our rights at Tiananmen Square." Urkesh was a hero to them, but he had to flee China and currently lives in Taiwan. Even today, we don't know whether the dead numbered in the hundreds or thousands. But either way, Deng Xioaping's government effectively buried the democratic movement.

We know equally little about the uprisings in the 1990s in other parts of East Turkestan, where the Uighurs in particular rebelled against discrimination and oppression, except that they were stamped out with brutal violence. In the media, which has been controlled by the state since 1949, all you ever hear are voices droning on about the tremendous successes of the Chinese government. Nothing about how they banned Uighurs from holding large gatherings, such as football tournaments, or from building a new mosque in the Baren Township because they decided it was "subversive". There they immediately introduced drastic measures to "encircle the dangerous criminals". The fall of the Soviet Union, on the other hand, could not be hidden from anyone.

When the USSR was dissolved on 21 December 1991 in Almaty, replaced by a Commonwealth of Independent States (CIS) in which all the Central Asian republics were sovereign members, we celebrated in the village. Many people took the opportunity to travel across the border to see their Kazakh relatives, either upping sticks and moving, or simply exchanging information and ideas. Beijing, meanwhile, relentlessly insisted that this declaration of independence had been the wrong decision, doing its best to stifle any hopes of independence in their own country.

Writers, intellectuals, and singers from Kazakhstan streamed into our province, giving concerts or presenting their work at other cultural events. People queued outside the bookshops to buy novels. It was the only way we could get our hands on Russian literature, including books by Maxim Gorky or Anton Chekov, as well as other foreign books.

Like my father, I was hungry for knowledge, devouring these classic novels, and eager for more information on Western countries. Maybe I could travel there one day, if I became a famous actress, TV journalist, or host? In those relatively relaxed political times, our compatriots were still running radio and television stations, even though the media was and had always been the "throat and tongue" of the Party.

The government was keeping us deliberately ignorant, preserving the illusion that we were free. For a long time, Kazakhs felt like we were independent in our region of East Turkestan: a distinct group. We still had room and air to breathe. We hadn't noticed that we were already living in a gigantic prison, the walls of which were already closing in around us, slowly becoming taller and more difficult to scale ...

1993–1997: my student years

The older we got, the more our parents worried. Every year, another one of us went off to university and moved to another city. But how were our mother and father supposed to pay for it? And who would look after their girls in the big cities, hotbeds of sin where the law of the jungle prevailed? Where suddenly everything was about money and greed? The whole country was changing at breakneck speed, flying in the face of all the old values. It was too much for the older people, especially when this new way of life came to their own village.

"You need to keep a constant eye on your daughters," my father instructed my mother. There was no need: she already was anyway. "Be careful you don't put a foot wrong," she stressed to us. We would never have dared do anything immoral that might sully our family's honour. It never even crossed my mind to commit a sin. I found boys completely uninteresting. All that mattered to me was my career. I wanted to give my parents even more reason to be proud of me, and I knew I'd be better able to support them later in life.

After I left school with top marks, I was the only one in my class to get a place at the university in Ili. Instead of assigning me to study Western medicine, the authorities had put me forward for traditional Chinese medicine. When my father took me down there to enrol, it wasn't yet that difficult for Muslims to get a spot at university. Some of the heads of department were indigenous, and the city was 90 per cent Kazakh. These days, the Chinese have turned us into a minority in our own land.

I was seventeen years old when I set off by myself on the 600-kilometre trip to faraway Ili. As on my first visit, I gawped through the bus window at all the skyscrapers, gazing at the traditional teahouses huddled beneath them, where women offered handmade noodles from steaming urns to hurrying passers-by. Elaborately decorated signs hung everywhere above the streets and shops, announcing "Welcome" in large Kazakh letters, while the same word was printed smaller in Chinese underneath. Today, the only signs are in Chinese. They've erased our words entirely.

In those first few months, I found urban life hard: the crowded streets, the din, the unfamiliarity. I was a simple girl from the countryside among 6,000 students, 30 per cent of whom were Chinese compared to 70 per cent of the lecturers. At night, sleeping with eight strange girls in a bunk bed, I felt very far away from my village and my parents. The girls above me and beside me were Chinese.

I kept getting homesick, feeling it tug at the pit of my stomach. I thought longingly of the mountains, of the scent of wild rue in our house and on our horses. Horses are very significant to Kazakhs: our language alone has fifty words for the colours of their coats and markings. There was usually a long queue for the building's lone rotary telephone, so I started writing a letter, taking care not to smudge the words with my tears. "I miss you all so much ..."

The student halls were like a tiny cosmos unto themselves, with a shop and a restaurant. The atmosphere was fiercely competitive. If you were an indigenous person wanting to get ahead, you had no choice but to learn Chinese. Some of the Muslim students complained in hushed tones. "Why should we have to learn a foreign language? The Chinese should be learning Kazakh!"

At university, it was impossible to stay out of the foreigners' way, as we had done in the village. From the outset, the lack of trust between us was like a wall. When we were in front of the Chinese students, we watched our every word, but they never talked to us much anyway. Open discussion was taboo. Even mild criticisms of Beijing's authoritarian approach were usually met with arrogance. "You're just jealous because China is so successful!" We always felt like they were spying on us, so mostly we just kept to ourselves.

That said, I knew they weren't monsters. They were ordinary people with ordinary concerns. "What's the best way to make ends meet? How can I take some of the financial strain off my parents? How do I get good grades?"

If you scored well in your exams in Group A, you earned points and received financial support and grants from the state. Occasionally, you'd also be given vouchers for food. I never went hungry, because I earned so many points. Soon I wasn't just the youngest but the best on my course.

When the loneliness threatened to get too much for me, I'd hop on the bus at the weekend and visit my older sister at university in the neighbouring city. We'd comfort each other. Soon my little brother Sawulet joined us. He'd registered for mechanical engineering. During that first year, our mother visited us every two months, because it would have been too expensive for the three of us to buy a ticket home. We used to wait for her impatiently every single time, pacing back and forth on the balls of our feet at the entrance downstairs. She brought love, but also a bit of money and some traditional home-cooked meals — lots of it, in fact. Back home, my father would give a forlorn sigh every time he saw her with her bags packed, so she suggested he take a turn next time.

I soon got used to my new life, and I was lucky enough to find a best friend among the Kazakh girls: Gulina. (I've changed her name to protect her.) Unlike me, she was tall, with long fair hair, but our personalities were wired along similar lines. We felt like sisters. Both of us made sure to always fulfil our obligations, ambitious, restless, and determined to achieve the next goal as successfully as possible before moving on to another one … in that sense, we were both typically Chinese.

Happiness, however, was perpetually one step ahead of us.

Mao reborn

It didn't matter whether you were at the cinema or some other cultural event: suddenly, the Party was everywhere, bragging about the great things Mao had supposedly achieved for communism. Mostly they talked about idealism and the people's willingness to make sacrifices — they kept quiet about the terror and dread he left in his wake. I was sceptical, although I was still only vaguely aware from the older Kazakhs about the darker side of this story.

The sharper students lowered their voices until they were speaking so softly you could barely understand them. "This new cult of personality isn't a good omen," or "They're opening a door that leads straight back into the past," or "The Party is reinventing the past so they don't have to face up to it." Others scoffed indignantly. "If Mao wasn't great and good, they wouldn't say so in our books and on TV all the time." I used to lurk in the background during these discussions, listening.

When you're repeatedly being told how wonderful, socially beneficial and helpful communism is for all concerned, after a while you're not even sure what's true anymore. And the horrors of the past, which our parents and teachers had never properly explained to us in the first place, had faded like old black-and-white photographs, rapidly dissolving into mist.

The first few pages of every book I opened at university contained information about Mao, Lenin, and Marx. If we were writing an assignment or presenting it to our fellow students, we had to start by referring to their ideologies. Otherwise it was impossible to get a high mark. Supposedly, 70 per cent of what Mao had done was good. He'd driven off the nation's biggest enemies. His mistakes — the other 30 per cent — were negligible, as the teachers would always babble, toeing the Party line.

"The great leader has taught us to be loyal to the community, to the Party, to the nation," I wrote in my next paper. It seemed obvious to me that everyone else would come first, and myself last. The community was more important than the individual. Still, why had Mao killed so many people in such a brutal way? Regardless, asking questions and understanding the answers brought no solutions, only new problems. I wasn't interested in politics. I just wanted to study in peace and stick to the national credo: "Be prosperous and successful!"

But whether you wanted to or not, you were constantly stumbling into questions you weren't allowed to ask. "Where did they get so many healthy organs?" Gulina gasped as we stood in front of our mortuary slabs, her eyes darting around in shock as we carried out our first practice operations. Everybody acted as though her question had vanished into thin air the moment it was spoken, pretending they'd heard nothing.

In front of us there were tables full of pristine livers, hearts, lungs … as medical students, we had a remarkable abundance of organs at our disposal. Wordlessly, we picked up our scalpels and focused on the task at hand. In East Turkestan, everyone was talking about how adherents of the "Falun Gong" religious community — demonised by general secretary Jiang Zemin — as well as other people in the region, were increasingly being abducted in broad daylight for this express purpose. It was well known that China carried out far more organ transplants than could possibly have been provided by voluntary donors. In 2009, health minister Huang Jiefu explicitly admitted that Beijing "harvested about two-thirds of the transplants from executed prisoners". The highly profitable organ trade in China is run not by criminals on the black market, but by the CCP itself.

Raking it in

At night, Gulina and I would sometimes lie next to each other in the narrow bed, wide awake and dreaming about becoming wealthy and respected. Rich people, we falsely assumed, could buy anything. Including freedom. I kept picturing how exhausted and ground-down my parents were. They'd scrimped and saved for their children all their lives, never treating themselves to anything. Another four siblings had followed after me and Sawulet, and their studies had to be funded, too. "I have an idea," I said one evening: I realised there was an excellent way to earn money while at university. "But my parents can never find out."

Basically, on the weekends I'd take the bus to the Kazakh border. There, I bought huge quantities of folders, pens, notepads, and other stationery at one of the countless wholesalers so that I could sell them to my classmates at a marked-up price during my one-hour break in the evening. As the top student I was held in high regard, so, from the outset, business was so good that I even expanded my offering to include gold costume jewellery for the girls.

In the end, my pockets were so full of yuan that I was able to contribute towards paying for my younger siblings' education. "Where did you get so much money?" asked my father, astonished. "I got it because I'm such a successful student and I work so hard,"

I said, without blushing: it was only half the story, but at least it wasn't a lie.

I was keen to avoid my parents' disapproval at all costs. It might have been dangerous if the truth got out, partly because I was a young woman travelling alone on the bus, and partly because I was haggling over prices and wares like a farmer at the market, in an industry dominated by men. My parents would definitely have been worried about my reputation. And it would have made them feel ashamed that they couldn't earn enough money; they would have felt like they'd got me into this situation.

Twice a year, towards the end of the semester, my siblings and I went back home to our village. On every visit, we found our once beautiful countryside defaced in some new way — the earth dug up with excavators, the mountain hollowed out with mines. The landscape was increasingly criss-crossed with roads and cars. And with every construction project, the softly murmuring spring produced less and less water for the village.

1997: the spring dries up

Beijing was deliberately sending more and more settlers to East Turkestan, part of a project to Sinicise even the outlying regions of China's most resource-rich province. It wasn't just the landscape that had changed. So had the behaviour of the villagers.

They no longer stopped on the street to chat. Their faces were closed, their minds as beleaguered as the overexploited countryside around them. Even within our own four walls, my parents had now forbidden us to mention our concerns.

The older people slumped into the doldrums. "Where the Chinese tread, no herbs grow anymore." That was how devastating their impact seemed to the elderly Kazakhs. There was a disaster in the offing; my grandfather was sure of it. Sadly, he was right.

Next time I came back to the village, the spring had dried up, and the villagers had no more drinking water. Then the water level in the river dropped, and it dwindled into a stinking rivulet full of fish floating belly-up.

In winter, the locals tried to fetch snow from the mountains to make up for the lack of water. Layer by layer, they chipped off the ice and transported it down on donkeys. "What on earth is going on?" My frantic parents could make neither head nor tail of it. Stroking his long white beard with his wrinkled hands, my grandfather shook his head, murmuring, "The mountains and the water are sacred creatures. One must never pollute them with rubbish and faeces the way the Chinese do. Water must always remain pure, or its spirit will be angry." My mother lowered her head. "So that's why it's abandoning us ..."

During this period, there were so many protests in East Turkestan against the increasing erosion of religious and cultural freedoms that in hindsight I'm not sure anymore what I knew at the time and what I've forgotten. I had no idea that, on 8 March 1997, several bombs went off on buses in Beijing while the situation in East Turkestan was being sugar-coated at the Party congress. The more pressure was put on people, the more vehemently they resisted. But Beijing responded with ever greater repression and violence.

Our family was used to suffering. We simply huddled closer together, as though in the middle of a storm, hoping we wouldn't get hit in the head by bits of flying rubble. But the minute it was over, we'd go straight back to work and milk the cows. All our energies went towards making everyday life more bearable by safeguarding ourselves against poverty and material deprivation. Unlike my siblings, I never wasted time thinking about starting a family. I wanted to pass my exams as quickly as possible and find a well-paying job.

In hospital, not all patients are equal

I passed with flying colours, and was immediately offered a highly paid position in the regional capital of Mongolküre (Zhaosu in Chinese), working in a large hospital as a doctor. "A young woman can't live in the city all by herself," decided my mother. What would people say?

My father thought it would be best if I moved in with a distant relative on my mother's side who lived in the city and offered me a room in his apartment. He and his wife were senior civil servants with a spotless reputation. I agreed, because it seemed like a good deal for both sides. I saved money on rent and food, and my relatives didn't have to spend much on help, because I'd lend a hand around the house and tutor their two school-aged sons.

I turned up for my first day at work with mixed feelings. Roughly 80 per cent of the employees were Chinese who the government had sent to East Turkestan. Would I be accepted by my Chinese colleagues as a valuable co-worker? As an indigenous person, I always felt like I had to be better than everyone else. Otherwise they'd immediately start saying, "The Kazakhs are lazy and don't have any brains."

I breathed a sigh of relief when I got home that night. "It's a good environment to work in," I told my landlady cheerfully, as she manoeuvred me into the kitchen and peppered me with questions. I dutifully prepared a meal for the family and laid the table. "I'm happy for you," said my distant relative, although she didn't look it. At first, I didn't pay any attention to her reserve: I was concentrating entirely on my new job.

When we were standing around a patient's bed at the clinic, discussing treatment options, my Chinese colleagues acted like we were friends. They didn't make their prejudices obvious, because I was an educated woman who knew their language and culture. I could still tell from their behaviour, however, that they considered themselves better than I was: superior and cleverer. We never seemed to be enough for them: too much of one thing, too little of something else.

They were simply echoing the language of politics. Beijing drew a sharp distinction between "us" and "them", planting negativity in the heads of the Chinese people. They grew up with it; it shaped their reality. And wherever prejudice is preached, violence isn't far behind. Soon it was us versus them.

Sometimes a sick Kazakh or Uighur would travel from their village to the city for the first time. Getting their bearings in the enormous hospital would be difficult, so they'd ask for help in their local language: "Please could you tell me where I'm supposed to go?"

The Chinese staff would never respond. They treated all indigenous people as though they weren't even there. Increasingly desperate, the patient would try again, describing their symptoms: "I'm not feeling well, my intestines are full of ulcers ..." But they would never be dignified with so much as a glance.

Eventually, the patient would give up and retreat to one side in resignation, waiting and waiting and waiting ... Meanwhile the white-clad staff would bustle past, ignoring them. Or they might whisper behind their hands, "Look at that dirty little ant." Sometimes the patient was a farmer dressed in simple clothes, but was that a reason to humiliate someone? Purely because they belonged to another ethnic group?

Whenever I noticed one of these abandoned patients, I'd go straight up to them and take their arm, guiding them to the right place. The first time I was confronted with this discrimination, I was outraged.

Arms akimbo, I tackled the issue head-on with my Chinese colleagues. "Why are you treating this patient so shabbily? This is a hospital. Our job is to care for all the weak and sick people who come to us, not to pick and choose between them!"

The response was usually one of surprise, followed by a question. "Oh! Was that one of your relatives? Is that why you want to support them?"

Shaking my head, I'd reply, "No, they're just ordinary people. They don't know the language and the rules here, that's why I want to help."

These were doctors and nurses: we were bound by a common code of ethics, according to which all human beings were of equal value. If the impact of the government's negative propaganda was being felt in a place like this — a place of compassion and love — then how bad was the situation on the street?

In shops, at the market, or in restaurants, indigenous people faced an even tougher row to hoe. Often we'd be met with a disparaging look from the Chinese owner. "What do you want in here?" They'd turn their backs or come straight out and insult us. "You Muslims have all been kicked by donkeys."

The gulf between me and my colleagues was even apparent when we occasionally invited each other round for dinner. Strangely, they'd always ask me questions about Kazakhstan, where a few of my relatives lived. This wasn't genuine curiosity: they simply wanted to have their prejudices confirmed.

"There's not such a wide range of goods available as there is in China," they would say, or "the Kazakhs are poor and sickly, they live in tin shacks and in slums under terrible conditions."

"No, no," I'd politely correct them. "Kazakhs live in big-city high-rises, just like people here." My colleagues tried to find out how I felt about the country. Was I a Kazakh patriot perhaps? Maybe even a traitor to the Chinese fatherland?

I did my best to make my remarks as anodyne as possible. "Kazakhstan connects Europe and Asia. It's the largest landlocked country in the world, and it offers lots of opportunities." They despised me for saying things like that. To them, Kazakhstan was under-developed, impoverished, and backwards. "The Kazakhs can't run their own companies, can't use computers, can't build machines …" It was solely thanks to Chinese aid that Kazakhs — just like East Turkestan — would soon be able to enjoy the fruits of progress and development. In retrospect, I wonder whether they were already putting together a file on me. In 2017, senior Party officials started using statements made by indigenous people during this period as evidence that they were "enemies of the system", which typically led to an arrest. According to the Party, anyone considered a friend of Kazakhstan was harbouring "treacherous sentiments" — reason enough to "de-radicalise" them in a camp.

Can you in the West imagine anything like it happening today? They served their guest tea and biscuits, deliberately questioned them about specific topics, and furtively jotted down their answers in order to denounce them to the authorities eighteen years later: "This person could be dangerous. Arrest them, lock them up, destroy them!"

If a Chinese person in East Turkestan started asking visitors questions about foreign countries, it wasn't usually well intentioned. Realising this, the locals soon learned not to discuss politics with the Chinese. But in the end, when they couldn't squeeze any more information out of us, a Kazakhstani passport stamp was all they needed. That was proof enough of "extremism".

My grandfather's death

I was taking a patient's pulse when a nurse called me outside to answer the telephone. My mother was on the other end. "Come home quick, your grandfather's not well." He had summoned all his grandchildren and relatives to his bedside, where he told us, "In a few days I'm going to die."

"No," we contradicted him in astonishment. "You've still got a long life to live yet!" It wasn't long since he'd been riding his horse through the neighbouring settlements, visiting friends. He'd never once seen a doctor, nor been prescribed medication. Even his teeth were still intact and dazzlingly white. Although he'd been born in 1897 and was one hundred years old, his death came as a shock for all of us. He'd already lived a long life, of course, but we'd have loved to keep him with us longer.

No matter how poor a Kazakh family was, they always held a big memorial feast to honour the person who had died. While the women sang the lamentation for the dead and prepared the food, the men my grandfather had chosen wrapped his body — after the washing and prayers were completed — in a white linen sheet. The others lifted him into a wooden coffin and buried him in his magnificently decorated tomb in our village cemetery on the mountainside, making sure he was facing Mecca.

Sadly, I had little time to mourn with my family: I was being called back to work. At the hospital, I found it difficult at first to concentrate on my patients. I was very aware of how important my grandfather had been to me and how much I missed him. It took several days until I was able to function normally again. There had been a quality about my grandfather that was as pristine and clear as the water that sprang straight out of the mountain.

A dead person's memorial is sacred to Kazakhs, because our

home is wherever our ancestors are buried. Would I even be able to find my grandfather's grave today? Twenty years later, Beijing decided anything Muslim was terrorism-related, so in 2017 indigenous people were instructed to remove all Muslim symbols — such as the crescent moon — from our relatives' gravestones.

Some Kazakhs, especially long-serving members of the Party, were particularly zealous about destroying their own family's graves, because they were trying to curry favour with the Chinese Party members. Of course, this led to serious conflicts within their families, and tore many relationships apart.

Numerous cemeteries that survived this wave of destruction were subsequently levelled by city excavators. In many large urban areas, the authorities defended their decision on the grounds of "needing more space". Elsewhere they forced our people to dig their dead out of the ground and rebury them in Chinese cemeteries. All traces of our ancestors were to be obliterated. It was a psychological atrocity and a terrible insult to us as Muslims.

The older people recognised long before we did that there were dark clouds on the horizon, heralding the approaching sandstorm. Danger was coming. Our generation simply came to realise it too late.

My first bankcard

My heart pounded excitedly as I was handed my first bankcard. I already had my monthly salary of 500 yuan in the account. Shortly afterwards, I started doing night shifts at the hospital as well, earning roughly half this amount again, which the teller — to my delight — gave me in cash.

I didn't need all this money for myself, so I hopped on the bus to see my parents and pressed the card into my baffled-looking father's hand. "Here, this is my monthly income. You can buy whatever you want." Full of gratitude, he spent the money on educating my youngest siblings.

I earned enough to afford pretty clothes and other luxuries. I was already considered one of the best-dressed people in my group of friends. The women admired me. "Oh, you have such a unique style," they'd say. It was true. I didn't necessarily go for more expensive fabrics, but I did wear unusual designs that I found in a shop belonging to a friend who sold Turkish goods.

All the women around me dreamed about wearing the same expensive brands and the same things, so they all ended up looking the same. I wanted to stand out from the crowd. I preferred bright colours while everyone else was wearing dark ones, and long skirts while short ones were in fashion. Friends would ask me curiously, "Where do you get stuff like that? We want one, too …"

When I glimpsed my reflection in a shop window, or when I hosted medical events, I occasionally thought about my old dream of becoming a journalist and travelling the world. Maybe I could do another course? But that would have been a bridge too far, so at some point I buried that dream. Apart from my soft spot for clothes, I didn't have the time to spend my money anyway.

After work, I was kept busy with the housework at my relatives' place. They were important people, constantly being invited to dinners or weddings, and most evenings and weekends they were out. They'd tell me, "We've just got to go out for a while — please look after our two sons and tidy everything up."

On the rare occasions when I did have time to myself, I had to ask my landlady for permission to go out. She knew perfectly well that I loved dancing more than anything and that I was a decent woman, so she could have just let me go, but instead she called my parents and aired her concerns. "What do you think?

Sayragul wants to go dancing in a club at eight o'clock tonight with a friend. I really don't want people talking about us because of her ... How is that going to make us look?" Our whole existence and our good reputation were centred under my parents' roof: we would never have jeopardised either of them.

Moments later, my mobile phone rang. It was my mother. Once I'd gone over with her exactly which girl from which family I was going with, which club I was going to, and what time we were all coming back, I heard her give several sighs. "Fine, but make sure you behave properly, and don't stay too long. Be back by around ten."

Although I'd been living away from home for years and was now twenty-two, my parents were still heavily concerned with protecting my honour, because even a tiny mistake on my part would have reflected poorly on them. Gulina and I painted our lips red and our eyes black, combed our shiny long hair, put on nice clothes and high-heeled shoes, and let loose on the club floor, dancing in the dry-ice mist under colourful lights to my favourite song by Modern Talking.

Even while I was on the dance floor, my phone rang and my mother asked, "Are you keeping track of time? Not that your aunt is getting annoyed ..." I ended up constantly checking my watch while I was dancing. Another ten minutes. Synthesisers and electric guitars. "You're my heart, you're my soul ..." In those days, the names of my favourite singers, Dieter Bohlen and Thomas Anders, were the most important things I knew about Germany. Today, apolitical songs from the West are once more banned in China. The West, along with its freedom of opinion and its pluralism, is yet again considered the enemy. Dissolute, debauched, and reprehensible.

Preparing for difficult times ahead

I poured all my energy into working at the hospital, but after shifts I was expected to prove myself yet again by cleaning, cooking, and tutoring until late at night. It took me a long time to realise that I would never be able to do anything right in the eyes of someone like my domineering landlady.

Perhaps her dissatisfaction was rooted in the fact that politics in China taught people from pre-school age onwards — particularly through the use of songs — to serve the government, the Party, and the community faithfully, but never themselves. This may be why some of them disparaged anyone who had remained honest, unwittingly holding up a mirror to them.

Despite these problems at the apartment, I remained dedicated, conscientious, and ambitious, repressing whatever was bothering me after work. I held myself to extremely high standards. As a child I had learned that the more effort I put in, the more I would be valued and loved. And I always wanted to be one of the best — I wanted to grow and develop every day.

"You're allowed to go out tonight," my landlady generously informed me. "Your father's not here to see," she joked, "so you can be back by midnight." After I'd left, elated, she called my mother on the phone, waking her up, and told her about my visit to the club, despite having given me permission. "It's ten o'clock, and Sayragul still isn't back …"

Of course, my mother got into a flap and started calling me repeatedly, but this time I wasn't paying as much attention. I was busy dancing, and it was so loud in the club that I didn't notice. It wasn't until I was on my way home shortly before midnight that I finally heard the phone ringing. I was assailed by a torrent of words. "Where are you? I couldn't sleep. I've been waiting for you to phone me back. Why didn't you call? Your aunt is very upset. What's she going to think about us now?" I was caught utterly off-guard that my mother even knew about my night out, and immediately felt guilty.

"Mother, calm down ..."

"How can I sleep soundly, Sayragul, if you're not at home?"

After that, I decided to give up going out altogether. There was no way I could let my behaviour reflect badly on my parents. Disobedience was out of the question for me. I felt bad for days because I'd come home so late and caused trouble for my family.

After a twelve-hour night shift, I'd do the washing for the whole host family, buy food, and cook, until at last I dropped into bed like a corpse. When other people were around, the lady of the house would praise me, putting her hand — dripping with golden jewellery — on my shoulder and saying to her guests, "She's such a lovely, helpful relative. We're glad to have her with us." It did make me feel good, but two minutes later I'd be back at the mercy of her capricious moods.

"You've got to work harder, study more with the boys so they get better grades!" Or: "Do a better job cleaning the apartment!" She'd say this even though I'd helped the boys as much as I could, and everything was so shiny you could see your reflection in it. The injustice was hard to swallow. Maybe I wasn't good enough? I remained trapped in self-reproach, going around in circles in my head and finding no way out. I never talked back; I always tried to suppress my anger. Otherwise the situation would have instantly become untenable.

The family viewed me as a tool, one that made them feel stronger. In retrospect, my time with them was good practice for what happened to me in later life, when I was faced with ever-higher hurdles and obstacles to overcome. In a society like

China's, you have to be hard on yourself. You have to tackle problems on your own.

Since I've been living in the West, however, I've wondered whether there were some things I shouldn't simply have taken lying down. Yet everything I ever did for my parents I truly believed was for the best. For Kazakhs, family is more important than anything else. I have never regretted anything I did for them. I never felt exploited, or that my siblings got better treatment. In fact, I often doubted whether I'd really done enough to help.

Still, when it came to that apartment in the city, I should have packed my bags, moved out, and put my freedom to better use. But lost time cannot be regained.

Starting over

My father showed up unannounced at the apartment one day, his face ashen. He looked defeated. "Your mother is very ill. Could you come back home and look after her?" My older siblings were nearly all married or living elsewhere, and the younger ones were still in school and also needed looking after. It was a tricky situation for me.

Unsure of what to do, I showed my father my work schedule. "Look, the shifts are always assigned a month in advance. I can't take the bus back and forth every day." The hospital was about fifty kilometres from the village. There was only one way out. "I'd better quit," I suggested.

My father shook his grey head heavily. "I can't make that decision for you, sweetheart. I'd never force you to take a step like that." I didn't have to think long. I could earn decent money anywhere, including in my parents' village. But if anything happened to my mother because I hadn't helped her in time, I'd never forgive myself. After nearly two years, I gave up my job as a doctor, even though I was earning a high salary, loved my work, and was a valued employee.

There's an unwritten rule among Kazakhs that children never abandon their parents. Usually, it's the youngest son or a daughter who lives with the family to care for their ageing parents.

Luckily, I wasn't the type to sulk or spend very long moping over what I'd lost.

Back home

My mother was in a bad way. She had dull, nagging stomach pains, and could barely get even soup down. I was horrified to find her lying in bed so emaciated and weak. Gingerly smoothing her pillow, I watched over her that night as she slept fitfully. "I need time to look after her properly," I told my father the next morning. I needed a job with flexible hours.

Nobody in the village was employing doctors, so I quickly retrained as a teacher. The process was straightforward, because locals who could speak Chinese were in demand everywhere. From that point on, I taught Chinese to Kazakh children between the ages of six and thirteen at Ahyaz School. I was deputy head.

Meanwhile I was shuttling my sick mother back and forth to doctors at big-city hospitals, but nobody could help with her stomach ulcers. After a while, I found a traditional Mongolian healer. "It's caused by bacteria," he declared, prescribing various herbs and teas. After a week, she recovered.

This may sound strange to people in the West, but in our village we heard only snippets of information about 11 September 2001, when Islamic terrorists attacked the World Trade Center in New York and the Pentagon in Arlington. In hindsight, it's clear that Beijing's subsequent global war on terrorism gave them a flimsy reason to clamp down on East Turkestan more brutally than ever. Islam merely served as a suitable pretext.

While indigenous people had previously been given a choice whether or not to join the CCP, from now on the government made it mandatory for all young people at public institutions. So on 1 July 2001 I became a Party member, even though I certainly didn't want to.

It was easy for Beijing to start by branding the Uighurs in East Turkestan as Islamic terrorists, because there were indeed pockets of deeply religious people among them. The government used them strategically to pave the way for the oppression of all Muslim minorities.

How can anyone destroy their own house?

The Chinese had their eyes our region, not just because of its strategic location, but also because it was home to vast reserves of crude oil, uranium, gold, iron ores, and the largest coal deposits on the planet. East Turkestan is the heart of the arms, mining, and cotton-growing industries.

The military had long since pulled out of our village, but since early 2000 Chinese construction workers had been plundering the mountains for raw materials. They mined dark-coloured minerals that they stored and processed in the empty barracks.

"Anybody looking for a well-paying job?" people from a new construction company asked around the village. That alone should have roused our suspicions, because the Chinese generally took the good jobs for themselves, and not a single one worked there. But our young men desperately needed the money. Day and night they worked, often three shifts in a row.

Our hale young lads rapidly deteriorated into invalids. The dusty air poisoned their lungs. They coughed their guts out. Their young bodies were as weak and cadaverous as the elderly, and the whites of their eyes turned yellow because their livers couldn't expel the toxins fast enough. Soon many of them were incapable even of the simplest jobs. And not a single one has ever recovered.

Piece by piece, Chinese companies have destroyed not only the village but also the mountain behind it, blowing it to bits with dynamite.

And they did it twenty-four hours a day. The thunderous crashing and banging was almost unbearable. Glasses trembled on the table. At the same time, one transport vehicle after another kept whizzing through the village.

In their eagerness to strip the mountain of its riches, the Chinese also resorted to chemicals. Suddenly, one day, a peculiar stench came wafting down from the mountains. The villagers were afraid. "It's poisonous," they whispered to one another. Not long after that, one of the rivers dried up, and the village was deprived of another lifeline.

Everywhere you looked, there was broken earth. "We've lost everything, our pastures and our animals," mourned the elderly, "our peace and now our sacred mountains, too." It was virtually impossible to stay. Plenty of local people fastened their rucksacks and moved away. We stayed.

The mountains and the landscape were sacred to us. I thought about my grandfather, who had so often torn out his hair in anguish. "This is our homeland. How can anyone destroy their own house like this?" Many people just cried softly and lamented the loss of Mother Earth, who had nourished our ancestors for centuries.

I stared pensively out of the window. When I was a child, the meadows had bloomed with wild tulips, fragrant herbs, and poppies as far as the eye could see. Countless birds and animals had lived in the pines and foliage. Where had they all gone? In the summer, the farmers had grown fruit and grains on our fertile soil, and harvested hay and straw for their cattle. By 2020, however, many of the fields were fallow and overgrown with weeds. There were hardly any farmers anymore, because the Communist Party had interned so many people in the camps. The Chinese began their invasion by investing, and destruction swiftly followed on its heels.

That same year, friends surreptitiously passed around the well-known novel *The Crime* by Kazakh historian Kajikhumar Shabdan. "Read this," Gulina whispered to me, "and you'll understand that there are two stories to be told about our country." One was about East Turkestan, which was true, and one had been made up by the Chinese, which said that Xinjiang had always been an inseparable part of China. Even as a little girl, I'd heard things like that and had always assumed there was a kernel of truth to them.

To my astonishment, I read that the Chinese had hung the severed head of a Kazakh hero from a bridge as a deterrent. I learned about the collapse of the East Turkestan republic in 1933, when England, China, and Russia had grappled for power in East Turkestan — part of the so-called Great Game. Ten years later, in 1944, Uighurs, Kazakhs, and other Muslim groups had proclaimed a new, independent republic of East Turkestan in Ili, until the president had unexpectedly and mysteriously disappeared.

We had been permitted only a fleeting glimpse of our true history. The writer of this famous novel had spent more than forty years behind bars, then was briefly freed before dying in Tarbagatay prison in February 2011, martyred because of his books.

The opportunity to come to terms with our own past — to be self-critical, to spend years exploring its causes, or to mourn — an opportunity that is taken for granted in a free country, was denied to us.

An eternal spinster?

Ultimately, I had no choice but to be optimistic. Otherwise I might have floundered or simply stuttered to a halt, because the authorities were continually throwing up obstacles. *You're still going to be successful,* I told my brain. I was still occasionally nagged by a doubting inner voice — but I suppressed it by focusing on the positive.

I was basically pretty lucky, I decided, because I enjoyed my new job with the Kazakh students immensely. And if I hadn't retrained to be a teacher, I would never have met my husband, Uali. In July 2002, I went on a four-week training course in the regional capital of Ghulja, where teachers from the eleven administrative divisions in Ili had been brought together.

Many years later, my husband used to love telling our two children the story of how we first met. "I was standing just outside the training centre with my colleagues when the cars pulled up with the teachers. I saw your mother getting out, and was spellbound in a heartbeat. Who is that incredibly fascinating woman, I wondered."

Uali even remembered exactly what clothes and shoes I'd been wearing. "She wore this very stylish long, colourful, airy summer dress, and high heels. And her long, shiny black hair fell loose all the way to her knees ..." He even recalled my build. "She was slim, delicate, and her face was beautifully made-up, with almond eyes ..."

I, meanwhile, paid no attention to the men by the door. I'd always had a gut feeling that I would die an unmarried woman. I didn't see myself building a family of my own: all my energy was devoted to my parents and siblings.

Of the thirty teachers in our room, however, I did notice Uali. Somehow, I could sense straightaway that he was a special person. His voice sounded oddly familiar, even though I'd never heard it before. And when I looked more closely, which I did infrequently and always in secret, I realised he was more attractive than the others, too — relatively tall, with jet-black hair and a round, friendly face. He wore a light black jacket, a red shirt, jeans, and black shoes. During the break, he tucked a small rectangular briefcase under his arm, which was a fashionable thing to have and to do at that time.

When the month was up, all the teachers returned to their respective schools. Uali sat next to me on the bus. He was supposed to get off after two hours, but stayed on for another four until we reached my village. *That's funny*, I thought. *Maybe he's got something he needs to do there.*

But he was still there that evening. And the next morning, I saw him again in the village, where he'd spent the night with some people he knew. Well, fair enough — it was a holiday. Now and again he'd call me. "Are you there? Can we meet up?"

"What are you still doing here?" I asked. I was sure he must have some business in the area. Why else would he be there? But Uali had something else in mind — I just hadn't noticed that he was interested in me as a woman. As a colleague, I wished him safe travels over the phone.

From August onwards, he visited me every week. All the villagers were agog, of course, watching as this dragged on for months. When Uali was with me, we chatted about ordinary things, such as our jobs and working with students. We were fundamentally very similar. He was a helpful, honest guy who always spoke his mind. Yet I still didn't feel much more for him than friendship.

Over the following weeks, I was very busy with other things, because I'd pooled my money with Sawulet's in order to completely renovate and extend my parents' house. Of course, as soon as anyone in our village did something new, the others would look on curiously and then do the same. There was hammering and banging all over the place.

When the construction work was complete, we put new furniture and modern appliances into all the rooms, including the internet and a large flat-screen TV. The whole thing took ages.

It wasn't until December that Uali plucked up his courage and told me he had deeper feelings for me. Today, I can't help laughing when I think about us sitting there in front of each other for a moment, both stiff, our cheeks burning.

Even though by now we were quite familiar with each other and understood each other's mentality and temperament, the first time he suggested marriage and politely pointed out that we were both old enough, I blurted out, "So I have to get married off now, do I?"

A second later, I was chewing my bottom lip, embarrassed. *Oh dear, what's the right thing to do here?* Maybe he was right? Lots of my friends were already married with children. And he was a great guy, no question. After I'd got over the initial shock, I laughed and told him I'd have to think about it properly.

I knew the rumour mill was already spinning out of control in the village. So why was I dragging my feet? Soon we were acting as though we were engaged, appearing together at parties and get-togethers. I was so happy during that time. I used to turn up the volume on Modern Talking in my room and just dance. What I didn't know — though nearly everyone else did —

was that there were two other young women chasing after Uali. Independently of each other, they both started plotting against me, spreading rumours that he would soon be marrying one of them instead of me.

The competition never sleeps

Kissing before marriage? Unthinkable in our culture! Kazakh couples don't hug or get intimate with each other like that. If we had, we would have felt incredibly guilty and indecent afterwards. The most Uali and I did was shyly hold hands and picture our future together.

One of the young women who wanted to split us up was a deputy mayor. She was maybe five years older than me, pretty, and came from a very well-respected family. Hardworking Uali had caught her eye the moment he started teaching in her village, Aksu, and rapidly built his own house.

During this time, she had cooked for him and done his laundry, never doubting that she was the only real candidate in the running. After all, she wrote poetry, sang, and had plenty of other artistic gifts. Who could resist that? But things had turned out differently than she'd imagined. She sent me a message via intermediaries that I should leave Uali alone immediately, because she wanted to marry him. I did not respond.

Not long afterwards, a teachers' conference took place in another town, and we both attended. Bumping into each other in the auditorium, we started chatting. "This man already made a promise to me," she explained quite matter-of-factly. I felt like an earthquake was happening inside me, toppling one building after another. "If that's true, then I won't hold onto him any longer," I replied, trying desperately to keep my voice from shaking, and my shoulders slumped. "I'm not the kind of person who breaks up a couple." The idea of something like that getting back to my parents was unthinkable! All their lives, my father and mother had instructed us girls to be modest and courteous. "Always think about what you're doing and weigh every word carefully." We were never supposed to let other people form a negative opinion of ourselves or our family.

After the conference, the two of us parted on respectful terms. But I stormed home, furious with Uali. "If you like this woman so much you promised to marry her, then we need to end this right now!" He shook his head vehemently. "No, no, that's not true. I've never hidden anything from you." He explained haltingly that she had indeed helped him round the house, but that she was like a family member — "not a desirable woman like you". "Good," I said, holding my head high, although I was annoyed to hear how happy I sounded.

Not long afterwards, I was in the town centre on school business and wanted to grab a quick bite to eat at a restaurant beforehand. I'd barely sat down and started twisting the noodles around my fork when my other rival — who I had no idea even existed — rushed toward me. She was a student from Ghulja, and her face was white with rage. "What kind of nasty game are you playing? Uali is *my* fiancé. *I'm* going to marry him. Keep your hands off!"

She was a tall, slim, very pretty girl. Much prettier than me. Her hair, like mine, was very long and dark, and fell loose down her back. It was clear, too, that she had plenty of spirit. Far more than I did.

"How many times to I have to tell you? He's mine! Let him go, or the boys will show you what's what!" She jerked her head towards a couple of yobs in shirts and jeans positioned by the door. I glanced cautiously around. The other diners were staring at me with interest. I tried to act as though her tantrum was nothing to do with me. In reality, I was extremely alarmed. The blood was thudding in my temples, but I did my best to keep eating, lifting my fork very calmly to my mouth, chewing and not forgetting to swallow.

"You'd better clear off! Otherwise my friends are going to beat you up ..." she snarled, one hand on her hip and the other on the back of her head. Other girls would have run a mile — but I'm not so easily intimidated. I was fearless. My father raised me always to stay calm, no matter what the situation. But my composure clearly made her blood boil. "Why aren't you listening to me?" Still acting utterly unflustered, I kept lifting the fork to my mouth and putting it back ... until, abruptly, she grabbed my plate of food and flung it to the ground in front of all the watching diners.

Everybody had heard. Everybody knew. It was an excruciatingly awkward moment. We were in the middle of a public place. My face must have been as bright red as a warning light. Everybody knew me. All this fuss over a man! Seething, I grabbed my jacket and marched off.

Back home, still boiling with rage, I sat down and wrote Uali a letter, practically jabbing the pen through the paper. "What was that ridiculous performance all about? If you have anything to do with this girl, you'd better come here right now and sort things out. Until then, it's over between us!" The words echoed inside me like a thunderclap, but inwardly I was still ranting and raving. "He *should* feel bad. Serves him right!" It was because of him I'd been made to look like an idiot in public. And where did that leave me?

For the next few days, I was rubbing my hands, picturing Uali tormented by remorse and begging me for mercy. But he didn't come. More time passed. The harder I tried to stop thinking about him, the more obsessed I became by those thoughts. What was I supposed do now? I kept seeing his handsome face in my mind's eye — I simply could not let it go.

Why hadn't he contacted me? Then, suddenly, I realised: I wanted this man, and no other. Jealousy coursed red-hot through my veins. At night, I lay wide awake, my heart pounding. I was restless, uneasy. I'd never felt anything like it before. Uali was the first man I'd ever longed to be with, the first man I'd been able to picture building a life with. Surely it couldn't be over, just like that?

I was desperate to talk to him, but my pride wouldn't let me. I kept taking out the piece of paper with his phone number and picking up the receiver to dial, then instantly slamming it back like a hot potato. For thirty days, we didn't exchange a word. For thirty days, we didn't see each other.

And then a boy with bulging pockets appeared in my room.

The messenger

The boy stood in front of me, an imploring look on his face. "Please, sister, there's someone outside who wants to speak to you, please go out and see him." I didn't think it was important — some bored neighbour, maybe — so I refused. "No, not now, I'm busy. I'll come later." But the boy, almost on the verge of tears, patted his crammed pockets. "Please, sister, come with me. He said you have to come or he wants all his sweets back."

At that I felt sorry for him, so I went with him to the front door, where Uali poked his head around the corner of the house, laughing.

"I've come to apologise," he said, while I was still walking towards him. "I did everything just like you wanted!"

Although inwardly I was jubilant, I raised my eyebrows nonchalantly and held my head high. Uali, disconcerted, began to confess. "Yes, I did know that girl, yes, I saw her a few times, but I never showed any serious interest in her." The higher I lifted my chin, the quicker the words spilled out of his mouth. "There was absolutely nothing going on with that girl, but I told her again even more clearly. Please forgive me!"

This man, frantically trying to find the right words, had everything I wanted. A good job, a good character — and on top of that he was such a lovable person. Far more prestigious catches than me wanted to marry him so much that they were still chasing after him. How could I let a great guy like him be snapped up by somebody else? Gradually, my face softened, and my eyes began to sparkle with joy. "Alright, let's get married," said my mouth, seemingly of its own accord.

We'd certainly taken our sweet time. Uali and I had first met in July 2002, but our wedding wasn't until June 2004. Perhaps it's true that women often subconsciously look for men who remind them of their fathers. Uali and my father did have a lot in common. Calm and level-headed, they were my best advisers and staunchest supporters. But as long as my father was alive, he was the closest confidant I had: with his help, I overcame all sorts of troubles.

When wedding planning gets complicated

Obviously, my parents — along with everyone else — had known for ages that Uali was interested in me, and they must secretly have been wringing their hands, wondering why it was taking him so long to propose. I was very strong-willed, too, and they weren't sure what decision I would make. So they just let things run their course and bided their time.

A Kazakh wedding is a highly complicated and drawn-out ceremony that consists of several parties. The bride never goes straight to her parents and tells them about her plans, so I sent my sister-in-law instead. Only then did Uali inform his relatives, who went to see my family.

One of my brothers spoke up enthusiastically at the meeting, because he happened to know Uali. "He's a really nice, upstanding guy. I'm 100 per cent sure he'll make our darling sister happy." After that, everyone else immediately approved my choice, set the bride price and the day of the marriage, and raised their glasses.

Where weddings are concerned, money is no object for Kazakhs. If you don't have any, you take out a loan. Both families pay their share and make their own preparations. After fifteen or twenty days, Uali's entire extended family paid us another visit. As a bridal gift for my parents, they were leading a small, gorgeous rust-brown horse on a halter decorated with fluffy white eagle-owl feathers, its ears pricked up curiously. Our engagement was officially announced, and we celebrated again with food, music, and dancing.

A few weeks later, Uali's parents organised the next wedding party in his village. I wasn't allowed to take part myself, only my relatives and friends. The groom's family and acquaintances gave him gifts such as money, TVs, and household goods to ease the transition into married life.

Finally, at my parents' house they started making elaborate preparations for my departure: hundreds of friends and relatives were due to be invited. The bride always moved to be with her husband. If it happened the other way around, the man would be laughed at and called a wimp.

It was a long, sad farewell …

Goodbye

The bride's send-off on 19 July 2004 was almost as big as the main wedding bash itself. On that day, I wore a white dress embroidered with tendrils and ornamental flowers. We celebrated with maybe four or five hundred guests and our new family in my parents' garden.

Several horses, lambs, and other animals had been slaughtered for the occasion: the tables sagged under the weight of all the lavish dishes. Throughout the party, the guests sang folk songs, gave speeches, and recited poems. For the evening, we'd also rented a large venue. It was mainly for young people to eat and dance, but my proud parents and in-laws joined us, too.

When it was over, I was allowed to spend a couple more days at home. Every morning the table was laid, and other acquaintances or relatives came over to wish me well in person.

On the last afternoon before I left my village, we were all deep in thought. Like my parents, I had been sure beyond any shadow of a doubt that I would stay with them forever. Tomorrow, however, I would be gone. Permanently. The atmosphere was gloomy. My parents' only comfort was that my little brother, Sawulet, wanted to move in with them.

At the final farewell ceremony, there were tears running down all our cheeks. While musicians played and sang long melodies, the guests handed me their last gifts for our new household. My voice was higher than usual; I spoke more quickly, and my eyelids quivered. Gulina, who had already been married for a while, squeezed my hand. Meanwhile my mother kept drifting restlessly to and fro, checking whether I was still there. She wanted to enjoy the sight of me as long as possible. The thought of letting me go was weighing on her heart, and I too hung my head, deeply dejected.

Early the next morning, Uali and his relatives took me to his parents' house in Aksu, followed by a long convoy of cars. Tradition dictated that my father had to stay at home. So he wouldn't feel so lonely, one of my younger sisters kept him company. Only my mother and my other siblings followed in the escort behind us. At the end of it was a truck loaded with my dowry.

It won't be long before we're together like a proper couple, I thought, full of nervous anticipation. Yet there were still many awful days to go before our wedding night.

The wedding itself

Over the four-hour journey on 26 June 2004, the mountains, trees and greenery gradually disappeared behind us, and the land grew increasingly flat, dry, and barren. Summers in Aksu were hotter than ours. I was familiar with the area from previous visits, because many of my mother's relatives lived round there.

We stopped outside Uali's parents' house. There was already a crowd of people gathered around the beautifully decorated tables in the large courtyard. My mother-in-law had warmed some animal fat over the fire for my arrival, so that she could greet me by touching my face with her greased hands. I smiled, because that meant I was welcome and would be treated well by the family.

At long last came the day of the wedding itself. I wore a long red dress, accentuating my slim hips. My head was crowned with a pointed red hat like a sorceress's, trimmed with beaver fur, its height symbolising the purity of the bride. A veil covered my kohl-lined eyes and red lips. Uali, meanwhile, wore a blue velvet suit embroidered with animal motifs. We were in love, enchanted with each other like characters from a fairy tale.

The final verse of the song still echoed as the musician put down his *dombra*. There were butterflies in my stomach as I knelt before him, thinking of my husband's ancestors, while all around us my relatives bowed. The singer carefully lifted the veil from my face with a long stick.

The party kicked off with our first dance as a married couple, and the evening was interspersed with performances, group dancing, competitions, and games. About two in the morning, everyone launched into the wedding song, while our relatives accompanied us to the house. This was common practice, but our arrangements that night were a little unusual.

The bride and groom aren't allowed to be together until all the guests have gone. Because my sisters and relatives were spending the night at Uali's parents' house, I slept with them in their room, and our wedding night had to be postponed. To be honest, I wasn't too upset about that, because I was wiped out, and I fell asleep the minute my head hit the pillow.

Today, looking at the wedding photograph taken on the edge of my parents' village, it scarcely seems real. We're both so young, so good-looking, and so happy, facing one another as we hold hands. In the background is Tian Shan and broad expanses of grassland.

We had no idea that traditional celebrations like ours would soon be forbidden.

Complications

As the bride, it was my job to get up first in the morning, and make breakfast for all the guests and serve them tea. Suddenly, my mother-in-law started shouting from the kitchen. "Sayragul!

Quick! There's an important call from home." There was such heartbreak in her voice that it made me queasy.

I grabbed the phone, but I could barely understand a word my sister said, because her voice was choked with tears. "Our father fell down, his whole body is twitching ..." The night before, our best dairy cow had been found dead on the ground. And the rust-brown horse — my bridal gift — as well as our dog had gone missing. My father had taken it so hard that he'd had a stroke that same night. His face was numb, his head twisted to one side.

The news hit us like a fox set among a flock of chickens. My family rushed home without even waiting for breakfast. I wanted to go with my mother, but our culture prohibited it. Uali and I couldn't visit my old home until we'd received an official invitation from my parents and they had slaughtered a lamb for the occasion. If we didn't abide by the rules, it would bring bad luck on all of us.

Usually, sticking to convention helped us cope with unpredictable situations, but in this case everything was topsy-turvy, and Uali and I were stranded at his parents' house, miserable. "I know this is a very difficult situation for you, Sayragul," said my father-in-law. He let us drive to Uali's house, which was closer to my parents' village.

"At least you'll be together, and from there it will be easier to get news from your relatives," my mother-in-law told me encouragingly.

I was so upset that a wedding night or romantic kissing was out of the question, even at Uali's house. The next morning, my brother Sawulet stopped by briefly so I could see my father before he was taken to hospital. His face paralysed on one side, he was struggling to tell me something, but all that came out were tears and incomprehensible noises. Distressed, I put my arms around him, and we both cried bitterly. "That's enough," interrupted

Sawulet. "You've got to stay in your own house now. If there's any news, we'll tell you later."

Days afterward, another brother told me, "They can't work out what caused it." I started feeling even more restless. Again, the phone rang. I was expecting news about my father, but instead they told me that, on top of everything else, my mother was now seriously ill, too. "What can I do? I can't just sit around at home twiddling my thumbs." Uali and I exchanged despairing glances.

We agreed that my older sister would take my mother to a 27th Bingtuan Division Clinic, which was known for having good doctors. On the way there, she picked me up. My mother was at least able to talk to me in the car, but she didn't have the strength to stand. "My whole body is lifeless," she sighed, her voice weak.

The clinic was staffed entirely by Chinese, but thankfully my sister — who had studied with one of the doctors — had a good relationship with them, so they treated us like everyone else. My sister stayed two weeks until everything was wrapped up, but I drove back after a couple of days, as soon as my mother was able to stand.

My head was spinning, and so was Uali's. We still weren't a real married couple, and we weren't allowed to kiss, because our wedding ceremony hadn't been fully completed. My relatives came up with the solution that saved us. "Just nip back to Aksu and get married a second time!" No sooner said than done. Once again, we invited our guests and cooked up a feast.

By now, my brother had called in a vet to examine the dead dairy cow. "Maybe someone poisoned it during the wedding celebrations," Sawulet wondered. But to everyone's astonishment, the young, completely healthy animal had dropped dead from a heart attack. So Sawulet buried it behind the house. The horse and the dog, on the other hand, remained mysteriously missing.

It's possible that someone took advantage of the situation and stole the horse, since virtually the whole family was away for the wedding; the dog might have run after it. But the cow dying, my father and mother falling ill — those were strange coincidences. I couldn't explain it.

My father suffered a second stroke in hospital. When he came home, he wasn't the same, so we turned to a traditional healer who helped both parents get back on their feet. At least, somewhat.

Endless anxiety

Since officially I still wasn't allowed to visit my father and mother — although I'd seen them outside their house — my father decided to solve the problem. "We'll slaughter a lamb and invite you here, as tradition dictates." After the meal, I was allowed to come over as often as I wanted, without any formalities.

Everything finally seemed to be on the right track, so Uali and I in Aksu cautiously attempted to steal a kiss — but we were interrupted by the phone ringing once again. It was already dark outside. This time, it was my mother on the line. "Come back quick, your sister's had a bad accident." When I told my husband, he stared at me in disbelief. Strangely enough, despite all the misfortune that seemed to be accruing around me, he never doubted that I was the only woman for him.

My sixteen-year-old sister, who had interrupted her studies and come home because of our wedding, was unconscious in bed. She'd been out on her moped, running a quick errand, when a car had ripped off half her heel. Apparently, the driver hadn't seen her. Witnesses at the scene had brought the badly injured girl home.

My mother, Uali, and I drove my sister, now groaning in pain, to the regional hospital that same night. The doctors shook their heads sadly. "We've got to amputate part of her foot. She'll have trouble walking for the rest of her life. My sister, overwhelmed with fear and pain, screamed, "My life is over!"

"No, no, everything will be fine," we told her, and decided to get a second opinion.

Online I found a Chinese surgeon based in Nanjing who thought she probably needed a different operation, but wanted to examine her beforehand. We didn't have to pay anything to bring him over, but if he carried out the operation it would cost us 20,000 yuan. We pooled our money.

The very next day, the Chinese doctor flew to Ghulja and waited for us at the hospital there. "With a bit of luck, she'll be able to walk again," he declared, after assessing the situation. But he couldn't guarantee it. While Uali and my mother drove back, I stayed by my sister's bedside.

Back home, my husband was sorting out a few formalities with the officials in Aksu so that I could teach at the same school as him. After all the stress and agitation, I only had five days to relax before I had to start my new job. Uali was the deputy head, while I worked underneath him. Our workplace was only ten minutes' walk from the house.

More than two weeks after our wedding and a cascade of unfortunate events, we found ourselves alone and undisturbed for the first time. It was 10 July when we finally sat down at the table and had a long talk. Afterwards, we hugged close and kissed, behaving like happy newlyweds for the first time. From the very beginning, Uali proved to be an incredibly loving and gentle husband. We were both ready to give each other everything.

A month later, my mother called me to ask a favour. "Could you give your sister a lift to the hospital for a check-up?"

This trip turned out to have a profound effect on my life.

A mysterious encounter

I'd ordered a minivan for the journey so that my sister could lie down in the back across four seats. Sitting was still impossible. My sister, previously such a lively girl, always chattering merrily away about something or other, had become very withdrawn since the accident.

When she did talk, however, she always asked the same question: "What's going to happen to me now? I'll be disabled, I won't be able to find work, and I'll be a burden to everybody." She'd always been slim, but now she looked as though the next breath of wind might blow her away. She lay down on the back seat, her expression miserable.

I sat up front by the window, leaving a seat free beside me. Along the way, another Kazakh got on: between forty and fifty years old, jet-black hair and eyes, his face as clever and wise as an owl's. I let the landscape slip past in silence until, after a while, I felt the man's eyes on me, like a finger on my skin. I turned to him resolutely. "Do you know me?"

He surveyed me, then replied, "It looks like you recently got married, and now you're having all sorts of problems at your parents' house. It's because when you moved out you took all the energy and strength with you." I swallowed. He continued placidly, "You were always the epicentre of that house. Without you, its stability has collapsed. That's why all these bad things keep happening."

I stared at him, wide-eyed. "How do you know that? Are you a shaman or a soothsayer?" I had no time for bad magic, but it was obvious that this man was different — that he possessed special gifts. Without stopping to think twice, I told him about my sister's accident and that she had to go to the hospital for checkups once a month. I asked him, "Will my sister fully recover?"

The mysterious stranger closed his eyes and leant back, groaning faintly, as though he was watching something sinister. Then he leant forward again and opened his heavy eyelids. "Your sister will be healed, but it will take a long time. She will start a family and be happy."

Deeply moved, I asked him for more advice. "What can I do to bring the situation at my parents' house back into balance?" Again he closed his eyes before giving me an answer. "The next time you visit your parents, you'll enter with a smile and leave with the smile." He paused briefly to let his words sink in.

"If someone hurts you, hide your pain from them. Even if they've done something terrible to you, don't let hatred into your heart. If you can do that, you will be strong and there will be no difficulty you cannot withstand." After a while, he added, "You should take care of yourself. Don't go with your sister every time. You're not alone, there are two of you."

I stared at him in confusion. He lowered his head, and I could tell from his posture that he'd finished talking. He got off at the next stop. Four days later, I discovered I was pregnant, at the age of twenty-eight. It was the best news Uali and I had had! We were unbelievably happy. Everything that man predicted has come true. My younger sister did recover, but it took her two years to be able to walk again properly. She has a good job and a suitable husband, as well as two children.

After this encounter, I tried to be more laid-back about everything. Previously, if a Chinese official tried pushing me around — "Come back tomorrow, we're processing the Chinese applications first" — I'd have seen red. I wouldn't have been able to let it go. Similarly, when someone close to me was sad, I was too quick to feel the same pain they did.

From then on, I've tried to smile even when I'm being

maltreated. I hid the pain of saying goodbye from my sobbing mother and said, "Come on now, I'll be back soon." It did me good.

It might sound strange, but without that piece of advice to guide me, I would never have endured what happened in the years to come.

Envisioning a golden future

Our brick house was in the centre of town, right on the street, next to a bazaar. In the summer, it got as hot as an oven under that red tin roof, but in winter it wasn't ice-cold even when the temperature dropped to minus 24 degrees outside. Sometimes Uali and I lit several coal ovens to heat the three rooms. Outside the house, there was quite a large courtyard, and behind it a beautiful garden with apple trees and a stream, where we planted vegetables.

As my belly grew rounder and rounder, Uali and I hatched plans for the future. "When we have children, we're going to give them a better life than we had." We both agreed on that.

A working couple from a Muslim minority wasn't allowed to have more than two children — that had been law in China since 1992. The Chinese themselves were only allowed one child, which made a lot of them envious. "It's not fair! How come the locals are allowed more children than we are?" In those days, the proportion of Chinese in the area, despite Beijing's resettlement program, was just 20 per cent. Not that high. Today, the figure is nearly four times that.

"Yes, let's work hard. In the future, we'll run a business and earn lots of money." I rubbed my hands, pleased. With more than 500,000 inhabitants, Aksu was an excellent spot for a business.

Unlike the other large towns, it had a good infrastructure, and the municipal facilities were very well built and well organised.

On 19 April 2005, I felt an intense pang in my abdomen. Only my mother went into the hospital room with me: my brothers and sisters as well as my in-laws waited nervously with Uali in the corridor outside. It was a difficult delivery. I was in labour for nearly thirty hours, and by the end I was exhausted and bathed in sweat.

During the delivery, my mother nipped outside to update my countless relatives with news. But the next time, she simply clapped her hands in the corridor and said, "Go home, this is going to take a while!" They'd hardly left, however, before an old Kazakh tradition suddenly popped into her head. "If someone goes home during the birth and comes back later, they have to leave something personal behind. Otherwise an accident will happen." Immediately, she dashed outside to fetch everyone back, but one of my younger brothers was already on the motorway. "Where is he? Bring him back!"

He'd switched off his phone, so he didn't get my sister's call until he was back home two hours later, hanging up his jacket in the hall. "Come back quickly!" Bewildered and anxious, he scratched his head. "Why? You only just sent me home!"

"Hurry up!" ordered my sister, without explaining further. My younger brother was convinced something terrible had happened to me, so he got behind the wheel in tears and hurtled back at breakneck speed. He kept picturing me dying, and was desperate to see me before I breathed my last.

Stricken, he ran into the hospital, where the others immediately reassured him. "Just leave some sort of personal item behind and you can drive back home."

"No, no, I know something's happened. You're lying, you're not telling me the truth. I've got to see my sister." Everybody tried to soothe him. "There's no problem, we only called you back because of the tradition." At last he doubled over laughing, pressed his watch into my mother's hand, and got back into his car.

"We'd like to do a Caesarean," the doctors had suggested by then, but my mother had serious reservations and encouraged me to keep pushing. "It's better not to let that happen — it should be a normal birth." By the time my younger brother was unlocking his front door two hours later, my daughter was born. Without an operation. So he got back into his car and stepped on the gas.

The whole family were beside themselves with joy over the birth of Ukilay. The twentieth of April happened to be the very same day that my mother had been born, fifty-six years earlier. We didn't care whether it was a boy or a girl, only that the child was healthy. Gulina gave birth to her daughter on the same day, too, although she'd been married two years longer than I had. For twenty years, Gulina and I were twins in spirit.

Today, I avoid all contact with my closest friend, because I don't want my presence in her life to put her in mortal danger.

CHAPTER THREE

Mouths Taped Shut

Tightening their grip around our throats

To the west, workers had already laid the foundations for a complex of buildings. We were setting up a small farm, hoping to make a living from the animals. Later on, Uali and I bought an additional piece of land from the neighbouring plot. By the time Ukilay was two years old, we owned four horses, thirty lambs, and four head of cattle.

Our produce proved hugely popular at the markets. Local and Chinese traders alike were warning their friends and relatives against buying products made by Chinese manufacturers, whether food, clothing, shoes, or other items. "Why?" we asked at first, confused. "All the Chinese things contain poisonous chemicals or plasticisers that cause long-term liver damage and make you sick and infertile," everybody told us. That was why the rich Chinese preferred to buy goods from Europe or Turkey for themselves and their children.

Business was good, so our next step was to open a clothing shop for children in a neighbouring village, hiring a sales assistant there. In Aksu itself there were already similar shops — the competition was too fierce. In the village, however, the parents were glad to have us.

Year on year, we built up our profits. In the spring, I had a great time organising and compèring at the Kazakh Nauryz festival. My father composed songs, and one of my musical brothers released a successful CD.

My family was happy, but relations between the Uighurs and

the Chinese were increasingly tense. The Kazakhs in our area were more moderate; there were no revolutionaries among us, so Beijing couldn't blanket-brand the lot of us as Islamic enemies of the state. Still, they were noticeably tightening their grip around the throats of all Muslims in East Turkestan. In 2006, Beijing issued new legislation around what they termed the "bilingual" system, which was a disaster for all of us. Previously, indigenous people — especially in the countryside — had spoken only their mother tongue. Chinese meant nothing to them.

But under the new law, 80 per cent of all new hires in schools had to be Chinese. Effective immediately. If they advertised for, say, twenty new jobs, they would automatically give eighteen to the Chinese and only two to us Muslims. In reality, it wasn't long before virtually 100 per cent of all teachers were Chinese, just like all other public-sector workers.

At our school, a multi-storey building with a large courtyard, almost one thousand children were affected by this sweeping decree. At this point, nearly 97 per cent of the students were Kazakhs, with the rest Uighurs and Muslim Dungan. There wasn't a single Chinese child.

Suddenly, lots of long-serving local teachers found themselves out on their ear, including academics and writers who were left to scratch out a living as security staff. The younger teachers were offered retraining by the government — but it cost money, and took several years before a local was able to teach Chinese as a subject. Those who overcame this hurdle were, from then on, only allowed to teach in what to them was a foreign language.

Uali and I discussed this catastrophe with other local teachers every day. "Where is all this going?" The legislation affected not just our future but that of all our children. Until now, families had naturally spoken their own language at home. "Will our children soon forget their culture and identity? Will this make them Chinese?" some of the mothers wondered, giving voice to the concerns of everyone present.

"We are all one nation," droned the Party officials. On a business trip to Ürümqi, Uali noticed a poster that stuck in his mind. Displayed in a corridor, it broke down the demographics in our region by ethnic group. First on the list were 17 million Uighurs, followed by 3 million Kazakhs.

These days, Beijing usually says there are 11 million Uighurs and 1.2 million Kazakhs. What happened to the other millions? By pursuing a ruthless policy of assimilation, the government has made countless people disappear and turned a colourful, diverse region into a homogenous Chinese state.

The children can't stop crying

During this period, my mind often strayed to my grandfather, who had described the atrocities committed by Mao. Sometimes I'd feel a cold shiver run down my spine. This time, I thought, things would probably be much worse than before. But the Party was still trying to convince us that everything it did was in our best interests. No one in the province would be left behind. Everyone would have a place to sleep and enough food to eat.

"Teach the children to love the Party!" our bosses instructed us. Suddenly, our little children had to carry so many Chinese books to school that they could hardly lift their satchels. In areas such as ours, where there were still more Kazakh teachers, we taught at least one lesson a week in our language, but soon we had to stop that, too.

It didn't help that the Party overloaded the children with so much homework that they'd sometimes have to stay up till one in the morning. How were they supposed to cope? They didn't speak a word of Chinese, but the assignments and books were all printed in these strange characters. It was particularly difficult for ordinary families living in rural areas, because the parents didn't understand any Chinese either. The pressure at school was so intense that the children's behaviour was increasingly disturbed.

In class, I was faced with six- to thirteen-year-olds who were utterly exhausted, ground down, and buffeted by fits of tears. Every day, there were new letters and new words to learn, faster and faster ... it was enough to send them insane. Imagine a class where most of the thirty-six to forty students spend the entire time crying with despair. It was hard for me as a teacher, because I was soon at my own limits, and I had no idea how to help them keep up with the pace.

I did my best to comfort them every day. "The bad times will pass, don't worry. You'll learn it all, you can do it!" Meanwhile the same problems were playing out in the adult world. Our whole society was under enormous stress.

"Maybe we should emigrate to Kazakhstan?" Uali and I kept wondering. But by 2006 it was no longer straightforward for indigenous people to move abroad. Previously, you could take your children on your own passport. Now, however, they had to have their own, but the officials constantly delayed issuing them. It was a difficult process getting a passport for a child.

Retraining a second time

It rapidly became obvious that the government was interested not just in its teachers' Chinese-language skills but in replacing locals with their own people. I was directly affected.

I was called in to see the head. "I know you've already retrained as a teacher, but I'm afraid you can't keep working here, because you're actually a doctor. If you do want to stay, you'll have to do another retraining course."

This change in the law would force me to spend two years at a pedagogical institute in Ürümqi, roughly 1,000 kilometres away. A fireball went off inside my head. They were going to separate me? From my infant child? Never! I quickly averted my face so he wouldn't see how badly the news had affected me.

What kind of mother would willingly leave her less-than-two-year-old child? Alone in a cold and heartless world? Ukilay needed protection, care, and the deep devotion of a loving mother. The thought of being parted from my little daughter nearly broke my heart. And anyway, how could I ask Uali to shoulder yet more responsibility? The farm, the shop — they both needed someone to run them.

At least the new law didn't affect my husband, because he was already a fully qualified teacher. And I was employed on a permanent basis, so the school agreed to continue paying my salary while I was away — although I was still inconsolable. "How am I supposed to live without my little Ukilay?" I covered my face with my hands, and wouldn't remove them.

Seeing me like that, Uali swallowed. "Don't worry," he tried to cheer me up. "I'll take her to work with me. My staff will look after her." At that time, my husband worked in an archive housed in the basement of a school building away from the main block, so it wouldn't disturb anyone if Ukilay cried every once in a while.

Once, when I was so upset that I didn't know what to do, I got into the car and drove to my parents' village. "Father, can I speak to you in private?" I asked him. He picked up his walking stick, gently took my hand, and led me out into the garden, where we were safe from eavesdroppers. He was the only one I could be open with about my frustration with the merciless policies of the Chinese.

With a trembling hand, he brushed the tears from my face and praised me. "You're my cleverest child and my most beloved treasure. Don't let yourself be beaten down by these people. Show them how ambitious you are and that you won't fail at their tasks." Slowly, I lifted my head.

I was one of life's natural high-achievers. Usually, I was passionate about striving to be the best, but I was already missing my daughter as I pressed a goodbye kiss onto her soft lips. I tried to grit my teeth and grab the bull by the horns.

At least we had plenty of friends, acquaintances, and relatives I could visit in Ürümqi. After the move, however, the pain simply would not go away. I walled myself up in my sorrow. Several times a day, I took the picture of my daughter out of my pocket and stared at it longingly, tears running down my face.

When Uali called and told me hoarsely that Ukilay had been rushed to hospital with severe pneumonia, I booked a flight home that same night. When I got to the clinic, he was nearly as white as the walls. My little girl's cheeks were glowing, but she threw her arms around my neck and hugged me as though she never wanted to let go. Nor did I. She was coughing, but I had no choice but to tear myself out of her thin arms and fly back.

Sometimes I'd lie awake in bed in Ürümqi, picturing Uali, Ukilay, and me building a new life over the border in Kazakhstan. After 2008, indigenous people were allowed to travel there as tourists, but public-sector workers like us were forbidden from moving to a foreign country.

On 12 May 2008, a cry went up at the university: "There's been a terrible earthquake in Sichuan!" Roughly 65,000 people had lost their lives. "What happened, exactly?" I asked. "Loads of schools collapsed on top of thousands of children," my fellow students told me.

The problem wasn't really the earthquake — it was shoddy,

botched construction work and corruption. As usual, Party officials covered for each other, whitewashing their own failures. They fed the media heartwarming stories about doctors and aid workers who had sacrificed themselves for the CCP, turning a day of pain into a day of celebration. Parents who protested were quickly got out of the way.

The government ordered a nationwide moment of silence. Heads bowed, I and the other students stood, still in shock, on a square outside the university.

Today, far more innocent people have lost their lives in the government's "vocational training centres". But their deaths are not enough for the CCP to order even a single day of mourning. They won't even bow their heads.

That's how little the lives of their own citizens are worth to them.

"I don't care what anyone else says, I want this baby!"

I left my retraining program with a diploma, but also with stabbing abdominal pain. The doctors suspected gallstones, prescribing strong painkillers delivered in the form of injections.

When I had a follow-up appointment in April, the doctor shook his head. "You've got to do something." I stared at him, puzzled. "You're pregnant, and for the last three months you've been taking a medication with serious side-effects. It's very likely your child will be severely disabled." Then he looked at me over the edge of his glasses. "Wouldn't you prefer to have an abortion? Talk it over with your husband at home. Then we'll sort out an appointment."

I cried the whole way back. When I got home, Uali put his

arm around my shoulders and handed me one handkerchief after another. "If that's what the science tells us, and the doctor says so, then we'll have to have the child aborted." But I dug my heels in. I knew I didn't want that.

One after another, I turned to my sister, my mother, and my friends and acquaintances for advice. They all agreed with Uali. "If that's what the science tells you …" Another month had passed, but I just couldn't go through with it.

Maybe the reason I was so desperate to cling onto the living creature growing inside me was because so much of our everyday lives was dictated from the outside. This time, however, it affected the deepest, most internal things about me. My body and my soul, my life and my love. And I didn't want anyone else telling me what to do.

Perhaps, I thought, they were all wrong. I sent several blood tests to renowned doctors in other cities. Unfortunately, they all confirmed the first doctor's prognosis, and repeated what he'd said about the abortion. But I didn't want to believe it.

From the outset, the pregnancy was a tremendous psychological burden, especially on top of our already long days. At seven in the morning, we dropped off our three-and-a-half-year-old daughter at kindergarten, picked her up at lunchtime for a quick meal at home, and then handed her back over to the carers, sometimes until nine o'clock at night.

Even if the whole world was against me, I was determined to have my second child. Uali kept shooting me reproachful glances. "What will we do if the child is born disabled? How will we keep our jobs? All our problems will be our own fault …" He kept on like this for two months until he finally stopped, partly because I wasn't listening to anyone anymore, and partly because we'd been struck by another twist of fate.

The greatest loss

My beloved father had never fully recovered from his stroke. After several stays in hospital — Uali and I took turns keeping him company there — he died at home on 16 February, at the age of seventy-two.

Four men carried his body in a wooden coffin to the Muslim cemetery. Their route led them past the new cemetery that the Chinese had built for themselves. In the depths of our grief, my family and I had thought, for a brief moment, *There's no point living anymore*. After the burial, silence set in. Apathy. Darkness.

I saw my father in my mind's eye, the way he'd been when I was a little girl. I saw him rounding up the whole village community to build a school. Even the children had helped out, shaping bricks out of clay and building the walls. That school had embodied our sense of national pride; there, the teachers had taught in Kazakh, passing on our culture and traditions. Overnight, the Chinese had trampled everything. They'd destroyed our education system and seized the village school. Today, they teach only in Chinese, even though my father intended the school for our people.

After he died, I was left with a profound sense of unease. Intellectually, I could deal with the loss, but I was powerless against my emotions. Just like my grandfather, he had sensed very early on that disaster was looming for our people. That's why he'd constantly tried to teach me strength. "Don't cry in front of other people, sweetheart. You can't let them see weakness. You've got to accept things the way they are, but stay strong and upright." Fundamentally, he was always telling me the same thing: the same advice the mysterious healer had once told me in the taxi. After that, I tried even harder to take it to heart.

All my life, my father had been my most important source of support. And now, abruptly, he was gone, shaking everything to its core. He was irreplaceable. Later, whenever I visited my widowed mother, I would slip away with an excuse. "I just want to have a quick walk." Strictly speaking, tradition forbade women from visiting the cemetery alone, but I went to see my father's grave anyway. It was beside my grandfather's.

I stood silently in front of his tombstone, my hands folded over my pregnant belly, and asked him for advice, just as I had done for so many years gone. Those conversations with him did me good, because I saw him with the eyes of my soul. I knew he was listening to me, that he was always with me. Even today, my father appears in my dreams and brings me comfort.

A supportive spirit

Sometimes Uali would find me alone in the bedroom, deep in conversation with myself. "Okay, Father, I promise you I'll be strong ..."

"What are you doing?" he'd ask. "Who are you talking to? If you go on like this, you'll go mad. You've *got* to stop." But I think the opposite was true, and it was my father who was stopping me going out of my mind. I told him, "My father was the only one who gave me strength."

Over the next few weeks, whenever someone whispered something into my ear about getting an abortion, I locked myself in my room and refused to eat. By now, Uali understood, and left me in peace. We were both happy when we felt the child move. "Feel that," I'd say to Uali, and he'd put his hand on my belly. "What a strong kid!" he'd say, with a broad smile.

We were constantly reassuring each other. "I'm sure the child will be healthy …" But a moment later we'd doubt ourselves, and be anxious. "How will we cope if …?" Social expectations were extremely high. Meanwhile we were stuck in our hamster wheel, oblivious to everything except the need to keep running.

Six months had passed, and I was still searching in vain for a doctor who would tell me something I hadn't heard from all the others. This time, I had an appointment for an ultrasound with my GP, who was a good friend. When she saw my huge belly, she was horrified. "What? You still haven't had an abortion? The child's still in there?"

And I replied, stern and exhausted: "Don't talk so much. Just tell me how the baby's looking." The doctor moved the scanner over my belly and described what she saw on the screen. "Yes, he's alive. He's got feet, legs, arms, and all his organs. His body is fine, but it's extremely likely that the medication has caused serious brain damage. Do you really want to give birth to an intellectually disabled child?"

Did I know, she asked, what that would mean for our lives?

Self-criticism in three steps

One political campaign followed hard on the heels of another. Since the year before, every public-sector worker had been obliged to undergo a three-step process of self-criticism in front of all their colleagues. In the first step, we had to write down all the mistakes we had ever made regarding the state or the Party, from our birth to the present day. It didn't matter whether we wrote it down at school or at home — the important thing was that we got it done in three days. Every workplace set up a separate office specifically for this purpose, where we would hand in our list.

In the second step, we had to find ways to put our transgressions right. "In the past, I have failed to systematically instil the Party line into the students. From now on, I will be extremely careful to guide the children onto the right path," I wrote. Others noted, "From now on, I will pay my Party fees on time."

At first, my husband and I found it difficult to come up with believable offences and explain them in a plausible way. If you confessed to lapses that were too minor, you would immediately be taken to task by your Party colleagues. "You're an oppositionist. You're taking the mick with these 'mistakes'."

Then followed the third and most challenging step. We had to confess our guilt in front of all our co-workers. The entire staff would be gathered into a single large meeting room. The Party members would choose several teachers from the audience. "You, you, and you, stand up and do your self-criticism."

The chosen teachers would have to read through their list of transgressions out loud. It took ages, because the list started at birth — so most people had accumulated quite a few. "In the past, I haven't always followed the rules of the Party 100 per cent, but in future I will pay the utmost attention to all the guidelines." It was unbelievably humiliating to stand there like an idiot in front of about one hundred people.

It was mortifying enough to go through this experience, but to add insult to injury they would cut your salary or deny you important additional financial benefits. If you were particularly badly affected, it could mean the end of your career. Promotion was impossible, and you were forbidden from receiving prizes or participating in competitions.

As Party members in senior positions who spoke excellent Chinese, Uali and I were not controlled quite as much as the others were, thank God. But Party officials kept meticulous records of all these written confessions, and subsequently brought them out again and again as evidence if they wanted to show that a teacher was unreliable. "Now you're contradicting what you said before," they would admonish someone. "You're a liar, and you've got to be punished ..."

As soon as Uali and I realised that they weren't using these documents to help people improve, but purely to control them, we secretly warned all the local teachers — *You've got to be careful about what you write* — and helped them fill out the forms correctly.

Some of my compatriots weren't as proficient in Chinese, and didn't understand what was being demanded of them. If one of them stumbled into a rash confession, we immediately apologised on their behalf to the relevant authorities, hoping to protect them from punishment. "This teacher doesn't speak very good Chinese, so he didn't phrase what he was saying properly."

Some colleagues confessed things such as, "Ten years ago, when I'd just started teaching, I didn't teach the students Chinese, even though that's their most important language." Or, "Once when I was ill I missed an important Party event." All these confessions were absurdly contrived. Soon everyone was copying from everyone else, because we knew if we gave different or varying answers, we would stand out. And standing out from the crowd was reason enough to be punished.

The best option was to admit errors in teaching or in dealing with other colleagues. You could never confess to wrongdoing when it came to Party policies or the state. If you said, "I always thought Xinjiang was an autonomous republic and that we should be allowed to speak our own language," you'd be labelled a subversive. That could lead to execution.

Beginning in 2016, Party officials started using these documents to justify the mass arrests of my countrymen and -women. The practise of self-criticism helped prepare for the subsequent wave of incarceration: years in advance, they'd already put together lists of the first people to be arrested.

It was this duplicitous long-term planning that enabled them to lock up more than 1 million indigenous people within the span of a few months.

Burning with shame

"Sayragul Sauytbay!"

When my name was called at the next meeting, it hit me like an electric shock. I leapt to my feet at once, despite being heavily pregnant, and addressed the packed hall in a loud voice. "I'm a bad person ... I have made mistakes ... I regret them deeply." There was awkward silence among my colleagues. It was worse than pity.

I was burning with shame. It was all so unfair! I overcame every difficulty, no matter how great, and devoted all my energies towards the school. Normally, teachers worked eight-hour days, but we were kept busy for twelve to fourteen hours at a stretch. I was working my fingers to the bone and I'd done nothing wrong, but I still had to confess my faults in front of everyone.

It wasn't just psychologically stressful, it was unbearable. After this session of self-criticism, I felt awful for a couple of days — I felt like the authorities had played me for a fool. It took me a while after every time to recover from the humiliation.

Uali ran his fingers through his hair. He didn't know what to say. Then he blurted, "What an absurd situation! You've got to make up a lie, then confess that lie in front of all these people and pillory yourself with it." Our Chinese colleagues also had to write down their every deviation from the Party line, baring all and criticising themselves just as we did. But when it was their turn to speak — which rarely happened — they were confident and self-assured. "What is all this? Why are we being asked to confess anything? We've done a good job." Unlike us, they were allowed to get away with saying so.

Indigenous people, however, lived in constant fear of insults and opprobrium. We kept our lips clamped ever more tightly shut, determined not to talk back, and took pains to follow the rules of the Party more scrupulously than ever. We wanted to prove to them that we weren't bad people. We wanted to do everything by the book, always, so that we wouldn't be excluded, despised, insulted, and threatened.

Senior Party officials treated us like children who needed firm but fair leadership, using a mixture of flattery and threats. *Feel the goodness of the Party, follow the Party, and ensure stability* was their credo. They pretended that all these measures were merely there to protect us from "chaos".

Initially, we were convinced that the Party must have a legitimate reason for trying to impose peace and order. Why else would they do all this? Surely not to grind down our self-confidence? To turn us into submissive, clueless conformists? The idea seemed so monstrous that it made no sense to anyone. We even made excuses for their actions. "They must have good intentions. They're genuinely trying to improve our work," said Uali. And I nodded thoughtfully. At first, we reassured each other, encouraging each other to be hopeful. "This is just a passing phase. Everything is bound to be alright soon." But it wasn't.

Deep down, all the local teachers hated this process of belittling themselves in front of the Party, but we did our best to hide it. While our Chinese colleagues continued to defend themselves, we were already used to being treated like second-class citizens. And even when you know that's not true, you still feel guilty — even though you have done nothing wrong.

While our Chinese co-workers worked hard, too, they passed on the most unpleasant tasks to the locals. They weren't subjected to the same burdens as we were, because they belonged — as the Party was continually reaffirming to them — to the "ruling class".

In the beginning, the relentless unfairness made me and Uali angry and disappointed. We felt the slow seeds of hatred begin to take root. But this only made us feel even more like shadows of our former selves, and I remembered the words of the mysterious healer who had warned me that unbridled hatred was ultimately self-destructive. Speaking alone to my father in the evenings, I swore to myself that I would stay strong.

Blood flows through the streets

"Another riot. This time in Ürümqi." Lost in thought, Uali put his hand to his mouth and turned away again distractedly. A Uighur girl from East Turkestan, employed as a migrant worker in Guangzhou, had been raped by several Chinese men. Her relatives had complained to the relevant authorities, but were ignored. It led to a brawl between Chinese and Uighur youth that culminated in an uprising on 5 July 2009, when thousands of Uighurs held a large-scale demonstration to protest against discrimination and unremittingly harsh treatment by the government.

It wasn't long before a big military convoy packed with soldiers headed to the city centre. Friends on the scene reported afterwards, "We saw it with our own eyes: some of the soldiers put on the same clothes as the Uighurs and blended in with the crowds of Uighurs and Chinese. Until then, not much had happened."

But these plain-clothes operatives were carrying sticks and knives. They mainly attacked their own Chinese compatriots, trying to stir up more conflict and give the other soldiers an excuse to crack down. Lots of innocent passers-by were killed.

Someone we knew had a sister who had just been treated for a serious illness at a clinic in the city. She had been discharged with a clean bill of health that very day. The woman was walking down the street, cheerfully telling her mother the good news over the phone — "Everything's fine again now ..." — when suddenly the conversation was broken off. This was the exact moment when the soldiers rolled their tanks into the crowd, crushing the woman under the treads. They never found her body.

By the time they were finished, the streets were running with blood and littered with body parts. There were so many corpses that it was difficult to tell whether they were mostly Chinese, Uighurs, Kazakhs, or other indigenous groups. By the next morning, the clean-up crews had wiped away every trace: it was like it had never happened.

On 6 and 7 July, after this incident, the CCP sent plain-clothes officers door to door at night, prohibiting Han Chinese families from stepping outside for the next two days, or from opening the windows or drawing the curtains. Other ethnic groups were not informed. They went about their business like always, suspecting nothing. What followed next was a widespread "purge" in which many innocent Uighurs and Kazakhs were killed.

A friend from Aksu lost two sons. One was trying to work at his brother's restaurant. The younger one, meanwhile, was in the city helping his friend find a suit for his wedding. The older son died on the street; the younger was murdered in the shop. This mother never saw her children's corpses either.

When word got around about what had happened, Uali and I as well as our friends all went to offer our condolences. She was distraught, of course, but then — abruptly — she refused to say another word about the loss of her sons. All at once, every mourner in Aksu fell silent, even though days earlier they'd been begging the police to return the bodies of their children. If you asked them whether the authorities had finally done something, they silently turned on their heels and walked away. The police must have threatened them with retribution if they kept talking about the dead.

The brutal incident was reported on TV, but was depicted simply as a riot by Uighur terrorists. They were continually coupling the words "Uighur" and "terrorist", linking them like identical twins so that people would think they were the same thing.

Most Kazakhs mocked the coverage. "How come there are suddenly so many terrorists in our homeland — apart from the Chinese? Where have they all come from? And where were they before?" It was broadly taken for granted in the Middle Kingdom — by Chinese as well as all other ethnic groups — that the Party and the government told lies.

Another good friend from Aksu, a Muslim Dungan-Chinese, saw a second, appalling side of the protests. His daughter had been unable to find a job anywhere, despite having a university degree, so he'd used his contacts to get her employment at a crematorium, where the Chinese preferred not to work.

The daughter had been there two months, and was perfectly happy. She was earning a good salary. After the demonstration, however, she refused to leave the house for four days. Her father was furious. "What are you playing at? I went to all that trouble getting a job for you." Crying bitterly, she told him the agonising truth. "I never want to go back there again. I saw things that are so horrible, you can't even imagine them …".

On the evening of the uprising, soldiers had brought countless human bodies to the crematorium on military trucks and dumped them out like rubbish. The daughter's lips trembled as she spoke.

"There were injured people underneath the dead bodies. They were still alive ..."

From the mountain of corpses came the sounds of people moaning for help, and hands stretching towards her. The police had simply kicked them back with their boots. Then they'd tipped them all into the furnace. Her father was so shocked by this that he kept repeating it to anyone who would listen. "They threw living people into the furnace. Living people ..."

Other witnesses reported similar information. It all fitted — like a piece into a jigsaw puzzle. It was clear now where the bodies had gone. No one doubted her story. We believed the state was capable of anything.

Anniversary of the People's Republic: a party no one wanted

"In two months, we'll be celebrating the sixtieth anniversary of the founding of China," the headmaster announced at a teachers' meeting. We had to start preparing in August so that everything would be ready for the enormous celebration by 1 October 2009. Nothing — absolutely nothing — could be allowed to go wrong.

Various work groups were busy planning the event from early in the morning until late at night, focusing on nothing else. It was very stressful for me. I was seven months pregnant. I taught my students all sorts of Communist Party songs and texts. Every line had to be memorised.

If only this were over already, I kept wishing to myself. I was so drained. In the evenings, I would stroke my belly, hoping the stress wasn't hurting the baby. Would the child be in pain when it was born? Would it ever be happy?

The day before the ceremony, all the teachers gathered outside the school to clean up and decorate the buildings and the street. Kick-off was shortly after sunrise, with ranks of people cheering and waving flags.

There were hours of communist songs and Chinese dances, while a voice blared from a loudspeaker: "Xinjiang is an inseparable part of China. Thanks to China's helping hand, Xinjiang has been transformed into a flourishing region." At its core, the celebration was nothing but more repetitive propaganda for a unified China.

My legs were heavy and my belly felt hard. The baby wasn't moving. My mouth sang: "My mother merely gave me my body, but the Party illuminates my heart ..." The celebration went on until late at night, and then we had to clean everything up again. It was immensely stressful and anything but a source of enjoyment.

Uali and I had given up discussing the diktats of the Party. Accepting the inevitable, we did our best to complete each new task, desperate to stay out of trouble.

The crazy mum with the cute baby

In December, my mother and sisters came to visit us in Aksu. It was late by the time they left. Hardly had the door closed behind them when the first contractions set in. My husband and I quickly made arrangements at home and spoke to the employees on our farm, before one of them drove us to hospital through the fog.

At seven in the morning, the driver, Uali, and I shook the porter awake, and he ran to call the doctors. Meanwhile I was pacing up and down the corridor. Anyone who didn't pay in advance didn't get treatment, so at 7.05 Uali hurried off to the payment office in the other building, asking our employee to stay with me.

By now, the contractions were so intense that I called over a nurse. "Please, I can't take any more …". She led me into a nearby room, where the baby practically tumbled out of me. Nobody had done a thing. It was 7.10 am on 15 December 2009.

The doctor on call, who knew nothing about my baby's potential disability, went up to the driver in the corridor and held out his hand. "Congratulations on your new baby!" The man grabbed his phone and called the real father, who was in the middle of handing over the money to the cashier. "Uali, where are you? Your son is here."

"Wait, what? How did that happen so fast?"

One of the nurses picked up the infant to carry him into another room for examination, but I barked in a commanding voice, "Bring me that baby right now! I need to see him!" Both nurses were visibly taken aback to find me issuing orders in such an imperious voice while I was still recovering in bed, and they hastily pressed the infant back into my arms.

I wanted to check properly for myself that there was nothing physically wrong with my son. One, two three … he had all his fingers and toes. His nose and ears were fine. But he was sure to be intellectually disabled. Wanting to check his reflexes, I pinched his cheeks firmly while the nurses watched, feeling sorry for the poor baby and disgusted by his horrible mother. What on earth was this madwoman doing to the child?

"Why isn't he crying?" I wondered. "Can't he feel anything?" I pinched him again. Then I kicked both nurses impatiently out of the room. "Go away, both of you! You don't understand!"

The next day, the doctors gave me the results of their tests and told me that nothing was physically wrong with the child. "Don't worry," they said. It was easier said than done.

Two days later, Uali and I were at home on the sofa, gazing helplessly at our newborn. "What will we do if he can't live on his own? How is he supposed to survive in a world like this?"

His father stroked his chubby cheek and murmured rapturously, "What a cute baby."

There was a queue of visitors outside our door, and the telephone didn't stop ringing, but I didn't want to see anyone or accept any congratulations, because I still wasn't sure about my son's condition. It's customary for Kazakhs to introduce their baby to all their friends and acquaintances with a big party at home, but not until forty days after the birth. "Let's wait until then," I pleaded with Uali.

According to our tradition, a child isn't named until that point. In the past, this was due to a high infant-mortality rate. To our ancestors, newborns were messengers from the subterranean world whose spirits still called to them, their connection only waning after forty days.

As soon as I had recovered mentally from the psychological strain of the last few months, and the forty days had passed, I whispered my son's name three times into his ear — "Ulagat" — and proudly showed him to his grandmother, his aunts and uncles, and everyone else. "I really am a lucky child," I decided, cradling my little Ulagat in my arms.

What more could I ask of life? My husband and I loved one another, we had two wonderful children, and we had worked very hard to build a good life for ourselves. By now, we had opened a second clothing shop in another village, our house was the grandest one in Aksu, and there was a foreign car parked outside our front door: a blue Chevrolet.

In old photos from around that time, you can see us taking the two children to an event near Aksu that involved Kazakh racehorses. Our son Ulagat was five months old, and Ukilay was four. In the background, there are lots of street and shop signs. Not a single one is in Kazakh — all are in Chinese.

Still, when we sat down at the table in the evening and

took stock of our lives, we were satisfied. We had to ignore the bad, otherwise our hopes of better times to come would have been dashed. "It was a difficult start for all of us, but gradually things have come good," we decided. We were some of the most prominent, well-respected figures in Aksu. Relief overwhelmed us: everything was alright.

My husband's health was now my only real cause for concern. Uali was increasingly pale, jittery, and thin. It was like he was disintegrating. The word "break" wasn't in his vocabulary — he'd bring work home from school and slog away till late at night. The constant tension and anxiety about not satisfying his bosses, despite his best efforts, were sapping his strength.

Everything is free, but only if you're Chinese

Sinicisation was the word on everyone's lips in 2010 and 2011, when the government settled vast numbers of Chinese people throughout East Turkestan. It had a profound impact on our homeland. Chinese construction companies moved into every village where Kazakhs were living, building hundreds of homes at breakneck speed. One looked just as featureless as the next. And the remnants of our history and culture were erased along with the old buildings.

Unlike the local people's houses, these blocks not only appeared immaculate from the outside, but were also modern and meticulously designed. They were made available to new occupants by the state, free of charge. All they had to do was pick up the key and move into their new home. If someone wanted to set up a business or run a farm, the state would build them the buildings or stalls they required.

All at once, we were inundated with thousands of people from inland China. Most likely they came of their own accord, because the government even paid their moving costs. Although they received generous financial support, indigenous people received no funding whatsoever, and their mute accusations were increasingly visible in their faces. "We're always getting short-changed." Why were our needs less important?

We were also surprised to find that the "one-child policy", still in force at that time, apparently did not apply to the newcomers, because most of them had two children. "Maybe they're trying to replace us even more quickly," some of the locals speculated warily.

Friends who worked in computer technology were warning us ever more frantically to be careful. "You've got to watch out! Don't talk about politics at home, not even when you're alone." Chinese companies fitted bugs into televisions and other household items. Everyone was being spied on.

Life hadn't been normal for a long time.

The gloves come off

Recently, Uali had started berating himself more and more. "I don't know what's wrong with me! My brain just doesn't work anymore." During long days on the job, he would suddenly get confused and couldn't concentrate. At night, he lay awake, his mind whirring, but by morning his head was empty. It was our situation making him unwell — and there was no medication he could take for that.

So far, Beijing had preferred to use relatively gentle methods of separating us bit by bit from our own culture and traditions, making everything Chinese and stifling all other ways of life. Now, however, their policies turned brutal. They would use any means necessary.

Every once in a while, Uali would be unable to breathe. He was extremely hard on himself, scrabbling desperately to cope with everything thrown at him until all sense of happiness was stamped out. It was inevitable that we would make mistakes, of course, if only because we did so much more work than everyone else. But even as my husband became skeletally thin, he wouldn't stop driving himself. It was like someone was chasing him with a whip.

At his next appointment, the doctor admitted Uali to hospital. Before sending him home a few days later, he issued a warning: "First, you need plenty of time to get better. After that, you should find a job that isn't so stressful. If you keep going like this, you'll drive yourself into the ground."

When the children were asleep, we talked it over at the kitchen table.

"Why don't you spend a couple of weeks at home and relax?" I said soothingly, shifting my chair a bit closer.

"Won't that hurt us too much?" replied Uali doubtfully. He seemed preoccupied, as though he hadn't been listening.

"We already have everything we need, and we've got plenty of savings. I'll keep working at the school by myself. Maybe if you stay home you'll get better soon? I'll cook whatever you like for you. You'll see — your brain cells will be right as rain again before you know it."

"Yeah, maybe it really would be better if I quit," admitted Uali shamefacedly, bowing to the inevitable. From that point on, he focused entirely on our farm and running the business. And, lo and behold, his health slowly began to improve.

Yet *Faster! Higher! Further!* was the watchword for local employees at public-sector workplaces. In 2011, the Party chose our district, of all places, for five schools that would trial a new program. Our duty as head teachers was to improve the instilment of communist moral values in our students. Instead of doing a single flag ceremony on Monday mornings, we now had one every morning. The pupils and teachers were under even more pressure to perform.

As if that wasn't stressful enough, Party officials organised additional events at which they taught communist rules about the "great, glorious and correct Party". Everybody had to take part. Yet again, the children didn't understand a word, and again they were upbraided until the tears were running down their cheeks.

They introduced a new subject, "Xinjiang": a history lesson that was like a stuck record. *Xinjiang is an inseparable part of China.* And not just since Mao — apparently, we've been Chinese for centuries.

My teachers were supposed to read aloud to our students from the freshly printed textbooks. Thanks to the influence of the Chinese, we read, the primitive Uighurs and Kazakhs in this remote region with its backwards culture had learned to live like normal, civilised human beings.

Mouths taped shut

When our son Ulagat was three and a half years old, we sent him to kindergarten, just as we had done with Ukilay. After a while, however, he refused to go. He screamed and wailed, rolled around on the floor, and the minute we tried to put him on his feet, his knees would buckle again. "I'm not going back there ever!" Concerned, I tried to find out what was wrong. "Why not? It's so nice there, you can play with other children."

But the boy was inconsolable. "They shut my mouth, they don't let me talk." It took us a while to understand what exactly had happened. Between Ulagat's wild sobs, we learned that the

Chinese teacher had put sticky tape over his mouth, because he'd been speaking Kazakh to the other children. Uali and I exchanged a horrified glance. "The teacher always does that," said Ulagat helplessly. "I have to walk around with the tape on all day."

"That can't be true," said Uali incredulously, but neither of us was sure. Ulagat buried his face in my chest and clung to me. "It's alright, I'll talk to the teacher," I reassured him, stroking his back. "Everything's going to be fine." But he didn't believe me, and dug his head deep under my arm, as though he was looking for a cave to hide in. "No, it won't be fine. I'm never going back there!"

After making enquiries at the kindergarten, I discovered that it was true: all the Kazakh children who spoke their mother tongue spent the whole day with their mouths taped shut. The staff only removed the tape just before the parents came to pick up their children.

"No, I'm not standing for that," I fumed at home. Uali and I considered moving to Kazakhstan once and for all. Lots of other parents and people we knew had already left East Turkestan, or had packed their suitcases the moment they heard about the way their children were being treated. We'd been waiting for Ulagat's passport for weeks, but his papers still weren't ready. Without a valid passport, we couldn't travel.

After a while, we put the plan on hold for other reasons, too: we were running a highly successful business, and we had friends and family nearby. "It's true we can speak our own language in Kazakhstan, and we do have lots of relatives there, too," we said to each other, "but we'd have to start from scratch. It's not easy to find your feet in a foreign city." So we kept delaying our decision, which turned out to be a grave mistake.

At least we'd found a spot in a private kindergarten for our daughter. The rules there were less strict than in the state-run places, and Ukilay was allowed to speak Kazakh. She might have had problems, but she didn't talk about them.

At home, like all the local parents, we spoke Kazakh with our children. I read them numerous books in our language. And since we're a musical family, we liked listening to traditional music together, too, as well as dancing and playing instruments.

Ukilay had a particularly lovely voice and could play the two-stringed *dombra*. At this point, we were still allowed to teach children that sort of cultural skill. From the outset, however, we told them nothing about the religious rules of Islam. Otherwise, they might have started prattling away in school or kindergarten about their Islamic lessons at home, and we would have been locked up as terrorists.

The Chinese teachers would question indigenous children in school, deliberately targeting their home life: "How do you spend your free time? What do you talk about? Do you also read the Koran?" Then they sedulously collected all the information so they could take the parents away.

Had we explained to Ukilay and Ulagat that they were Muslims and had to pray regularly, it would have put all our lives in danger. Nor did we keep a Koran on the bookshelf. Our bosses had made it crystal clear to us that we had to follow the rules of the Party, never the rules of religion.

We taught the ten commandments to our children as though they were the normal rules of life, the way my grandfather had done. *You must not lie, You must protect the environment and not torment animals, You should never do anything to hurt anyone else.* Those were the rules of religion. The rules of the Party were exactly the opposite.

Since we couldn't find another kindergarten where they were allowed to speak Kazakh at short notice, we simply decided to keep our son at home. "Ah, why not? I'm at home anyway." Uali winked at the little boy. "You can help me out in the barn, can't you?" Ulagat leapt up in a flash, cheering excitedly. "Hurrah!"

Ürümqi: the third-most polluted city

As soon as Uali felt up to taking on new challenges a year later, he accepted a lucrative job offer in Ürümqi. Because he spoke flawless Chinese, he was much in demand at the Chinese construction firm who employed him: working from his computer at the office, he was responsible primarily for monitoring arriving and outgoing construction supplies.

Ürümqi, the regional capital, was a long way from where we lived, but there was a good connection by train and aircraft. I could visit him with the children almost every weekend and be there in under two hours. The company had given Uali a small apartment in the outskirts of the city. "Compared to working at the school, this is child's play," he told us. His work day was capped at eight hours, and his responsibilities were clearly delineated.

Still, even in Ürümqi we had regular conversations about moving to Kazakhstan. "Things are still pretty difficult right now — I can't just drop everything and throw in the towel," I pointed out. "I've got obligations to fulfil first." My promotion had come with even more responsibilities, and the job was twice as hard as before. I didn't want to accept that the stacks of paper on my desk were never going to get any smaller.

On our weekends in Ürümqi, we preferred to avoid the city centre. There were tower blocks everywhere, built much too close together. The streets were choked with cars, and you couldn't get away from the stench, the traffic, and the cries of hawkers. All the pavements were crowded — it was hard to move around with the children, because we were constantly being bumped and jostled.

Smog cast a pall over the city, covering it with a grey veil that blocked out the sunlight. Factory chimneys belched smoke in the background. Ürümqi was famous for a sad statistic: it was the third-most polluted city in China. Luckily, Uali's company and his apartment were somewhat outside it.

"Look, more giant posters," marvelled Ukilay as we stared out of the window in the taxi back to the airport. In fact, since Xi Jinping had become general secretary of the CCP in November 2012 and president of China in March 2013, there wasn't a single part of the country that wasn't plastered with portraits of him and propaganda images in the old-fashioned style favoured by Mao, featuring colourful paintings of peasants. *The people are happy!* and *China is strong, thanks to the Party!* The power of the Party and its leader was soon ubiquitous.

"Cracking down on terrorism" was Beijing's next priority. Xi was stoking fear ever more vigorously, increasingly demonising China's perceived enemies in order to build up his power base even further. More and more people were crammed into the prisons. As of 2014, nearly all five-star hotels were reserved solely for Chinese: it didn't matter how much money indigenous people had. Suddenly, they were making distinctions between Han Chinese and non-Han Chinese citizens at the train stations. They were allowed to go through without security checks, but the rest of us — considered untrustworthy — had to undergo several checks and were sometimes questioned for up to an hour. It reminded me of apartheid in South Africa and the racist Jim Crow laws in the USA, when white people and people of colour were strictly segregated.

At the beginning of 2014, life in Aksu became even more difficult for me. At home, I was gradually drowning in work, while my job at school was becoming more and more complicated and time-consuming, involving extra tasks, more organisation, and more coordination. Our own children were being neglected, so I told my husband on the phone, "It would be better if you came back and spent more time with Ukilay and Ulagat." It wasn't long before he was back with us in Aksu.

Finally reunited as a family, we cheerfully packed our bags on weekends to spend some time in the countryside and relax together. It had been ages since we'd had the opportunity to do that.

July 2014: a deep breath in wonderland

We loved going on trips with other families to the well-known spa resort of Akyaz. The valley, encircled by mountains, is in the middle of the Tian Shan mountains, only four hours from us and near my parents' village. Local people believed the place had curative powers. There were Kazakh-style felt houses built especially for visitors, and lots of horses. And no matter the time of year, it was always green.

Further up the mountains, Kazakh nomads lived with their animals, as they had done for centuries. The water of the River Akyaz glowed in the light of the sun, blue on one side and white on the other, the colours separated by a natural line that seemed painted by an invisible hand. The fairytale landscape attracted plenty of locals, and for a long time it was one of our favourite spots: one of the few places the Chinese hadn't completely ruined.

After 1998, however, a lot of Chinese people started to arrive: initially, to build mines and dig for gold; later, to set up businesses for the streams of Chinese tourists looking for rest and relaxation; and, finally, to charge local people admission fees to visit the places we had traditionally visited for centuries, which was an incredibly humiliating feeling. Still, I took a deep breath every time we got there: after all, this was the land of our ancestors.

On our last visit, we had seen some Chinese engineers taking soil samples by the river. "What are they doing there?" my daughter asked us, but we had no idea — only a dark sense of foreboding. There were too many Chinese looking for gold in our river, dumping mercury and other poisons into the water, and redirecting its course. As a result, the currents were even more powerful, and people and animals in the area started dying from the toxins leaking into the environment. In 2015, the authorities set up a restricted area: no one was allowed in. Since then, we've had no information about what has happened to one of our last ancient sacred places.

We were also enchanted by the beauty of a similarly dreamy mountain landscape nearer Ürümqi, one that again had been mostly home to Kazakhs for centuries. The Chinese had had their eye on Ulanbai for years, until eventually they seized it and started developing it as a tourist destination. Construction companies would usually go around before they started building, plugging their projects and making all sorts of promises to the locals: "You'll make good money, your lives will be great ..." Often, the farmers would believe them, selling their pastureland for peanuts. They realised too late that they would never see a share of the profits and that most of the jobs went to the Chinese.

This time, however, the Chinese encountered resistance from more urbanised, educated Kazakhs. In 2014, tensions led to a major clash in Ulanbai between Kazakhs from Ürümqi and the Chinese military. The incident was well documented in articles and even in several video recordings, in which you can see the Chinese razing houses and beating up women who are running away from them. Many of our compatriots ended up in hospital. The violence even led to a brief conflict between the Kazakh and

Chinese governments, although Beijing ultimately prevailed. In corrupt systems, even political concessions can be bought.

The state-run media reported on the resistance in typical fashion: "Beijing is attempting to bring prosperity to the country, but a few uneducated and aggressive troublemakers have tried in vain to stymie that."

For generations, most indigenous people have suppressed the pain of being subjugated for fear of punishment. And just like our grandparents did for our parents, Uali and I protected our children with silence, telling them nothing about the history and politics of our country. We accepted every slap to the face with resignation. Like slaves in chains.

We had never learned to think for ourselves, and never practised expressing criticism. In China, there was no free thought and no leeway given to try out other things independently. Since childhood, we'd been used to having minimal room for manoeuvre — it seemed like everything was laid out for us, so it never occurred to us to decide for ourselves what we wanted. Yet these limitations consisted solely of the fear they had instilled in us. The CCP was afraid we would find out what lay beyond those limitations.

Our characters, like our landscape, were in ruins. But how else can people in a society such as China's be expected to react? The Party had broken our spirits and our health. Looking back, it makes my blood boil. Everything we had done to please them, hoping they would let us live in peace, was a waste of time. All our efforts were for nothing. For nothing!

At the time, I wasn't aware of the tremendous weight on my shoulders. It wasn't until I reached the West that I found the courage to express my disgust with the CCP and openly distance myself — to say, "I'm not a Party member anymore!" And at that moment, I felt an enormous sense of relief, as though I'd taken off a rucksack filled with lead. It was as if I'd learnt to fly.

But I had a bitter road full of pain and misery ahead of me before I reached that point.

The three evils

It was like we were a powder keg, and the government had lit a long fuse. Suddenly, everything exploded all at once. There were so many protests and frustration-led attacks during this period that we almost stopped paying attention.

When several masked people launched a knife attack at a train station in Kunming in March, or when there was an attack at a vegetable market in Ürümqi in April 2014, for instance, I completely erased the incidents from my memory. Uighur terrorists had apparently set off bombs at the market, killing dozens of people and injuring more than one hundred.

Religious fanatics from abroad, the Party told us, were inciting Uighurs to commit acts of violence. "We will snuff out the flames of terrorism!" they announced. Every day, they talked about what they called the three evils: terrorism, extremism, and separatism. Hour after hour, they demonstrated their superior power on state television, parading images of counterterrorist activities: armed security forces stormed apartment blocks and arrested suspects who were later executed. Documents have since revealed that as early as 2014 the Chinese government was inviting companies to tender for projects to build the first camps for Muslims.

Hoping to stop Ukilay and Ulagat asking the wrong questions, I only let them watch children's TV. Our daughter was already in Year Four, and was a very hardworking student. To my relief, I had found a place for our son in one of the five kindergartens that I ran from 2015 onwards. I could keep an eye on him there. My children were always asking me, "Why aren't we allowed to speak our language in class?" I would respond concisely. "Because that's what the authorities want." After a while, they stopped asking questions.

Glued to the TV in the evening, Uali and I wrung our hands. China had seen its first horrific suicide bombings. In numerous speeches, Xi Jinping warned that terrorists who had gained experience in Syria and Afghanistan might carry out attacks in Xinjiang at any time.

We weren't sure whether terrorists were actually active in Xinjiang. There wasn't much evidence, so it wasn't clear who was behind the attacks and if they really did have connections abroad. "But even if it is true," complained Uali, "there aren't any Kazakhs among these radicals." Besides, what was the point of explaining? Our people weren't going to Afghanistan or Syria to fight: we were fighting for survival in our own homeland.

Generally speaking, Kazakhs in East Turkestan were in a better position than Uighurs in other areas. Fewer of us were unemployed or living in such poverty. The Kazakh government had good economic relationships with Kazakhs in East Turkestan, although Beijing had already started slowly trying to undermine this.

We never believed any of the government propaganda about the Uighurs. So many of them were our friends, fellow students, co-workers, and acquaintances. As Turkic peoples, we were culturally alike. Our language, culture, and architecture were similar. We intermarried. They were totally normal people like us, who worked hard and just wanted to live in peace.

It's possible that there were a few radicals among them, as in any other country, but that did not justify labelling an entire religious group as terrorists. To do so was anything but a wise response to the violence of individuals. Yet the Party never missed an opportunity to turn Muslim minorities against each other and whip up prejudice among the Chinese.

Even so, any halfway-educated person knew what the government's true intentions were. They were using the Uighurs like pieces on a chessboard, plotting their next moves. Xi Jinping was running a new televised campaign of intimidation against all Muslims. "The population of Xinjiang has a period of painful treatment ahead," it ran. There would be "no more mercy".

But how could we have predicted a scenario like this, one that has never before existed at this scale? One that not even the most brilliant thinkers in their most horrifying visions of the future had ever described? The inhabitants of Xinjiang were facing the establishment of the biggest surveillance state on the planet, one that could call upon big data and the most modern information technology the twenty-first century had to offer.

It was the end of all self-determination.

Passports revoked

"All public-sector workers must hand in their passports," the authorities demanded. "Why?" we asked, shocked. Their reasons were brief: "It's harmless. We're just modernising some of the technology to make our jobs easier. We want to re-register all the data." When some people still hesitated, they tried to be reassuring: "You'll get your passports back quickly."

By now, however, many indigenous people were sceptical — we suspected that the authorities had other intentions altogether. Maybe they wanted to stop us travelling abroad? To trap us in our own country? We kept asking the same questions, trying to postpone handing over our passports. They responded by setting a deadline at the end of April. Anyone who missed it would be punished.

Since Uali was in early retirement and no longer working in the public sector, he was allowed to keep his passport. But with a queasy feeling in the pit of my stomach, I handed over mine. Of course, it wasn't just locals who had to do this; the Chinese did, too. However, as I stood in the queue, I watched as they gave the Chinese back their passports while they took ours away.

That night, my husband and I lay face to face. "I hope I'll get my passport back soon," I said anxiously.

"Everything will be fine," Uali told me, brushing the hair from my face, but his voice sounded like he didn't believe it. "Go to sleep!"

We had no idea that the border guards had already received instructions from the government not to let public-sector workers travel without special permission. Even with my passport, I wouldn't have been allowed to cross.

Apparently, they were trying to stop people like me revealing state secrets or information about the oppression of minorities in Xinjiang. Nothing frightened Beijing more than negative stories being leaked about China, damaging its image and booming economy, and slowing its rise to the pinnacle of global dominance. The Party magazine *The Search for the Truth* required leading Party members to communicate only positive stories about the Middle Kingdom internationally.

My husband and I didn't want to spend another day in this vast open-air prison. Our minds were made up. We were moving to Kazakhstan permanently. I fought doggedly for months to get my passport back, laying out my reasons to the officials: "I just want to make a brief visit to Kazakhstan to see our relatives with my family. Then we'll come straight back."

But they kept putting me off with excuses.

Time to say goodbye

In the past, we had sometimes gone years without feeling the painful impact of Beijing's politics in our everyday life. Then months. Then weeks. Soon, just days. And now every second counted.

At night, Uali and I stood under an apple tree in the garden. "Our children don't have a future in our own country anymore. You've got to try to get your passports as soon as possible so you can escape to Kazakhstan," I whispered. "If things keep going at this pace, it won't be long before the three of you can't travel either."

Rather than thinking about myself, I had decided to put my family first. Uali swallowed. The Adam's apple in his thin neck bobbed up and down. He lowered his head, and after a long, pensive silence, he said, "Yes, maybe you're right. I should travel on ahead with the children." I took both his hands and spoke to him beseechingly. "I'll follow you as soon as I have my passport."

I was still clinging to that hope, like a drowning woman to a frail twig. The next day, Uali informed the relevant officials that he was taking the children to visit relatives for two months. They were still not allowing me to leave. "Right now, it's difficult to get a travel permit for you," they said. "Let your family go on ahead by themselves. You can always join them for a few days afterwards."

It was risky, but we told both children we'd decided to turn our backs on our homeland forever. "In Kazakhstan," we said, "life is better. You're allowed to speak your own language there." We didn't want to lie to Ukilay and Ulagat. The plan was for Uali to rent an apartment in the capital city, Astana, find a job, and enrol the children in school.

In July 2016, we finalised all our preparations and packed our bags. I was the one registered to use the vehicle, so if we were travelling a long distance I had to drive. I got behind the wheel and drove my family eight hours to the border crossing at Khorgas. There were no hold-ups on the motorway, but only the usual checkpoints on entering and leaving the city. These days, you wouldn't get that far, because even on short trips they've started scanning the faces of everyone in the car at regular checkpoints.

Even from a distance, we saw the enormous complex of buildings at the border, a bit like an airport. I parked in a carpark, near the entrance. Uali and I got out without a word and hugged. For the benefit of the children, we were acting like we were saying a completely normal goodbye — as though I was just popping over to the baker to buy bread. But it still hit them hard. They stayed sitting in the car for ages, crying.

I felt like sobbing, too, but I cleared my throat, coughed, and pretended to have something stuck in there. I couldn't let them see their mother sad and deeply afraid. My voice scratchy, I told them, "You're going on ahead now, and I'll join you soon." At that, Ukilay and Ulagat cried even more loudly. "I've just got a few things to do, but I promise you I'll come as soon as possible," I said, adding, "I'm not leaving you alone. After all, I love you more than anything in this world."

The children knew that was the truth, and they followed us into the large terminal, which was teeming with people. Uniformed guards and cameras were everywhere. Just like at the airport, only people with the correct papers were allowed through the checkpoint.

Uali held my clammy hands, tears welling up in his eyes. "The most important thing is that you try to get your passport back as soon as possible," he said firmly. "Don't worry about getting our money or our possessions out — just leave everything." Inside, we were both torn: we hoped that I would join them soon, but we knew that might be impossible. It was hard to take our eyes off one another, but we did our best to put our children's minds at rest; besides, time was short.

Holding hands with both children, Uali walked away beyond the barrier, while Ukilay and Ulagat kept turning around to look at me, tripping over their own feet. I waved until at last the three of them had disappeared into the crowd. Then I got into the car and drove back.

Outside our house, I cut the engine and ran into the empty apartment. Stopping short in the hall, I collapsed onto the floor like a loose bundle of rags. There was a brief silence. Then I started screaming and wailing. I'd lost everything! It was all gone! Eventually, I stopped moving and sat upright. My voice shrank into a whisper, then fell utterly silent. I froze like that, unable to move. "Father, forgive me for being so weak …"

CHAPTER FOUR

Worse Than a Mental Hospital: the world's biggest surveillance state

A tyrant from Tibet comes to East Turkestan

In August 2016, the president appointed a new Party secretary for East Turkestan. The man chosen for the task was Chen Quanguo. Over the previous seven years, he had been responsible for destroying the culture and way of life of indigenous people in neighbouring Tibet. Many people knew his history. Visitors from Tibet told everyone that it was his inhumane policies that had driven monks to douse themselves in petrol and publicly burn themselves alive.

The news spread like wildfire through Aksu: "That mass-murderer is coming to Xinjiang!" All our friends were talking about it. "What's going to happen to us now?" they wondered frantically. We were all terrified.

Meanwhile Party officials were kicking the propaganda machine into high gear. "This man is a master of organisation and a great leader of the people. He has brought great prosperity to the developing country of Tibet within a very short span of time. When he comes to Xinjiang, all of you will profit from the economic boom!" They tried everything they could to make him palatable, but it only made us more panicky. We knew that the truth was always the exact opposite of the line the Party tried to sell us.

When the news of Chen Quanguo's first decision reached us, we turned pale. "The rest of you have to turn in your passports, too," they told us. "Including children and the elderly." At that moment, all hope within me was briefly extinguished. *I'll never get out of here*, I thought.

Every fifty to one hundred metres down the roads, small concrete bunkers sprouted out of the ground like mushrooms: checkpoints. Police officers and auxiliary personnel in black, blue, and yellow uniforms were on every corner, stopping passers-by and demanding to see their papers. There was barely any point in putting your ID away anymore, because you had to pull it out again a minute later. Travelling one hundred metres soon took an hour. Then, abruptly, they informed us that all citizens had to report for a health check.

Anyone who did not cooperate was instructed to go to the police station.

We were astonished when — after an AIDS test and blood samples — we were told to report to the nearest police station for an eye scan. They'd sent them our healthcare data without asking permission.

"The third generation of ID cards is coming out soon, so we need specific information," they sighed, before making a short video recording of every single person. "Please smile, now look sad, turn left and then to the right ... and while we're at it, let's take some voice samples, too."

Why would they need samples of our voices for a new ID? "It's for your own safety," they emphasised. People were so afraid that they tried to sugar-coat the situation, grasping for an explanation that would reassure them. "If they're using the latest methods," they rationalised, "then it makes sense that they'd need that sort of information." Using all the data they had gathered, the state was soon able to track every step taken by every single person in East Turkestan.

During this period, organ harvesting started to become a worrying issue in our area. In the city of Kuytun, people had found the bodies of two Dungan-Chinese children under a bridge. Their organs had been removed. Video recordings of the family screaming and crying beside the brutalised little bodies rapidly found their way onto countless forums. Yet by the very next day, all trace of the footage had been expunged. Around the same time, passers-by in Ürümqi had stumbled across two female students, one Kazakh and one Uighur, whose bodies had been cut open and then carelessly discarded by the perpetrators.

Who were we to the CCP? It was a question of none of us dared to ask out loud, because nobody could bear to hear the answer. I watched expressionlessly as workers installed dozens of cameras in every single state-owned building, including at the entrances and in the playrooms at our kindergartens. Why were they doing that?

Shops and tailors that had long sold or made traditional clothing were forced to close. Police confiscated their goods, dragged the owners to court and then to prison, and put the workers into camps.

Meeting in secret: setting up vocational training centres

It was about seven in the evening. I hadn't even taken off my shoes when the telephone rang. "You need to be at a secret meeting in Zhaosu in two hours," a Party member informed me. No further explanation. I hurriedly tidied my hair before jumping into the car and setting off. Arriving around nine, I found 180 other senior Muslim public-sector workers gathered outside the main offices of the county Party committee. We shook hands in the wintry chill and introduced ourselves. "And where do you come from?" I asked the people around me. It was so cold that our breath was foggy. All of us held senior positions at hospitals and educational institutions, and had been hastily summoned from the surrounding towns. Nobody knew what to expect.

Looking back, I'd say this meeting took place in early November 2016, but I can't be sure exactly what day it was. I used to be able to store several ID numbers and complicated strings of digits in my head for weeks — even if I saw a phone number as I was whizzing past it on the motorway, it would be lodged in my memory. But now? After my traumatic experiences in the camp, memories sometimes slip through my brain like it's a sieve. My mind is so crammed with junk that nothing else can squeeze in. I can't tell my story in a tidy, well-ordered way. I keep forgetting things that later pop into my head, so it looks like I'm getting tangled up in contradictions.

They collected our phones and handbags as we went inside, then guided us into a hall filled with chairs. Running the meeting from the podium were five or six high-ranking security officers in various military uniforms, as well as other important figures from the Party leadership. The main topic of the evening was as follows: "How do we achieve stability in Xinjiang?" The second question was: "What is the most effective way to combat religious extremism?"

One of the officials was the director of the education authority, an extremely ugly Chinese woman by the name of Yang Tianhua, who gave a shockingly offensive speech. She was of medium height, with a dark braid down to her hips. "In the future, we will eradicate all malignant thought contaminated with ideological viruses from the minds of indigenous peoples!" I glanced around, irritated, but everyone was staring at her as though spellbound.

As a senior official, she wore the typical blue communist uniform: jacket, blouse, and trousers, plus a metal badge pinned to her chest bearing the Party insignia, a small red flag, and a gold hammer and sickle. In recent years, teachers and school heads had also been forced to wear this outfit — not just for official events, but during the workday itself.

Towards the end of the meeting, the other Party officials matter-of-factly explained how they planned to "deradicalise" Muslim separatists. "In order to achieve our goal of stability," they announced, "we are going to set up re-education camps." It was as though our brains had to translate this horrifying statement before we could absorb it. They didn't provide exact figures or any real information on the size of the camps, but they did emphasise that it would be on a large scale. People in the room started fidgeting as though they were sitting on hot coals.

It was the first time we'd heard anything about these camps. The person who read out the statement was holding several documents in his hand, but only shared a few snippets with us. It was obvious he'd left most of the information out. Nor did he fully answer our questions afterwards. Something was wrong. A murmur swept through the room like a wave.

People in the audience kept raising their hands to make sure. "We don't quite understand what's being set up here. What does 're-education camp' mean?" A senior military official hastened to reassure the troubled crowd. "Don't worry. It won't affect well-respected people like you, of course. These are merely a few simple measures to support less-educated indigenous people — to help them retrain and learn new jobs. They're perfectly ordinary training centres."

Before we were allowed to leave — by now it was coming up to twelve o'clock — the Party bosses stressed that everything we had heard that night was to be kept strictly confidential. Nobody was allowed to discuss the meeting. We were instructed to hand in our phones and bags at the entrance outside, un-asked, at all future meetings. "It is strictly forbidden to take notes or photos, or make video or sound recordings," they emphasised. By two in the morning, I was back home. Everything was dark.

There was no one to tell about the appalling things I had heard.

Unannounced inspections

Countless other secret meetings with senior officials have taken place since that night — sometimes at the town hall, and sometimes at various government offices. At one of these, they focused on the one-child policy. Everyone who ran a kindergarten or a school was ordered to find out which of their employees had broken the rules since the introduction of the policy in 1980 and had more than two children. This was even though all those couples had already been punished — so we didn't understand the point of starting all over again in 2016.

One insane measure followed another. The next time, I was told to make sure that every apartment of every one of my hundred employees was inspected. As each house was searched, I filled out a form that included several questions about the furnishings. "Are there religious items such as a prayer mat or foreign articles from Kazakhstan or Turkey?" Then I had to go through their bookshelves with a colleague to record the individual titles. Obviously, these inspections had to be unannounced. Anything from a foreign country was suspect, taken as an indication of terrorist activities.

It cut me to the quick every time, but all traces of our culture were condemned — ornaments on the wall, for instance, or colourful tassels or decorative knives with gilded hilts. I did my best to be present during as many of these visits as I could, trying to shield my compatriots as much as possible and list as few of the articles as we could get away with. "It's better if you throw away or destroy certain things. Otherwise they could put you in danger," I urged them. We even lifted up the corners of the carpets and checked the manufacturers. "It's best to remove all the labels so you can't tell it came from abroad."

I wasn't worried that my local colleagues would get me in trouble with the higher-ups for giving this advice. Most of them had known me for years, and respected my fairness. Anyone who worked hard in my kindergartens was rewarded, regardless of whether they were Kazakh or Chinese. Everybody knew my intentions were good. In any case, Muslims were a majority here, so most of the staff were affected by these measures, too.

If I happened to be doing an inspection with one of my few Chinese employees, I would tip off my indigenous colleagues in advance as a precaution. As a result, there wouldn't be much to take issue with during the search itself. We would dutifully take our photos and fill out the forms together.

Cutting off contact

"Muslim terrorists are trying to topple Xinjiang into chaos." You heard it on the radio, on the TV, and from senior Party functionaries at work. Yet the chaos in our homeland was caused not by terrorists but by Beijing and the Party itself.

Living in East Turkestan, it increasingly felt like we were waiting for a massive volcanic eruption. More and more people were disappearing from the streets. The police would drive around the neighbourhood, arresting friends and acquaintances. Nobody ever returned. Soon there were virtually no young men to be seen. What on earth was going on?

One day, the authorities started rationing sugar, because sugar could be used to build a bomb. Of course, Kazakhs don't use much sugar anyway, unless someone's baking a cake, so it didn't really affect us. What did affect us, however, was when the authorities suddenly started sending someone once a month to check the electricity meter in our homes. If you were using more energy than usual, they interpreted this as a sure sign you were doing something illicit — you had to be preparing for a terrorist attack. Imprisonment, in these cases, was the only option.

In schools and kindergartens, convoys of workers arrived to top the walls with barbed wire. They put up watchtowers and fences too high to climb over. The whole place started looking like a high-security wing. Even our doors were fitted with steel reinforcements. And everywhere, on every corner, in the playrooms and the corridors, the cameras were watching.

I gazed pensively out of my office window into the courtyard below. Before my colleagues parked their cars, they showed their IDs to the security guards. Every day, the same game. You showed your papers and trotted out your little speech: "I confirm that I work here." This procedure alone took nearly half an hour.

The only pleasure I had left were my telephone calls with Uali and the children. We communicated via WeChat, a Chinese app similar to WhatsApp, almost every evening. "The kids miss you so much," said Uali. "The little one cries for you all the time and asks when you're coming back."

"Put them on the phone," I demanded, and made a promise to Ukilay and Ulagat one after another. "I'll have my passport soon, then I'll come to you." I tried to sound as confident and relaxed as possible.

The next time I called, Uali told me how bitterly cold it was in Astana. "It's minus forty here. The children can't stand it here much longer — partly because of the icy temperatures and partly because they feel like they're too far away from you. We're going to move to Almaty." It was closer to the border with East Turkestan, and the climate was milder.

"Mama, when are you coming?" The children were wailing in the background. Uali turned around to soothe them. "As soon as we're near the border, your mother can be with you in just a few hours." But I could tell how tense he was. "Sayragul, please tell them that's true." Ukilay and Ulagat laughed with relief when I confirmed what he'd said. Then Uali took the phone, went into the other room by himself and started speaking in hushed tones. "Please try and get your passport as fast as possible so you can be with us for the holidays in January."

"Yes," I replied. "I'll try."

After that, all contact was broken off. In November 2016, the authorities cut all communication between Kazakhstan and China via WeChat, phone, or the internet. Nobody was allowed to keep in touch with the outside world via those technologies.

All those apps were now banned. We had to delete them immediately, or face draconian penalties. Not long afterwards, they forced us to lug our computers, laptops, and mobile phones down to security stations, where officers checked the contents of every device. The night before, I spent ages staring at the message on my screen — *We miss you...!* — before deleting our last texts.

The following day, I filled out a form listing all my customer numbers, everything installed on the machines, and every program I'd downloaded onto my phone and computer. But they had a host of other questions, too. "How many people live in your household? How many animals do you keep? How many electronic devices do you own?" When I handed in the piece of paper, the Chinese official told me, "From now on we can seize and check any phone, landline, or computer at any time." It was obvious from his crooked grin how much he relished his power.

It wasn't until I reached the West that I learned they used these opportunities to install spyware like Fengcai (which roughly translates to Bees Collecting Honey) on our mobile phones. They used these apps to gather incredibly intimate data, neatly sorted into categories such as text messages, contacts, calendars, and photos. They searched everything for suspicious key words like "Taiwan" or "Islam", which would immediately alert the security services. Even people simply travelling into Xinjiang would unwittingly have their phones tampered with in a similar fashion.

Heading into work, I felt the colour drain from my face as I showed an officer my papers. Who would he see me as today? A spy, a traitor, or a kindergarten head teacher? From January 2017, the police redoubled their arrests of people with relatives or friends abroad.

I was considered a "suspicious element", since my husband and children had stayed in Kazakhstan. If I was arrested as the wife of a "spy", the officials would find the telephone numbers of my mother, sisters, and brothers on my phone, and then they would be implicated as well. Trying not to put my relatives in unnecessary danger, I avoided contact with them as much as possible from then on. I didn't even dare call my mother anymore to ask how she was.

Loneliness had crept into our hearts.

Political re-education

Nothing was the same after that. Our lives were turned upside down. After collecting the indigenous population's passports, they changed any name that sounded Muslim or religious, and renamed the person something simple, usually Chinese. Hussein suddenly became Wu.

It was decided we needed a new look to go with our new names. Every Muslim man wore a beard, but unless he wanted to be arrested, he now had to shave it off. One seventy-year-old neighbour refused. One day, a few Party members barged into his home, tied the old man's hands behind his back, and forcibly removed his white beard. The man kept shouting the whole time, "What are you doing? You're cutting off my beard, but it will grow back." They put him in a camp for seven years.

Our social life was obliterated. Nobody dared stop to chat on the street anymore. Nobody wanted to celebrate as a group at a restaurant or meet up at a café. And anybody brave enough to throw a big traditional wedding or invite lots of people to the funeral of a relative had to submit their guest list in advance and state the names of the organisers. All of a sudden, there were cameras everywhere; the streets were full of police, and the tea houses were almost empty.

If you wanted to meet up with friends, you had to ask the police or the relevant security agency for permission in advance. It took days to receive an answer, which would usually tell you that the event had to be over by 9.30. If you wanted to invite people for a meal at a restaurant, you had to give your name and submit to an interrogation by the police, who would ask you why you had organised it.

Nobody wanted to stick their neck out. No more than two or three people were allowed to eat together at a restaurant, if they happened to meet by chance. Who'd want to go out under those conditions? Most people stayed at home, silently loathing the government and its despotism. Police cars patrolled the streets twenty-four hours a day, sirens on and lights flashing. No respite. Nobody was allowed to speak out.

Officers in uniform might show up unexpectedly at any time to drag people away. Some they shook awake in the middle of the night; others were informed in advance that they would be brought to a re-education camp in the next couple of days. Several people hanged themselves in their homes before they could be taken. Many children were left behind with no one to look after them, so the CCP took them to an orphanage. Others died on the street.

Outwardly, the Party continued to speak in euphemisms about "vocational training centres" where indigenous minorities would "become qualified" and "graduate from school". But why were the police dragging people away in handcuffs at night if they were merely taking them to a school? Everybody knew people were tortured and murdered in those camps. "You can't pull up every weed lurking among the crops one by one," Chinese inspectors in yellow body armour laughed mockingly. "You've got to spray chemicals if you want to annihilate everything."

We were all in a constant state of fear, waiting for heavily armed men to burst through our front doors. *When will I be taken?* I made preparations, like everyone else. I stuffed a pair of shoes, a nightgown, a toothbrush, and a change of clothes into a bag I hung on the wall behind the door, so that if I was arrested I could grab it on the way out.

When I think back, it feels like I was living in a warzone. During the Second World War, soldiers gunned people down like dogs: that was how they were killed. Killing in the twenty-first century, however, was different: we were perpetually being tortured psychologically. The government was waging a special kind of warfare against an entire population. They're killing us slowly, even now, piece by piece. Every morning, a part of you dies. Inside a few months, our lives had turned into a nightmare.

The world looks away

At some point during this shambles, a delegation of high-ranking officials from Xinjiang were invited to Beijing. It was decided that, from 2020 onwards, the borders of East Turkestan would be sealed. Nobody would be allowed to leave, and no one would be allowed in without supervision. That privilege would be reserved for certain public officials.

One of the politicians at the meeting announced the decision, and the news soon spread online, communicated in sombre Kazakh: "We have been informed that the whole of Xinjiang is to be closed off." I was stunned. I had no one left to talk to, so I spoke quietly to myself. "It's like North Korea."

The next day, we all received the same news again, but this time it was crossed out with a red X. Reports marked with a bright red cross were how the Party responded to the leak of classified information. They added a warning: "This rumour is untrue."

We were all required to read it and pass it on. This way, it reached the few people who hadn't already heard about it. Essentially, the Party had just made this "confidential" information public. And we all knew that if the government claimed something was a lie, then it had to be the truth. It made our blood run cold.

Not long afterwards, we received the next crossed-out bulletin: as Kazakhs, we had to be careful, because there was an anti-Chinese organisation in Kazakhstan called Atajurt. Anyone connected to this organisation or its chairman would be arrested immediately. From this point on, all Kazakhs were kept informed that there was an organisation in Kazakhstan that was documenting human-rights abuses in China by systematically questioning people who had escaped. "At least they haven't forgotten us," I sighed, relieved.

Yet I was still losing sleep over the first report. What would happen to us in 2020 if the Party imprisoned us in our own country? There would be no one to witness the crimes they were committing. Would they kill all the minorities and free thinkers? The idea of being so completely alone and isolated from the rest of the world was paralysing. *Who gave Beijing so much power that they're allowed to arrest, torture and murder us, unchecked and unpunished? Aren't there any other countries that could intervene and stop these atrocities? Why is there no end to the constant stream of arrests, day after day? When will it all stop? Why does no one in the world see us? Why isn't the international community protesting?* I kept racking my brains, but I had no answers.

If the world keeps its eyes averted, I thought feverishly, *they'll end up exterminating millions of people — a whole ethnic group — at a single stroke. Genocide.*

And then my front door burst open.

CHAPTER FIVE

Total Control: interrogations and rape

January 2017: the first interrogation

Before driving home around eight o'clock, I'd checked all the kindergartens. I was just making myself something to eat in the kitchen when I heard a noise at the front door, then a stampede of approaching footsteps. A moment later, three heavily armed Chinese policemen were blocking my escape route.

For a split second, the room began to spin; my mind raced. *They're going to put me in a camp!* I was certain of it.

"Come on," one of the men ordered me.

"Where are we going?" My voice was as thin as a breaking thread.

"You don't need to know. Come with us!"

I was still holding my phone, but a moment later one of the officers grabbed it off me and handed it to someone else. I didn't have time to change: I was still wearing my blue Party uniform from work. They didn't let me put my coat on or pick up the bag I'd packed for just such an emergency. Suddenly, everything went dark. They'd slipped a black hood over my head from behind.

Outside, they shoved me onto the back seat of their car, and the next moment I was jammed between two armed men. The third was at the wheel. My heart was icy. *Are they going to lock me up for good? Will I ever see my children again? What do they want with me? What did I do wrong?*

The journey took about an hour. When they jerked the hood off my head, I was in a small interrogation room. Where was I? Maybe in a secret police building? I had no idea. In the middle was a dividing wall made of glass, while two Chinese police officers — a man and a woman — were seated on the other side. He asked the questions; she jotted everything down. In front of me was a table, and on it a microphone with a button.

The questions pelted down. "Why did your children and your husband leave for Kazakhstan? Where do they live? What are they doing there?" If I hesitated for even a second, the woman would jump on it instantly. "Why aren't you answering? What kind of devious ulterior motives are going on inside your head? Are you an enemy? Talk!" Endless accusations, barked like orders. "What was the purpose of your family travelling there?" I chose my words carefully, worried that putting a foot wrong in this minefield would cause an explosion. "They only wanted to visit Kazakhstan. We've got a lot of relatives there. But then my children really liked the area, so they decided to stay and go to school." When they realised I was sticking to my story, they tried to find other things to pin on me. "Do you have something against the Chinese education system? Is there something you don't like? Is that why you sent your children to school in Kazakhstan?" "No, no, I'm not against anything," I protested, feeling like a fish squirming on a hook. I didn't want to give them any grounds to bring charges against me.

The two of them kept checking my phone to see who I'd been in contact with. "What is your husband doing in Kazakhstan? Does he have connections to any political organisations there? What enemies of China is he working for?" The man kept reformulating the same questions. "He went to Kazakhstan with the purpose of working with some kind of separatist organisation, didn't he? You can't pull the wool over our eyes. We know everything, we have people everywhere, including in Kazakhstan."

I responded truthfully. "I don't know!" Gradually, however, my temper got the better of me, and I lost my cool. "If you know everything, and you can do all these things, then you can find out for yourself!"

Eventually, they gave me explicit instructions to bring Uali and the children back. "Your husband has been a Party member since 2007. He's a traitor. You should divorce him," they told me. "He *has* to come back and hand in his papers." After that, my family would never be allowed to leave the country again.

The interrogation lasted four hours. Then they put the hood back over my head and pushed me back into the car. On the journey back, the man next to me growled, "You will tell no one about this interrogation. Understood?"

"Yes," I heard myself reply. At one o'clock in the morning, they finally dropped me back home.

Standing in the hallway, I was gasping for breath like I'd just run a marathon. I was filled with disgust. For years, I'd spent every day working for the Party and the government, slaving away and kowtowing morning, noon and night; I'd done everything they asked, to the best of my ability; I'd never put a single foot wrong. Yet the Party was treating me like dirt. Why? What was the point of all this? I hurled my jacket onto the floor.

There was worse in store for me, I knew. I could sense the fiery rage in my heart turning into all-consuming hatred, so I pulled out the photo of my father and sat down on my bed, confiding all my troubles and listening to his advice. *Never lose faith in the future. The most important thing is that you're still alive. You'll see, there are better times ahead. Keep your chin up!* I could either give up and die, or fight — and maybe survive. From then on, I went to bed every night fully clothed.

By the end of that year, they'd hauled me in another seven or eight times. Every morning when I woke up at home in my bed, I thanked God I was still alive.

A year of psychological terrorism

In March 2017, the CCP made Xi Jinping — "chosen by history" — president for life. In doing so, they elevated him to the blood-stained throne formerly occupied by Mao. There was no one in the country as powerful. Xi, then sixty-three years old, acted the part of the kindly, self-sacrificing yet strict father in propaganda, while the Party was the caring mother. Meanwhile the indigenous population was shown no mercy.

The night-time interrogations always followed the same pattern. Suddenly, I would find myself surrounded by police — in the bathroom, the corridor, the living room, around my bed. The hood would already be over my head. Only the interrogation rooms and the faces of the officers were different every time.

Sometimes there was only one person grilling me. When there were two of them, however, one would usually stand next to me, watching while the other asked the questions. Those men were sinister. Terrifying. My mouth was dry and my heart raced, shallow and rapid. They enjoyed watching me tremble. During one of these interrogations, they hit me. On the head and in the face. As hard as they could. And not just once. I didn't let them see how much it hurt, but eventually the tears came of their own accord. Each time I would crawl back out from under the table, straighten my back, and take my seat.

"Are you still in touch with your family in Kazakhstan?" or "Did you tell them to come back yet?"

"How can I do that? We're forbidden to contact them …" They were bellowing at me so loudly all the time that I barely dared to raise my voice above a whisper. Then they started beating me again until my cheeks were swollen. I kept howling back, "How should I know what they're doing?" Soon I was back under the table. "You've got to get them back immediately!"

Next time, they were bitterly angry with me. "Did you know your husband and children have received Kazakhstani citizenship?" I was genuinely surprised. "No, that's news to me." And although I was afraid, at that moment I was inwardly elated. *At least my loved ones are safe*, I thought. *The Party can't do anything to hurt them now.* The officers started berating me again. "Be honest: you knew, didn't you?"

They probably assumed that the ceaseless interrogations would grind me down, like grain beneath a millstone. That as soon as I got back, I'd find some way to contact Uali and beg him to come home — that I couldn't stand being terrorised any longer. Later, they would force prisoners like me to call their relatives living abroad during interrogations and feed them lies to lure them back to East Turkestan. Things like: "Come home quickly, your mother is seriously ill."

In China, family is a common means of gaining leverage. They will threaten students, pensioners, or even relatives who have been living abroad for decades: "If you don't come back now and de-register properly, your parents or your sisters back home will end up in jail." But anyone who does return to protect their relatives from harm soon finds themselves in handcuffs. I realised now that I was being held in Xinjiang as a hostage.

At all the interrogations they asked me similar questions. It was clear they'd discovered where and how my husband and the children were living. "You know all about this, you're just lying! Do you think we're idiots? Why don't you tell us the truth?" A few hours later, the police car dropped me off outside my front door. Before I got out, they gave me back my phone.

When I switched it on in the apartment, I saw I had seventy missed calls from my mother. "Why haven't you got in touch? Where are you? I'm so worried! Please call me!" All of them had come in during the last interrogation. My mother had to wait until midnight before I finally called back.

"Where have you been all this time? I kept calling, but you didn't pick up. Has something happened?" Her voice sounded so anxious that my heart ached more than my bruised body. I had told no one about those night-time interrogations. Yet my mother sensed something wasn't right. "What happened, my child?"

Trying not to upset her, I spoke gently. "Everything is fine. I just had to work at the kindergarten tonight. And I forgot my phone at home. I'm sorry it's so late, but I only just got home."

Her voice sounded different than before, as though something inside her had broken. "Go to sleep, my child. Relax! You need to rest."

June 2017: secret meetings

The most senior positions in East Turkestan were occupied by Chinese, and they were endlessly legislating to forbid more and more things. We were crushed under the weight of all these prohibitions. It was like a landslide, squeezing and smothering us until we were gasping frantically for air, unable to move so much as a finger on our own.

I sat bolt upright in the auditorium among the other head teachers I knew from Aksu, listening to the unbearable. Nobody was allowed to share religious content, such as Koran verses, via their mobile phone. Tibet and Taiwan were taboo from now on. "Official documents must be handed over to the relevant office in person, not via computer or telephone," they informed us. That made it easier for them to cover their tracks. "If we catch any of your staff doing any of these things in future, we will hold you responsible," they warned us menacingly. Inappropriate behaviour

Above: Ukilay looks after her younger brother at her grandparents' house in October 2010.

Right: Sayragul's daughter, Ukilay, is highly artistically gifted, like her whole family. She demonstrates this in July 2014 by dancing on the mountainside in her mother's home country.

Sayragul Sauytbay at her desk, working as a teacher at the school her father built for Kazakh children.

Above: Mother and daughter visit a place traditionally sacred to Kazakhs on Children's Day 2010.

Above right: Daughter and son in July 2014, on a hill in their home city.

Right: Sayragul Sauytbay at college, May 2007.

Above left: Sayragul Sauytbay was an outstanding and ambitious student with extremely high grades. At a regional academic competition in the Autonomous Prefecture of Ili in May 2004, she won first prize.

Above right: Sayragul Sauytbay quickly made a name for herself in her home country, hosting and running major events. Here, in March 2006, she sings at the Nauryz festival in Aksu. Kazakh culture is close to nature, deeply bound up with ideas of faith and social ties. It brings to life the history of the whole ethnic group, so ten years later the Chinese government has banned the celebration of any culture except its own.

Setting up a festival at the school in Aksu in June 2011. Sayragul Sauytbay performs as a singer.

Above: Days before fear: playing in the snow outside her parents' home in January 2002.

Above right: Sayragul's mother and one of her sisters take Ukilay to school in Ahyaz on 1 June 2007, to take part in 'Children's Day'.

Three exceptional people who risk their lives to protect the rights of others: human-rights activist Serikzhan Bilash, lawyer Aiman Umarova, and the chief witness, Sayragul Sauytbay. Pictured here in March 2019, all three are taking part in an Atajurt event in Almaty.

Ulagat with his maths teacher.

Prisoners in a camp, where torture and brainwashing are rife. Uighurs as well as Kazakh human-rights activists describe them as 'the Communist Party of China's fascist concentration camps'.

Sayragul Sauytbay with her son, Ulagat, before the Kazakh City Court in Zharkent.

An event organised by Atajurt. Desperate Kazakhs who have lost relatives in the neighbouring region of Xinjiang, which is kept strictly hidden from the outside world, hold up photographs of their loved ones, hoping for news.

Left: The largest peaceful protests ever witnessed in this autocratic state took place during the trial in Kazakhstan. People were all over the streets, raising their voices in support of the Kazakh chief witness and wearing T-shirts with the words 'Freedom for Sairagul' printed in three languages.

Working from witness statements, Sayragul Sauytbay made a sketch to illustrate how people are tortured in underground water prisons. Shackled at the wrists, they spend weeks with their bodies immersed in dirty water.

Sayragul Sauytbay with Melania Trump and US Secretary of State Michael R. Pompeo at the ceremony for the International Women of Courage Awards on 4 March 2020 **(above)** and with her family **(left)**.

Sayragul Sauytbay and Alexandra Cavelius after their last interviews in Sweden.

on the part of our employees was to be reported immediately. It was unmistakeable: they were telling us to denounce them. Like my other colleagues in senior roles, I never denounced anybody. Instead, I'd warn them in secret. "Watch what you say! Don't talk about Tibet anymore, or you'll get us all into big trouble."

Again and again, we saw the Party dredge up ancient history to paint people as traitors to their country. Between 1988 and 2000, there had been a brief wave of religious freedom, and many mosques had been built. Countless individuals had donated money or a piece of jewellery, helped out with construction, or given a lamb to the workmen.

"You will find out who was involved," they instructed us. Seventeen years later, we were being ordered to question hundreds of employees about their participation. Their instructions can be roughly summarised in three steps. First: Ask nicely. Second: If the person insists they are innocent, force them to disclose information about another colleague. Third: If the person isn't willing to speak, pretend you have official evidence against them.

Preparing my evening meal at the table that night, I found myself muttering agitatedly out loud. "How pointless! How unnecessary!" I noticed too late that I had chopped the peppers and potatoes virtually into pulp. It wasn't until much later that I understood why they were doing all this. Diligent as honeybees, they were gathering justifications to put indigenous people in camps. This way they always had a reason for imprisoning someone behind those silent concrete walls. Only, the reasons were as random as they were insane. Muslims weren't innocent until proven guilty anymore: soon it was the other way around.

Propped up on my elbow at my desk, my chin resting in my hand, I rapidly took stock of the situation. All my older employees were bound to have donated something or been involved somehow. How could I warn them without my Chinese colleagues getting wind of it? Noticing a truck drive into the courtyard with a large delivery of medical supplies, I was struck by an idea: moments later, I was rushing downstairs to round up the people I was worried about.

"You need to help me unload the truck!" We had already come up with a secret code for emergencies so that our Chinese colleagues wouldn't immediately figure out what was going on. If you wanted to warn someone, for instance, you said, "The weather's turning cold tomorrow." Occasionally, we also exchanged secret notes, which we used to pass on brief or coded messages.

"This all needs to go to the basement!" I told my teachers, because I knew they hadn't installed cameras in there yet. As we unpacked weighing scales, eye tests, and measuring devices and put them on the shelves, I hastily brought my colleagues up to speed. "I'll tell the authorities that none of you were involved in the fundraising," I explained. If the Chinese interrogator tried to pretend that I had given them their name, they shouldn't believe them. I clasped my hands pleadingly. "Don't confess anything, or we'll all be taken away. Permanently."

Three days later, I and the other head teachers handed in blank lists to the authorities. The next morning, we were all given a warning and told to investigate more closely. Again, we didn't offer up any names. Straightaway, we were summoned to another meeting. "You're all liars!" one of our bosses harangued us. "We know exactly who supported building the mosques. The imams gave us a list of donors. You're going to have one last chance to give us the names yourselves!" As we left, they issued a final warning: "Lie again, and you'll be arrested." This time, they only gave us one day.

That night, I sat at my kitchen table for ages, thinking. I'd known my older employees for years; some were close friends. *If I denounce them and put their names on the list to save myself, what will be left of me as a human being?* I wondered. The next morning, I submitted a blank list.

Again, they gathered all the head teachers and brandished the pieces of paper in front of us. "A commission will begin investigating tomorrow. And woe betide anyone who's lying ..."

Next morning, there was a long queue outside the offices of the education authority, and I joined the others at the back. Everybody was holding a list. When I noticed that some of them actually contained a few names, I whispered, "What are you doing?"

They defended themselves, hissing back softly, "Didn't you hear? They know the names anyway. If we deny it, we'll end up in prison ourselves."

Speaking under my breath, but still sharply, I shot back, "Oh really, they've got lists? Seventeen years ago there weren't any detailed computer records, and the imams would have got rid of the handwritten lists ages ago. The ones who actually collected the donations would either be dead by now or have moved away. It's an empty threat!"

Gradually, the mood changed. People in the queue started discussing it among themselves. "She's probably right." And: "We're such idiots!" They went straight back to their schools and drew up new lists. Without any names. If a commission did come, we decided we would all stick to the same story: "We're innocent. If you have any proof, please show us." In the end, it turned out there had never been any such list of donors. But they arrested the people anyway.

According to the data in the China Cables, 15,683 people in East Turkestan were interned within a single week.

Worse than a mental hospital

"All these measures have been put in place because of the risk of a terrorist attack," our bosses told us. Sometimes my staff and I had to spend several nights in a row at school so we could be available at any time. All night long, Chinese inspectors in yellow body armour swarmed through the building like a feral swarm of wasps, searching. If one of them showed up at the office and couldn't find the person they wanted to speak to, that was reason enough to march them off for "refusing to work". The stress was indescribable.

One-third of my teachers were assigned to stand guard in the building. Another third were banded into a security force armed with truncheons and told to patrol after dark. The final third were busy in the surveillance room, keeping a twenty-four-hour watch on CCTV footage of the whole area. Other than their colleagues with truncheons, they never saw anyone. Every two to three days, they would switch duties.

As a head teacher, it was my job to supervise the whole process. Occasionally, Party officials would allow us a few hours' sleep, and we set up a guard room with about five cots for this purpose. Some of the teachers on guard duty ended up so exhausted that they nodded off where they stood. Suddenly, however, the "yellow jackets" would pounce on them, screeching, "What are you doing? You're on duty! Take him to the camp!"

If one of my colleagues gave in to the call of nature while one of the inspectors happened to be looking for him, they'd start demanding, "Where is he? Why's he sitting on the toilet when he's supposed to be on guard duty? He's defying the state!" Then they'd grab him on both sides and drag him off to the camps as a subversive. Crazy, isn't it?

My main office was situated in the largest kindergarten: the other four buildings were smaller, located three or four kilometres apart. I stayed there until midday, preoccupied with bureaucratic red tape and paperwork, and then I'd hop in the car and drive from one kindergarten to the next, checking that everything was in order.

As head teacher, I was responsible for everyone and had to be constantly available. If a child was injured in an accident or a member of staff made a mistake, they'd hold me accountable and lock me up. So I was always on the go, all night long — rushing around behind the wheel, one building to the next. It was like I was doing endless laps around a roundabout, never reaching my goal.

Some of my teachers had to take up position outside the entrance at 7.00 am, standing ramrod-straight like guards outside the Queen of England's palace, wearing helmets and holding their truncheons in front of their chests while the children streamed into the building. Other members of staff were on the street, brandishing their truncheons at cars and mopeds. "Where are you going? What are you up to? Turn back around!"

No sooner were all the children in the building than our guards would hurry in after them, scrambling to take off their gear as soon as possible and reappear at the front of the classroom on time, now in the guise of teachers. As soon as the bell rang, they dashed off again, picked up their helmets and sticks, and kept watch in the schoolyard. Soon they weren't sure whether they were teachers or soldiers. Did we even have time for lessons anymore? We were all so incredibly confused.

In a system like that, the only thing that gets you through is tunnel vision. You have to be under strict control at all time, carefully monitoring others to make sure they're conforming, too. Lack of sleep ground us down relentlessly. Many people got sick.

We weren't even allowed to eat in peace. My teachers ordered fast food, and would spend their shifts on guard duty snacking on bags of chips. This, too, was grounds for arrest. "We don't care if you're on a break," the inspectors lambasted their victims, "or if you're sick or tired. When we're there, you've got to do your jobs." Life at school was worse than in a mental hospital.

If the higher-ups did give me a break, I'd run home for two or three hours, shower, change, and rush back. The CCP turned us into compliant, obedient drones. We accepted their orders. If they told us something was wrong, then we simply took that at face value, even if the order was rescinded the next day. We were absolutely under their control, thoroughly manipulated and unable to think for ourselves. We were puppets.

How did I cope for so long? First, I'm not the kind of person who's easily steamrolled. Second, despite the wretchedness of the situation, I never stopped hoping that I would one day get my passport back — that I'd one day see my children and my husband again.

The final nail: physical control

If anyone had assumed things couldn't get any worse, they were wrong. In October 2017, the authorities instituted a program for Kazakhs and Chinese called "Becoming a Family", designed to teach us more about Chinese culture. Indigenous people had to live with a Chinese family for eight days once a month — or, alternatively, Chinese people could live with us. The Chinese were allowed to choose which option they preferred.

The authorities assigned one Muslim from our area to every Chinese household. As usual, they dressed it up in the Party's sweet, cloying jargon, pretending that the whole thing was being done out of consideration and for our protection. "You'll eat breakfast, lunch, and dinner together, just like a member of the family," they told us.

You had to eat whatever was put in front of you. If they shovelled pork onto their Muslim guest's plate, so be it. Hosts had to document all shared activities by snapping a photo on their phone and sending it to the authorities. "Aha, they've eaten dinner together," the officials would nod, ticking that off their lists.

If my teachers were on guard duty, they had to give the authorities plenty of advance warning: "I'm afraid I can't do my family duty that day. But I'll make it up later." The important thing was that you crossed off your eight days per month. And what did that look like in practice? Well, during your lunch break you'd rush off to your host family's home, cook, then head back to work. In the evening, you'd do the Chinese family's housework and spend the night. If it was a Saturday or a Sunday, you'd spend your free time with them. For us Muslims, that usually meant doing their chores — mucking out pigsties, cleaning, caring for the elderly. And at night we had to go to bed with the hosts.

The following month, the authorities would send us to the next Chinese family, or another Chinese person would be standing on our doorstep. Can you imagine what that was like for young girls, wives, or single mothers like me? The men were given the same rights of access to our bodies as to those of their wives. That was the final nail in their appalling plan: to take away our control over own bodies. We're talking about the rape of an entire ethnic group on a vast scale.

If a woman or a girl resisted, the Chinese host was supposed to complain to the authorities. "She's not fulfilling her duties!" Then the police would snatch the girl and take her to a camp, where they would teach her to be more obedient.

At night at the kitchen table, I chatted softly to my father. "If I work even harder, make myself indispensable, then they can't send me to a Chinese family for eight days — I'll get out of it ... Father, what do you think?" But I couldn't hear his answer over the blaring sirens of the police cars outside, bathing me in blue light as they passed.

A campaign of "friendship" that sows hatred

Outwardly, the campaign was designed to promote friendly relationships with the indigenous community. In reality, it was sowing hatred. We lived in a constant state of panic. Every day, every minute, every second we were afraid. The photos and video recordings taken by Chinese families were intended solely for the authorities, to prove they were adhering to the program, so I've no idea how they found their way overseas. People must have shared them and passed them on.

You can find countless such images online, showing indigenous women in the arms of Chinese men. Sometimes they're lying next to each other in bed, the sheets just barely covering their naked bodies. There have been instances of women who killed themselves out of shame because the photos were seen by their relatives.

I saw some of them myself when I got to Kazakhstan. Video recordings, for example, showing two Chinese men getting drunk and tearing off a grandmother's headscarf, laughing, or constantly refilling the glass of an elderly Muslim man with a white beard and forcing him to drink. One shows a girl around fourteen or fifteen. By the end of the recording she's very drunk, and is made to dance for the Chinese. Her mother and father sit silent and motionless on the sofa, looking on as one of the men kisses their daughter. The authorities used these recordings as evidence that a Chinese person had adequately fulfilled their role in the Muslim family.

The region around the Altai Mountains was known for its rebellious population. News of two cases in the area, which is situated in the far north-west, made its way to Aksu. At one school, four hundred Muslim students refused to eat pork, and all of them were arrested.

On another occasion, a Chinese person was assigned to a Muslim family that included a grandfather and his sixteen-year-old granddaughter. After a while, the man wanted to have sex with the girl. The grandfather told him he had a right to do so, but that first he wanted to show him his best horse outside. Like all Kazakhs, this old man was a first-rate rider. Swinging onto the back of his horse, in a flash he lassoed the man around the neck, then dug his heels into the horse's flanks. Galloping away, he dragged the man behind him through the sand until he was dead. As punishment, the elderly grandfather and his entire family were taken to the camps.

And then, for the first time, the "friendship" campaign found its way to my doorstep.

"Let's figure this out ..."

Sitting at my desk, I stared fixedly at the man's address. I knew he was an affluent, single businessman in Aksu. How was I going to get through the day? A Muslim woman alone in a house with a man whose intentions I didn't know? Our honour and our pride are sacred to us. By that time, they were the only things keeping us going, cherished at our very core.

That night, on the way there, with a sick feeling in the pit of my stomach, I kept running through in my mind how to save myself — what was the smartest tactic here? I was concentrating so hard that I didn't even notice my feet turning towards the apartment block, my legs carrying me up the stairs to the second floor, or my finger pressing the bell. Shocked, I took a step back when the door opened.

"Oh! It's you!" said the man, astonished. He was tall, roughly thirty-eight years old. He knew me, too, of course, because I was also a well-known figure in Aksu, and had run and hosted quite a few major events. Clearly, he wasn't aware which Kazakh the authorities had assigned him, and he greeted me politely.

First he invited me into his kitchen, where we had a cup of tea together: this was required by the guidelines, which he had already received in writing. My cheeks were burning, as though I'd been sitting too close to a fire. I had to take several deep breaths, and then everything I was feeling came tumbling out in one go: "You know us Kazakhs and our culture, and you know the way we live now." His probing eyes rested on me while I fought for my honour. "I'm Muslim, and you're Chinese. We've both been forced into this situation. You know what an immoral position this is for a Kazakh woman like me." He nodded and agreed. "Yes. Right now, we need this new policy in Xinjiang. It will bring more stability. But I understand what you mean."

Then he invited me into the living room of his spacious, four- or five-room apartment, where we sat down opposite each other. Again, I watched him with anxious interest, like a cornered animal, gathering my strength so I could get out of this terrible situation. "Let's figure this out so we can both emerge unscathed ..."

Chinese participants in the campaign were obliged to fill in a form every day, detailing the duties their Muslim guest had performed: having breakfast together, having lunch together, and so on. The piece of paper was on the table between us. I tapped it with my finger. "Please show me some sympathy and say I've done all those things." Nervously smoothing my trousers, I rushed to describe my situation. The words spilled out: it was like I couldn't breathe if I didn't blurt them all out at once. "I'm a wife and mother living alone, a head teacher —" He cut me off impatiently. "Yes, yes, I know you. I'm aware of who you are."

Moving stiffly, I drew my purse out of my handbag. "How much do I need to pay you?" I could see from his thin smile that I had judged right. "If you give me 20 yuan a day, that's fine," he replied. It wasn't a huge sum: you could maybe eat at a restaurant twice for that amount. Wordlessly, he rolled up the notes and listened as I continued. "I'll pay you that sum every day. In return, I want to leave the house around midnight and go home. I'll take the back exit. Nobody will see me. The next morning, I'll come back early, before sunrise."

"Agreed," he said, his expression unmoved. For a moment, I sank back into the armchair, taking a deep breath of relief. I showed my gratitude by immediately setting about fulfilling the other expectations of the campaign, one chore after another: stuffing his dirty laundry into the machine, ironing his shirts, mopping the hallway …

When I was done, we sat back down at the laid table. "You only have to eat what you want," he told me, taking out his phone, "but let's take a quick photo as evidence." He walked around the table. "Okay, now take some of that pork and act like you're eating it …" I lifted the fork to my mouth and held it there until he'd snapped enough pictures. He'd also documented all my other jobs and sent them straight to the authorities.

He was one of the Chinese people who adopted only those parts of the system that they felt benefited them. The rest they accepted as long as it didn't harm them or stop them earning money. Many of his compatriots were silent accomplices of the system: they had bought into the "Chinese dream" that the Party was always talking about, and were intoxicated by the idea that they would soon be part of the world's ruling elite.

After about seven hours, I crept downstairs like a cat in the middle of the night. Outside there were guards and cameras everywhere. Putting one foot cautiously after another, I kept glancing anxiously over my shoulder, taking a circuitous route home via small passageways and side streets. Every shadow looked like danger. Was that someone clearing their throat? I pressed myself up against a tree, holding my breath. There was a long, fearful silence. Under normal circumstances, it was only a kilometre, but I took so many detours I walked at least three times that far, until at last, feeling like the devil was nipping at my heels, I dashed the final few steps into my house, shut the door behind me, and leant against it, gasping for breath.

Without switching on the light, I tiptoed into my bed. Sleep was impossible — my heart was thudding too loudly. Early the next morning, while it was still dark, I hurried back to his apartment block via the same meandering route. Although no one hit me or mistreated me, those eight days were torture. Every night, I dropped twenty yuan onto the Chinese businessman's table, and I was finally allowed to leave.

The Party and the government used that campaign to destroy our young girls. Who could they confide in about the awful things that had happened to them? Anyone who was open about the abuse ended up in a camp. In any case, our culture forbade any discussion of rape. They had besmirched the honour of our girls and women, even though we ourselves were blameless.

Many of my young female co-workers at the kindergartens came to me sobbing, throwing their trembling arms around me and crying until the collar of my Party uniform was soaked with their tears. I tried to find the words to comfort them, but everything sounded mocking in my ears. So we were silent, our heads resting on each other's shoulders, until our eyes were red.

So far we had put up with all their cruelties. Not being allowed to speak our own language anymore, not being allowed to practise our traditions or be who we truly were. Yet this humiliation was beyond everything else. They were violently forcing themselves into the core of our being, trying to subjugate us, to break us. I can't even find the words — how do you describe a situation that's indescribable?

Nobody outside wanted to talk anymore. Trust within families had been destroyed, because the Party exhorted everyone to denounce everyone else. Betrayal was often the only way to save your own life or your own job. A twenty-four-hour hotline had been set up specifically for this purpose. Following orders, I gave this number to all my employees. They also installed a brand-new postbox outside the kindergarten entrance, with a sign encouraging people to anonymously report suspicious activity.

There was no shortage of reasons to defame someone. Some Chinese people got jealous because a Kazakh had, on the basis of better education or performance, been given a more senior job than them. The Party had now provided those people with a highly effective means of getting rid of unwelcome competition. All it took was one complaint. For instance: "The local manager is damaging friendly relations between Kazakhs and Chinese. He's keeping us Chinese down and favouring his own countrymen." The accused would soon find his papers stamped with the words "dangerous nationalist", and he would be taken to the camps for re-education.

As head teachers, we no longer had any room for manoeuvre at work. Every task had to be done according to a strict timeframe and reported to the higher-ups as complete. Colleagues were no longer allowed to exchange any personal information. There was no scope for compassion, no *You look pale, can I help you?* Instead, we were supposed to harangue people. *Have you completed all your tasks yet?*

Slowly but surely, people all over Aksu were developing psychological problems. I didn't see anyone who had completely lost their mind or gone berserk, but nor did I see anyone behaving like a normal individual. Lots of business-owners, for instance, lost the will to keep running their shops. People sank into apathy. Everything stagnated; life turned sluggish. "Why should I earn money if I could be sent to the camps tomorrow?"

The following month, the rules of the "family" campaign were tightened. The authorities had got wind that many Kazakhs were paying bribes to avoid spending the night in a stranger's bed. Keen to close the final loophole, inspectors started calling Chinese families in the middle of the night and ordering them to put their Kazakh guest on the phone. Everyone had to keep their phone on them at all times so that the officials could locate them anywhere. Finally, they stationed uniformed guards overnight outside Chinese families' front doors. If you were a female Kazakh trying to go home, you'd end up with a black hood over your head.

I was lucky. I wasn't affected by the stricter regulations, which came into force in October 2017. Not long afterwards, I was sent to a camp myself.

A secret visit in the night

I happened to overhear a few snippets of a friend's conversation. "You'll never guess — an old married couple in the next village got permission to go to Kazakhstan for a funeral!" The news hit me like a bolt of lightning. Officially, indigenous people were only allowed to cross the border if they could find a relative who would guarantee their return — using their life as collateral. Unofficially, travel was forbidden. Still, I instantly sensed an opportunity to get a message to Uali through the couple.

But how could I persuade these strangers to help? And how could I get there without someone catching me? Two days before they set off, I secretly rented a car, which I parked far away from my building. I couldn't let anyone recognise me, so one night I took a jacket and a pair of trousers from Uali's wardrobe, hid my long hair under his hat, and jumped behind the wheel, dressed as a man. I knew I was in mortal danger, of course, but my life was increasingly dangerous anyway.

On the outskirts of the village, I switched off my headlights and pulled up near a cluster of trees. I made the final stretch on foot, in the dark, keeping off the road. There were no lights on in any of the houses. I tiptoed into their courtyard like a thief and knocked on the couple's door. Two drowsy but frightened senior citizens answered.

"Please, it's important," I hissed, the words coming out in short bursts as I puffed and wheezed. Their hands clapped to their mouths, they glanced all around before hustling me indoors. Without even taking a breath, I blurted everything out at once: "My husband is living with our two children in Kazakhstan. I've not had any contact with them for ages." I held out my letter like a beggar. "Could you please give them this?"

They were eyeing the envelope as though it was a poisonous snake. "No, it's too dangerous!" they said, their voices hoarse. Still, I was at least able to convince them to take a piece of paper with Uali's telephone number. "Please, call him when you're in Kazakhstan, and ask where he's living and how the children are doing." The conversation lasted no more than five minutes, and then I was back in the darkness outside.

A week or two later, a Kazakh woman I didn't recognise came to pick up a couple of children from the kindergarten. She waited in the garden for me until all the parents had left before approaching. "Excuse me, I'd like to speak to you about these two children." Then, leaning close, she quietly introduced herself as the daughter-in-law of the elderly couple that had gone to Kazakhstan. "My relatives weren't allowed to go home," she hissed. Apparently, there had been problems with their papers at the border.

I answered out loud, "The children are very hardworking!" She smiled and replied, "I know," then added softly, "Your husband has bought a house in a village near Almaty. Your children are going to school there. They're fine."

"They should keep plugging away at Chinese," I emphasised in my loud voice. Nodding eagerly, she quickly took the opportunity to pass me my husband's new address.

Finally, I had discovered where Uali was living. Now I just had to find a way to reach him in Kazakhstan. *Maybe I'll be out of here in a few days*, I thought. In fact, however, I had no chance of escape. My pursuers already had me in their clutches …

CHAPTER SIX

The Camp: surviving in hell

Late 2017: arriving at the camp

Towards the end of November 2017, I was disturbed late one night by the telephone ringing. Who could it be? Suspicious, I lifted the receiver to my ear. "Take a taxi into Zhaosu city centre immediately," instructed a male voice. "Someone will pick you up there."

"Why should I go there?" I asked uneasily. "Who are you?"

"Don't ask questions!"

But the words tumbled out of my mouth. "Why should I go anywhere at this time of night?"

"You shouldn't ask questions. You're being taken for retraining."

"What kind of retraining?"

"No need to worry. Tomorrow you'll be taking part in a seminar in another city."

Was that true? Why did I have to set off for retraining in the middle of the night? But maybe I was getting het up over nothing, and it was just another secret meeting. It took about an hour to reach the address they'd given me, clutching a bag with my toothbrush and basic essentials in my lap. "We're here," said the driver, stopping in the middle of a wide street. It was midnight. As agreed over the phone, I pulled out my phone underneath a streetlamp and texted the number they'd dictated to me: "I'm here."

Frightened, I lowered my phone and hunched my shoulders. It was too late to run away. Anyway, where would I go? They could find me anywhere. Then I saw the lights of a police car.

The doors burst open, and four policemen with machine guns jumped out. Seconds later, they had grabbed me by the sleeves, thrown a hood over my head, and shoved me into the back seat. I'd been taken in before, of course, but this time I knew: *It's finally happening. They're taking me to a camp. My life is over.*

As I sat in the back between the armed officers, fabric covering my face, I started to cry. For a while, I lost control of myself: my body convulsed, my tears ran, I sobbed and sobbed. The policeman next to me kept jabbing his rifle into my side, snapping, "Stop that! Why are you wailing? Keep quiet! If you don't stop, we'll really give you a reason to howl! You want us to pull over?" At that, I froze. I knew they could do anything they wanted to a woman.

The journey took about two hours. Suddenly, the car started driving very slowly, then stopped. I saw nothing, but could hear the front window being opened. "We're dropping someone off," the driver said. Then they parked the car, forced me out and dragged me away, gripping my upper arms.

Heavy doors were unbolted, opened, and closed behind us. Our footsteps were more muffled: we had to be inside a building. My knees felt weak; my legs could barely carry me. Two or three times we paused, and one of the officers repeated, "We're dropping her off." Panicking, I tried to figure out what was happening. *Those are checkpoints, and what's in store for me here is worse than a prison.* I clenched my jaw to stop my teeth chattering.

Once we'd entered a room, someone jerked the hood off my head. It was so bright that I blinked in the unexpectedly dazzling light. Gradually, my eyes adjusted, and behind a desk I saw a Chinese military officer with various insignia on his epaulettes. A colossus of a man, he was in his late forties, medium height, with a broad, ugly, frog-like face and glasses. On his head he wore a cap with more military insignia, and tall lace-up leather boots on his feet. *Maybe a colonel with some kind of special unit,* I guessed, but my chest was so tight I could barely think.

It must have been about three in the morning by the time I sat down opposite him. Between us were the heavy table and his computer. Not bothering with a greeting, the man outlined the situation in sharp, clipped military jargon: "You are in a re-education camp, and you will work here as a teacher …"

My head began to whirl. Not as a prisoner? As a teacher? Why me, of all people? What did it all mean? Was I saved or doomed? "From now on, you will be giving Chinese lessons to the other inmates," he instructed, gazing at me the way a cat looks at a mouse. "And you will not refuse to take on other tasks as well."

He shoved a document towards me. "Just to be clear: you will tell no one what you have seen and heard here. Sign this!" I barely had time to skim the beginning of the three or four pages.

The rules of my new job were listed one after another:

> This contract is strictly confidential.
> It is forbidden to speak to the prisoners.
> It is forbidden to laugh, cry, or answer questions
> without permission.

It was a struggle to put pen to paper, because it was written in black and white that anyone who made a mistake and broke a rule would face the death penalty. My heart sank even further.

"Sign it!" he barked. I had no choice. I signed my own death sentence. My hand was shaking as though all the fear in my body had collected inside it.

"Give her the clothes," the colossal man ordered a subordinate. As I turned towards the guard, my eye was briefly caught by the signs on the wall: the twelve guiding principles of Xi Jinping, which were ubiquitous in the offices of all senior figures, and were also displayed in my kindergarten.

It included things like: "Everybody must speak Chinese ... everybody must dress like a Chinese person ... everybody must think like a Chinese person, regardless of whether they are Uighur or Kazakh ... everything you do must be in the service of China ... no indigenous person is permitted to have foreign contacts ..." All of it could be summarised in one sentence: anything remotely different has to be made Chinese. It was supposed to sound like paternal advice, but was phrased like a series of orders.

Carrying a military-style camouflage uniform in my arms, I followed the guard into the hallway. Afterwards, I saw the officer another couple of times when new prisoners arrived at the camp. He was probably one of the higher-ups in charge of special assignments. I would end up going to his office from time to time to drop off some forms about the health of particular prisoners.

The first night

When you're in a state of shock, adrenaline makes certain areas of the brain switch into high gear. From that point on, I committed everything to memory with absolute precision, because I knew I was one day going to tell the world about it. From the outset, I clung to that thought like a lifebuoy.

Ahead of me and slightly to the left was a small hall. Inside was a glass-walled sentry box. On the left, a corridor roughly twenty-five metres long branched off from the hall, with twelve cells on either side. Later, I noticed that men and women were kept on separate sides.

The door of each cell was triple-locked and secured with an additional iron bolt. Two guards were assigned outside, working in shifts, 24/7. The reason they went to such extraordinary lengths was because they were terrified that prisoners might break out and bring their atrocities to light.

I averted my eyes as I was led right, in the opposite direction, down an equally long corridor. Here, too, there were cameras on both sides. Every two metres. Not a single nook or cranny was left unobserved. There were no windows anywhere. This half of the storey housed the administration block: six offices, one behind the other.

After a few metres, we stopped outside the fourth door, which — unlike the prisoners' cells — did not have a hatch in the middle through which to pass food. Evidently, I was going to be treated better as a teacher than the inmates.

On the bare, roughly six-metre-square concrete floor was a plastic rollout mattress as thin as two shopping bags, plus a flimsy pillow and a thin plastic blanket. A camera was in every corner. "Go to sleep now!" they ordered me, before the barred steel door slammed and the key turned in the lock.

For a moment, I just stood there, staring at a small double-barred opening on the wall in front of me, so high up that I couldn't see out. *How long do I have to stay here? What's going on?* I was racking my brain feverishly for answers I didn't have. Since I had been repeatedly interrogated by the secret police already, I assumed they hadn't yet found a reason to arrest me. But now I had a nasty thought.

They must have brought me to the camp under the pretext of wanting me to teach so that I would finally slip up and they could lock me away in this place for years. *Don't cry, don't talk, don't show emotion …* Thinking of the rules I'd signed, I realised how easy it would be to make a mistake — but I didn't want to give them the satisfaction!

I lay down on the plastic blanket and stared up at the ceiling, where a fifth wide-angle camera was pointed at me. Every millimetre of this grey concrete bunker was being recorded. The light was glaring. It never went out.

Daily routine

Shortly before six, a loud, screeching bell shrilled through the building. Where was I? I started awake, my pulse racing, saw the camera above me, and felt as crushed as when I fell asleep. A moment later, someone was banging at my door. "Get ready! Quick!"

In front of me, on the left, partitioned off by a hip-height wall, was a toilet area with a hole. A camera was pointed at this, too. On the right, by the door, was a small sink beneath another camera. I hastily turned on the tap, but only a thin trickle came out. I splashed my face and cleaned my teeth. There was no soap or comb.

I'd slept maybe two hours, but minutes later I was standing bolt upright like a guard outside my door, hands by my sides, wearing my camouflage uniform and matching peaked cap, with the jacket buttoned up to my chin.

At six on the dot, all the doors on both corridors opened automatically. For a moment, I was winded. From the open doors of the prisoners' cells came an abominable stench of sweat, urine. and faeces, wafting across the hall and permeating the whole block. The blue-uniformed guards in the wing opposite wore masks whenever they entered the cells.

At this point, I didn't yet realise that the regulations stipulated each individual should have one square metre of space. In reality, however, they would cram up to twenty people into sixteen square metres: approximately four hundred prisoners per floor.

They only allowed one plastic bucket with a lid per cell, which served as a toilet. The prisoners were only allowed to empty it once in a twenty-four-hour period.

If, after five hours, the bucket was full, the lid had to stay on. So even if the prisoners' bladders were bursting or their bowels were rumbling, they had to wait until the bucket was empty. Over time, this led to terrible organ problems in some individuals, and the air was so foul it made everyone extremely nauseous.

My attention was diverted from the prisoners, who were lining up outside, because I was directed to join a queue of about six administrative workers and other employees. At times it was longer or shorter, depending on the meal break. Conversation was forbidden.

It rapidly became apparent that several very different groups of workers were employed on this floor, ranging from the cleaning women in simple suits with jackets to high-ranking officers who wore black balaclavas like bank robbers, revealing only their mouths, eyes, and nostrils. Even the Chinese employees were clearly afraid of these masked, machine-gun-brandishing men in their tall leather boots. I soon found out first-hand what their job was.

Every single procedure in the camp was organised down to the most minute detail. It was like an anthill. I'd estimate that around one hundred people were employed on my floor, working in shifts. I was the only teacher, and the only Kazakh in a relatively senior role. Otherwise there was probably one indigenous person for every twelve Chinese employees, but they were always in more junior positions.

Accompanied by two guards, a group of employees moved about twenty-five metres towards a double door, behind which we made a sharp left towards the kitchens. At the end of the corridor there was a window-sized aperture in the wall, through which a Chinese kitchen assistant pushed plates of food towards the people in front of me. It smelled great, and looked like a decent meal. My stomach growled.

To my disappointment, as an indigenous woman I was given one piece of steamed, mushy white bread and a small ladle of cooked rice water with a few floating grains of rice. Similarly, the Chinese staff weren't penalised even if they made the same mistakes I did: too hesitant, too nervous, too hasty …

We marched back to our rooms in rows. Before I hurriedly gulped down the bland, unsalted soup, the guard remarked insolently, "If we knock, bring the clean ladle back to the kitchen with the others. If we don't, you'll use it to get your food tomorrow." They always locked the door behind them.

At seven, two more guards led me into one of the offices near my cell. Nobody was allowed to move around the camp unaccompanied: there was always at least one armed guard following on my heels like a shadow.

The lesson plan

Unlike the previous office, this one was appointed with cheap chipboard furniture. Another Chinese man was waiting for me behind his desk to explain my job. I could never remember any of their faces, because they were different every time. Presumably, they simply switched people to different departments in the building: a security measure to prevent contact and conversation among colleagues.

"Sit down," the man ordered me, pointing at a chair. Brusqueness was the standard approach in the camp. "During the lessons, you will speak only when instructed." For men like him, violence was a legitimate means of strengthening Chinese society and maintaining the respect it was due.

He raised a warning finger. "You must never say anything except what is written in these instructions." He waved the bits of paper in the air. I would never be allowed to express my own opinion or to act independently. Turning to the door, where a guard was stationed — dutifully raising and lowering his head, hanging on the officer's every word — he added, "Men like him decide what is allowed and what is not!"

He then leaned forward and handed me a multi-page document that specified in meticulous detail how I was expected to behave. I was to stand as motionless as possible and always speak in a sharp, snappish tone of voice. I was only allowed to approach the guards in specific ways.

I had already learned outside the prison walls that the art of surviving in a surveillance state entailed keeping a low profile and putting on a rigid mask. That way, the swarm of informers didn't have as much scope to read something reprehensible into your behaviour.

"Repeat it back!" The man questioned me on the code of conduct as though I was a schoolchild, and then explained the topic of that day's lesson. "Open it!" The first four pages of the lesson plan dealt with an extract from the resolutions passed at the nineteenth Party congress. Taken together, the legislation was the length of a book, so I was only supposed to teach part of them to the prisoners every day.

"Keep turning the pages!" ordered the officer. The next two were about Chinese customs and traditions. How did the Chinese bury their relatives? How did they celebrate weddings? "This is your second topic of the day," he told me.

He then gave me half an hour to get my mind around the content.

I had to understand the meaning of the legislation myself and

memorise parts of it before I could teach it to my students —
who included everyone from academics to people who couldn't
even read. I was allowed to take only a few notes to use in class.
Simply reading aloud was not permitted.

After absorbing so much information in such a short span
of time, I was extremely tense and nervous. *I hope I don't forget
any of the details*, I thought anxiously. Then they'd lock me up
like an animal, too, trapped in one of those stinking cages. I tried
frantically to block out everything else and concentrate wholly on
the task ahead.

"That's enough," growled the officer, glancing at his silver
watch. "Stand up and summarise all the topics!" It was the only
way he could be sure I had understood everything the way I was
supposed to. "Wait!" Taking out his phone, he photographed my
notes. I was not allowed to handle any pieces of paper without
them being checked. At the end of the day, they made sure I had
returned all written materials to the office. No evidence, however
minor, could be allowed to leave the building. Nothing, absolutely
nothing, could make its way outside.

Every day — sometimes in the morning, sometimes at night
— I was taken into an office and given my new lesson plan. Each
time, a member of staff would appear from the stairwell behind
the glass wall, carrying notes not just for me but for all the other
teachers on the other five floors as well. Once I realised that, I
quickly worked out that at four hundred prisoners per floor, plus a
basement, there must have been about 2,500 people held in total.

"Take her into the classroom!" The man ran a hand through
his black hair and waved me out with the guard. This time,
instead of turning left towards the kitchen after passing through
the double doors, we turned right, down a corridor. Along it were
three or four larger rooms, one of which was my new workplace.

I wouldn't leave that floor for the next five months.

7.00 am to 9.00 am: teaching the living dead

I'd scarcely set foot in the room before my fifty-six students rose to their feet, ankle shackles jangling, and shouted, "We're ready!" They all wore blue shirts and trousers. Their heads were shaved, their skin white as a corpse's.

I stood to attention in front of the board, flanked either side by two guards with automatic rapid-fire guns. I was so unprepared for the sight and so appalled that for a moment I almost tottered on my feet. Black eyes, mutilated fingers, bruises everywhere. A cohort of the living dead, freshly risen from the grave.

There were no tables or ordinary chairs, only plastic stools meant for kindergarteners. For an adult, it wasn't easy to sit upright, especially if you were in pain, like some of the men in blood-soaked trousers, whose haemorrhoids had burst.

Ten or twelve people crouched in five rows: academics, farmers, artists, students, businesspeople ... roughly 60 per cent were men between the ages of eighteen and fifty. The rest were girls, women, and elderly people. In the first row was the youngest, a schoolgirl thirteen years old — tall, thin, very clever. With her bald head, I'd first taken her for a boy. The eldest, a sheepherder who joined us later, was eighty-four.

Fear was etched into every single face. All light in their eyes had gone out. No spark of hope to be seen. I stood there in shock, feeling my mouth tremble. All I wanted to do was cry. *Don't make any mistakes now, Sayragul!* I screamed inwardly at myself. *Or pretty soon you'll be sitting on one of those kids' stools as well!*

One inmate after another spoke up. "Number one is present." "Number two is present." And so on until number fifty-six. After the roll call, the guards handed everyone a pen and a small booklet.

As the inmates were supposed to take notes, their handcuffs had already been removed when they went to fetch food, and now hung clinking loosely from one wrist. Over the course of the day, the prisoners filled out the exam questions in the booklets.

At first I couldn't squeeze out a single word. It was like my throat was clamped shut — but compassion was forbidden. On pain of death. Spinning on my heel, I grabbed the blackboard and started writing in chalk, speaking in a rough voice. When I turned back around, I kept my eyes fixed on the back wall. I couldn't bear looking into those faces. The walls were crudely plastered in grey concrete, like the walls of a factory.

There was a red line drawn on the floor in front of me, which I couldn't cross without permission from the guards — and then only if I had something important to do on the other side. It was a way of avoiding any familiarity or relationship developing between me and the prisoners. I was never allowed to get close to them. A table and a basic plastic chair were provided for me, but oddly the guards moved them aside at the beginning of every lesson.

Both women and men had to sit ramrod-straight on their stools, staring straight ahead. No one was allowed to drop their head. Anyone who didn't follow the rules was immediately dragged away. To the torture room. "He's doing it on purpose! He's refusing to fall into line and resisting the power of the state!" — that was the standard accusation.

From 7.00 am to 9.00 am, it was my job to teach these poor, maltreated creatures about the nineteenth Party congress and Chinese customs. "When a Chinese person gets married or has a family, it's different than with us Muslims," I began, keeping it as simple as possible. Many farmers had no idea, because in the mountains they'd never experienced anything except their own culture. For them, I had to explain every single step of these ceremonies.

"At Chinese weddings, the guests always have to say the same set phrases when they congratulate the couple," I added. "For example, 'I wish you both much happiness and I hope you have a baby soon.'"

They sat in front of me with dismal faces, those shaven-headed living dead, and there I was, teaching them ways to say congratulations in Chinese.

9.00 am to 11.00 am: checking

From 9.00 am to 11.00 am, I went through the material again so I could check it afterwards. "It's time for everyone to check their notes now!" a guard told me, and I translated for the prisoners. If anybody didn't understand something, they were supposed to ask. When a hand was raised, I first looked at the armed guard to my right, making sure the question was allowed. Once permission was granted, the shackled prisoner would ask his question in his mother tongue, assuming he didn't speak Chinese well enough. If so, I first had to translate the question for the guard and wait to be told if and how I should answer. I was constantly switching between Uighur or Kazakh and Chinese.

Occasionally, individual prisoners were called on by the guards to stand up and recite what they had learned. Those who made progress earned points. "If you learn well, you'll be released sooner," they were promised, so everyone tried to absorb the material as fully as possible; only the elderly and the sick, mostly between sixty and eighty, found it atrociously difficult.

Most understood little or no Chinese. You could tell how badly they were struggling: the characters danced before their eyes, getting mixed up and tied into knots. It was an impossible task — how were they supposed to cope? How were any of them ever supposed to get out? They wanted to scream and cry, but all of them knew they had to conceal their inner turmoil.

Later on, their answers would be checked by Chinese staff, who would decide who to move down. Anyone who broke the rules outside of class also lost points, which could eventually lead to them being taken to another floor. Infringements, according to the guidelines, were to be punished increasingly harshly. These included moving in the wrong way, not knowing something, or crying out in pain.

Like the woman who had undergone brain surgery before being interned at the camp, whose untreated wound grew large and weeping. Or the people who couldn't sit down after being tortured — reason enough to drag them off and torture them again. Those who were moved up or down were assigned a different uniform and a different floor.

I soon noticed that prisoners in different-coloured uniforms were being led away in groups. Those wearing red, such as imams or very religious people, were branded serious criminals. Less serious crimes were signalled by light-blue clothing. Those accused of the more minor infractions wore dark blue. On my floor, all the prisoners wore light blue, a colour that seemed uglier in my eyes with every passing day. One by one, the less educated and the elderly lost more and more points, until finally they were sorted out like bad peas. Their places were immediately filled with new prisoners.

11.00 am to midday: "I'm proud to be Chinese!"

At 11.00 am, the guards handed out one A4-sized cardboard box per prisoner, each inscribed with a phrase in colourful script.

"Number one" held his over his head and said it aloud, and everybody repeated it several times in a row. "I'm proud to be Chinese!" Then the next person held up theirs. "I love Xi Jinping!"

Those who were not Han Chinese were considered by the Party and the government to be subhuman. Not just Kazakhs and Uighurs, but all other races across the globe. Holding up the next box, I had to add my voice to the clamour: "I owe my life and everything I have to the Party!" Meanwhile the thought whirling around in my head was: *The entire Party elite have lost their minds. They're all completely nuts.*

My gaze wandered aimlessly over their faces, when suddenly I froze. That man with the bald head — I knew him! Yes, he was a Uighur who had been arrested in Aksu in summer 2017 for celebrating a religious festival. It had caused quite a stir locally. At that moment I could see him still, a decent family man, roughly twenty-five years old, bringing his children to my kindergarten. He'd been such a genteel, happy person. And now? Who was he now? Dead-eyed, open-mouthed, screaming, "Long live the Party!"

Suddenly, a guard jabbed me with his machine gun. "Why are you goggling at him like that?" Frightened, I shouted the next phrase even louder: "Long live Xi Jinping!" Inwardly, I gave myself a good few mental slaps. There were two guards in the room, not to mention several cameras. How could I have been so stupid?

On and on it went. The Party, its "helmsman" Xi Jinping, China. Everyone was screaming as though with one mouth: "I live because the Party has given me this life!" and "Without the Party there is no new China!" Their plan was to reshape us into new people, to brainwash us until every single person was convinced. "The Party is everything. It is the most powerful force in the world. There is no god but Xi Jinping, no other almighty country, and no other almighty force in the world but China."

There were, of course, some weak personalities whose resistance dissolved as though in acid after a while in the camp. But I don't think this method really works. Lots of the prisoners were simply doing whatever it took to get out of that hellhole. They only pretended to change, acting as though their faith in the goodness and strength of the Party and its leaders made them happy.

After the abuse they'd suffered, they couldn't possibly believe all that nonsense. Speaking for myself, I never lost my faith in God. Sometimes I risked a glance at the tiny double-barred window on the exterior wall. It was forbidden to look out, but you couldn't see much anyway. No patch of sky. Only barbed wire.

As soon as one group was finished, the next one was led in. Sometimes the first group would stay, too, so there'd be more than one hundred "pupils" in the room.

Midday to 2.00 pm: water soup and fresh instructions

From midday till two, the guards put all the prisoners back into their cells and the staff back into their rooms. Minutes later, I was in kitchen queue with the other workers, ladle in hand. This time, I was handed a small piece of real bread and bland vegetable soup that was more water than vegetable. Sometimes I'd even get a spoonful of honey. Every day, they alternated these three different meals, morning noon and night. For months.

The prisoners were virtually left to starve, although, unlike me, they were forced to eat pork every Friday. Initially, some Muslims refused. Their protests resulted in nothing but torture and unforgettable pain. After a while, these people ate the pork, too.

Scarcely had I cleaned my ladle than there was another knock at the door. That meant I had to be ready in a matter of seconds. I had to be in an office next door until two, preparing for the afternoon session.

2.00 pm to 4.00 pm: a song in praise of the Party

From two till four, all the prisoners were gathered back in a classroom to sing Party songs for two hours. First, we all launched into the national anthem. Afterwards, there was another "red" song. "Without the Party, these new children would not exist. The Party has created these new children. The Party makes every effort to serve all the nationalities in the country. The Party has saved this country using all its strength ..."

Hunched on their plastic stools, their notepads resting on their thighs, those poor inmates wrote down all the texts on the board. Writing, singing, writing ... learning a whole song in a single day was too much to ask, so we only practised one verse per day. Next day, as the prisoners trudged in chains to the kitchen, they had to sing the verse they'd just learnt.

We were living in the twenty-first century. The world was advancing at breakneck speed: only in China did we seem to be spiralling backwards into our murky past. Back into the old barbarism and savagery of Mao. The Party and the government had gone to great lengths to erase that period from our memory and from the history books; yet this silence had condemned us all to relive the same atrocities and the same mistakes.

Like the omnipresent Xi Jinping, Mao — his great hero — had wanted to shape a "new man" by subjecting suspicious individuals to a brutal process of "thought reform" in camps. Just as before, a new creation was to be born from our suffering. We would become passionate servants of the Party, free from all other convictions and ties, believing only in the goodness and holiness of the Party, committed to serving its epic rise to power and the great Party leader.

Today, I only have to hear a tiny snippet of the national anthem and I react aggressively. I start to boil up; I feel a burning loathing of the Party and the state. And I think of the tortured prisoners. Of all those innocent people transformed into soulless husks. Into patriots dedicated solely to the great rebirth of a superior ethnic group. Into the perfect Chinese. Every morning, the inmates had to repeat, "I am Chinese!" over and over. One thousand, two thousand, three thousand times. Before they were even allowed breakfast.

4.00 pm to 6.00 pm: self-reflection

In the eyes of the Chinese workers at the camp, the inmates weren't human beings: they were merely criminals with numbers. "If you hadn't broken the rules or revealed yourself to be a spy or a double agent, you wouldn't be here," they told them. That was how they justified the abuse. Anyone detained in the camp, they reasoned, deserved pain.

The next two hours were primarily about sitting still and reflecting on one's mistakes. This time, I remained in the background. The two heavily armed guards, plus two or three Chinese employees from other departments, planted themselves in front of me.

One of them raised his voice. "If you acknowledge your crimes quickly and try to make them right, you will be released sooner." In case they didn't understand Chinese, I had to translate it into Kazakh.

Evidently assuming that the prisoners didn't know why they were in the camp, the employees explained. They might, for instance, be guilty of praying, of holding quite ordinary religious views, or of harbouring negative thoughts about the Chinese language, Chinese customs, or the Chinese in general.

In fact, there were hundreds of different reasons why all these people had been arrested. A photo taken with the wrong individual was all it took. And there were plenty of those. Until quite recently, Kazakhstan and Xinjiang had been on good terms. During this period, lots of foreign artists, singers, and writers had travelled into the province. Hundreds of fans had had their picture taken with pop stars, or standing next to a poster of a celebrity. Now, such photographs were considered proof of subversive thinking, and used as grounds to "purify the mind of such treacherous ideas".

After running through the various types of crimes, the staff suggested ways the inmates could determine which ones they had committed. "You must ask yourselves: what did I do wrong in my former life? And how can I best express that?"

When an employee called on the thirteen-year-old in the front row, asking, "Why are you here?", she jumped up like a shot and answered in fluent Chinese. "I made a terrible mistake and visited a relative in Kazakhstan. I will never do anything like that again!" The rest of the time had to be spent in contemplative silence, while prisoners judged their past behaviour and acknowledged their guilt.

Anybody who maintained their innocence was not only punished, but found their relatives had been detained as well. And confessions had to sound believable. A man might convincingly claim, for instance, "I was a believer, and I went to the mosque." Even if that wasn't true, he had to try to formulate his offence in Chinese during those two hours so that afterwards he could write it down properly.

Prisoners spent late afternoons preparing their written admissions of guilt, which would be handed in that night. Nobody ventured to say a word. Everyone was quiet. There was no sound to be heard bar the rushing in my own head, like an impending flood.

6.00 pm to 8.00 pm: a break and an evening meal

From six till eight, it was time to eat. The prisoners lined up outside their cells: women on one side, men on the other. Down the middle of the floor ran a straight red line, framed either side by a blue line. They had to move unswervingly along this red line. Shackled at the wrist and ankle, they were only able to take small, shuffling steps. Anyone who stumbled or accidently stepped on the blue line was tortured. Once they reached the kitchen hatch, the guards unlocked their handcuffs on one side so that the prisoner could carry their food back.

Meanwhile I had to report to the office after my first day of class. I had made a mistake.

Mistake!

The door wasn't even closed, and already I was being grilled by a member of the administrative staff. "Did you recognise a familiar face among the prisoners? Why did you look so concerned when you were staring at that Uighur?" The staff in the surveillance room had caught my expression on camera. They were always on the lookout. How is she behaving? What's going on in her mind? Is she a traitor?" And the trap had been sprung.

For a moment, I was gripped by sheer terror. *It's over — it's all over!* I thought. I had signed a contract agreeing I would make no mistakes, or else I was dead. "No, no," I protested, trying disjointedly to defend myself — I could barely tear my tongue from the roof of my mouth. "That look on my face wasn't because of a person. I just keep getting these terrible stomach pains. They hurt so much there's nothing I can do."

"Sit down!" he ordered, and handed me a pen and paper. I was supposed to write a confession and sign it, avowing that I would never look a prisoner directly in the face again. No sooner had I laid the pen aside than I was told to repeat the promise out loud: "In the future, I will never behave that way again."

The next day, the young Uighur was missing. They had probably deducted points and demoted him to a red uniform. I spent many nights racked with terrible guilt. *They've sent him somewhere even worse*, I thought, *and it's my fault.* How could I have forgotten myself like that? How could I have dragged someone else down with me? I tore myself into a thousand tiny pieces, berating myself over and over until nothing good remained — and it made me loathe the Party even more.

8.00 pm to 10.00 pm: "I'm a criminal!"

From 8.00 pm to 10.00 pm, the prisoners were dismissed into their cells to "accept their crimes internally". This meant concentrating on them fervently and repeating their offences over and over in hushed tones. "I'm a criminal because I prayed. I'm a criminal because I prayed. I'm a criminal …" Heads turned to the wall, their shackled, upraised hands resting against the brickwork. For two long hours. Cheek by jowl.

Meanwhile I was busy doing paperwork in one of the offices, organising records or filing documents. Under constant supervision, of course. Once a week, I drew up a handwritten report on what I had accomplished, carrying out a self-assessment. "I performed all my tasks to my complete satisfaction." They only allowed senior employees to use the computers. I wasn't allowed anywhere near them.

My report was between one and three pages, depending on how much time I was given. I assume they compared it against the CCTV footage they'd recorded.

Sometimes they would send me to the medical area, just two doors down from my cell, so that I could sort patient files. Every prisoner was initially examined by a doctor. Their condition, their blood group — every detail that evidently mattered to them was meticulously recorded.

Once a month, the prisoners "donated blood". All the inmates would be lined up outside the medical area, waiting to be seen. I had to participate as well, but they did mine separately. I only met one nurse on that floor who worked there for several months at a stretch. Judging by her accent, she was from a city in the interior, like nearly all the other staff members. She was roughly twenty-one years old with short black hair, and wore a camouflage uniform, like me. Other nurses, doctors, and carers were always called in from outside in the middle of the night.

"Put the files of the prisoners with infectious diseases in a separate folder," she told me. The other medical staff called her by the nickname "Xiao Chen". Otherwise they rarely addressed each other by name, preferring to use their job titles: "Hey, medic, over here!" they'd say.

They paid special attention in the medical department to the files of young, strong people. These were treated differently and marked with a red X. At first, I was so naïve — only later did I wonder why they always earmarked the files of fundamentally healthy people.

Had they preselected these individuals for organ harvesting? Organs that doctors would later remove without consent? It was simply a fact that the Party took organs from prisoners.

Several clinics in East Turkestan traded in organs. In Altai, for instance, it was common knowledge that lots of Arabs preferred the organs of fellow Muslims, because they considered them "halal". Perhaps, I thought, they were trading in kidneys, hearts, and usable body parts at the camp as well?

After a while, I realised that these young, healthy inmates were disappearing overnight, whisked away by the guards, even though their point scores hadn't dropped. When I checked later, I realised to my horror that all their medical files were marked with a red X.

A second reason they might be systematically rooting out all the healthy, strong people only occurred to me after my release. There have been numerous reports of people being transported into central China and used as slave labourers. Any company that benefits from this has a moral responsibility. They should be checking their supply chains very carefully for any breach of human rights.

We know from subcontractors' lists, as well as from research by independent think tanks and other scholarly sources, that tens of thousands of Muslims from East Turkestan have been sent to factories nationwide. For these people, leaving the camp does not mean escaping state control: they are housed in isolated accommodation with other workers, in complexes surrounded by barbed wire. Companies in the West — including Bosch, Adidas, Microsoft, and Lacoste — benefit from this slave labour. Firms such as Siemens supply crucial infrastructure, among other things, to these camps. Innocent people are being arrested, monitored, and detained using foreign-made cameras and scanners.

10.00 pm to midnight: written confessions

From ten till midnight, every inmate spent two hours hunched over their notebook on the floor of their cell, writing down their admissions of guilt. If you put something like, "I committed a religious crime, because I fasted during Ramadan. But today I know there is no God," you had a good chance of improving your point score. Everyone had to hand in their work the next morning.

The system rewarded the best actors, the ones who were most convincingly able to pretend that they had "freed themselves from dirty thoughts". One sentence was particularly important, and always had to appear in a confession: "I am no longer a Muslim. I don't believe in God anymore."

Meanwhile I would be drawing up another report, or cleaning the corridors, various offices, and the classroom. Sometimes other employees would be assigned to the same tasks, but when it was my turn, I always had to work alone. There was no clear rota. Sometimes it was my turn every day. Sometimes I had to do it during the daytime; sometimes at night or in the evenings. For me, there was only one reliable rule: you don't get breaks.

As long as the prisoners were awake, the staff were trying to control their thoughts. Even when they were finally left alone, I don't know how so many people were able to rest in such a confined space. They had to sleep pushed up against one another, on their right sides, chained at the wrists and ankles. Turning over was strictly forbidden and would be harshly punished. I imagine it was like falling into a dark, bottomless pit — like dropping briefly into unconsciousness.

But my day wasn't over.

Midnight to 1.00 am: keeping watch

I was on sentry duty till one in the morning. At midnight, I had to stand in my assigned spot in the vast hall for an hour. Sometimes we would switch sides with the other sentries.

We were always positioned behind a line drawn on the floor. On rare occasions there would be a few inmates lined up there, too, but there would always be a guard by each of them. "We cannot under any circumstances allow a break-out!" they insisted. Not that escape seemed likely. All of the doors had multiple locks. Nobody was ever getting out.

If, by some chance, one of the prisoners *did* manage to escape, they continued, we were not to let the news spread around the camp.

I stared at the glass-walled guardhouse opposite. Behind it was the stairwell. I had quickly realised that there must be several lower levels, because administrative staff often took ages fetching things from "the bottom floor", even when they were ordered to hurry.

The stairwell was also near the "black room", where they tortured people in the most abominable ways. After two or three days at the camp, I heard the screams for the first time, resonating throughout the enormous hall and seeping into every pore of my body. I felt like I was teetering on the edge of some dizzying chasm.

I'd never heard anything like it in all my life. Screams like that aren't something you forget. The second you hear them, you know what kind of agony that person is experiencing. They sounded like the raw cries of a dying animal.

My heart almost stopped beating. I felt like casting myself on the floor and covering my ears, but I knew I couldn't even think about crying. *Otherwise you'll never see your children again,*

I reminded myself desperately. So I clenched my teeth as hard as I could, and retreated ever deeper inside my own mind. Deep enough that I saw only hazy outlines and heard only muffled sounds. From that day forth, I heard those screams every day.

1.00 am to 6.00 am: sleep

After I was relieved of duty, I curled up on the plastic mattress, drew up my knees, and pulled the blanket over my head. The cold oozed up out of the concrete floor and into my bones. Usually, in an attempt to stay a little warmer and more comfortable, I kept my uniform on.

Sleep was impossible, although I was utterly exhausted. The stench of the toilets, the screams still echoing in my ears, the unbearable things I'd seen — I was so profoundly shocked and frightened that every muscle was tense.

I lay motionless, unresting. I kept picturing the prisoners' grave faces in my mind's eye. Their mute resignation. Questions swirled endlessly through my head. *Why is this happening? Why don't these people care about our pain? How can anyone be so stony-hearted?* Our lives were worth no more to them than a beetle trodden heedlessly underfoot.

At some point, I drifted off, and two hours later the bell shrilled again. For days, life in the camp was exactly the same.

Artificial light twenty-four hours a day. Locked in a concrete coffin. Before long, you didn't know if it was day or night. Winter or spring. Had weeks passed, or months?

Some days were similar to the first. On others, I received strictly confidential instructions …

State secrets: the Three-Step Plan

Confidential information was always reaching the camp unexpectedly, usually in the middle of the night. Sometimes once a week; sometimes ten days in a row. A messenger would scurry out of the stairwell behind the glass wall and into one of the offices.

Which room the guard led me to and how many people were present seemed to vary depending on the importance of the message. I wasn't always told to attend, but I usually was. Not many people were privy to state secrets, so at most two or three senior officers would be present.

These government officials mostly belonged to a new authority, the name of which roughly translates as "National Security". They wore uniforms similar to the police and military, although more expensive and of higher quality. The most senior person in the room was given the information first, and then passed it to me.

I was supposed to sit and read it quietly while officers stood behind and beside me. As I read, they studied my facial expressions. The first time I was still clueless about what to expect, so my dismay was written all over my face.

Beijing likes to pretend that it's not responsible for what governors in distant Chinese provinces get up to. But these confidential papers were emblazoned with the words "Classified Documents from Beijing". The truth is that the camps in East Turkestan were set up on orders from Party headquarters in Beijing.

The documents they had pressed into my hands set out the government's Three-Step Plan:

> Step One: 2014–2015: Assimilate those who are willing in Xinjiang, and eliminate those who are not.

I felt dizzy. Planned mass murders? Each step consisted of a core idea and a bullet-point list of sub-items. As early as 2014, Beijing had started laying the groundwork by separating my homeland into two regions: northern and southern. The Uighurs in the south had been selected as the Party's first victims, because they were the largest ethnic minority. The northern region was populated mainly by Kazakhs, Kyrgyzstanis, and people of other ethnicities, who had been increasingly targeted from 2016 onwards. I was almost afraid to read on. Apprehensive, I hunched over the papers.

Step Two: 2025–2035: After assimilation within China is complete, neighbouring countries will be annexed.

Various countries, such as Kyrgyzstan, Kazakhstan, and Uzbekistan, would gradually be seized, including through the Belt and Road Initiative and generous lines of credit. The plan was to make these economically struggling countries indebted to Beijing. More and more Chinese would then move there and settle down and build factories, but also invest in media companies, publishing houses, and TV stations, paving the way for Chinese politics in those countries. On top of that, Beijing would send spies and informants into foreign countries to gather state secrets.

Step Three: 2035–2055: After the realisation of the Chinese dream comes the occupation of Europe.

My eyes were fixed on the sheet of paper; I almost forgot to breathe. This meant that China's campaign of terror might not end with the Uighurs or the Kazakhs: they were seeking to bring the whole world to heel. And if other countries didn't twig in time, it meant this nightmare would be repeated for them, too.

When I looked up, I realised from the officer's tight smile that he hadn't failed to notice my pale face and agitation. "Why are you reacting like that? What exactly are you reacting to?"

"I'm intimidated by your authority," I stuttered, apologising meekly. "And anyway, I'm not sure if I've understood the content correctly and whether I'm allowed to ask you."

Smugly self-satisfied, he lifted his chin and quizzed me on the content. "What did you understand from that?" If I didn't phrase my response using the correct Party jargon, he interrupted me — "No!" — and gave me the official interpretation. "Repeat!" he barked, forcing me to repeat his version.

The goal was to recruit the poor souls in "class" as foot soldiers, pressing them into service for the government's fantasies of global dominance. To bring them onto the side of the Party, so that ultimately the nation would be like a beehive: everyone would think alike, share the same beliefs, and work towards the same purpose. We were all supposed to work together to become the most powerful country in the world and "participate in the glory of the People's Republic's project". The prisoners were supposed to be the eyes and ears of the CCP.

Finally, they took the documents out of my hand, ordered me to stand up, and took me over to a metal bin in the middle of the room. In front of the eyes of the guards, one of the men took out his lighter and held it up to the paper. Another member of staff was filming a recording as proof, and didn't turn off his phone until the very last scrap had gone up in flames.

The snippet of information I had glimpsed disappeared. But it was only a fragment of what the colonels knew, information that was electronically transmitted and much more detailed. When there was nothing left but a pile of grey ash, they let me sleep.

Some people in the West don't believe any of this — it seems too monstrous to be true. But I've met another Kazakh survivor from a different camp who also learned about the Three-Step Plan. Clearly, they were teaching the same material in various camps, so there must be more witnesses to corroborate this.

Teaching assimilation: "How long do we have to stay here?"

The next day, class began with a song in praise of the Party. "The Communist Party has managed to re-educate so many people! This is good for the people as a whole, because we are one unified group!" After that I moved on to the Belt and Road Initiative.

I passed on the government's confidential information in small chunks spread out over several days. The guards in the room checked whether the message had got through by quizzing random prisoners. Only then would they let me continue teaching.

"This new silk road already connects Xinjiang very successfully with Africa, Asia, and Europe. This mega-scale economic and geopolitical project will transport not just our goods, but great Chinese policies as well."

The message to the prisoners was clear: any resistance to this vastly superior economic, political, and military power was futile.

They reacted anxiously to the part about assimilation in Xinjiang and the timeframe it laid out. During the question period, they raised their hands. "You promised to let us go within five or six months. Does this mean we'll be here for another ten years?" Or: "What do we have to do if we want to get out before 2035?"

As usual, I had to translate for the guards before I was allowed to answer. "If you do everything you're told, stay submissive, and continue to eat pork and do everything the Party representatives command, then you'll get out more quickly."

Was that really the truth? There is no clear answer. In the five months I spent there, not a single prisoner was released. And afterwards, in Aksu, I never heard of any friends or acquaintances being set free from a camp, even though most of the ones I knew had been locked up for years.

Even if a prisoner wasn't subsequently forced into slave labour, he or she would never be the same. With the best will in the world, I can't imagine that any of those maltreated people lived very long. The constant physical and psychological pressure would have scarred them to such an extent that they would have been incapable of feeling happiness during the brief time left to them. Their spirits broken, they were in a perpetual state of fear. Even a slightly raised voice set their hearts racing and made them uneasy.

Rampant malnutrition, abuse, infections, and medication meant that anyone who left those prison gates was deeply traumatised, with significant psychological and physical health problems. Many of them weren't themselves anymore; they were state-controlled robots.

Making the dead disappear

I've described one type of confidential document already — the type that ended up crumbling into ash. But some controversial subject matter wasn't intended for teaching, so they took a different approach. Not even the guards in the room were allowed to know what these documents contained, and thus one night I found myself standing motionless in a small office, silently reading Instruction 21.

Here, too, officers observed my facial expressions, trying to work out how I was reacting to the contents. But I'd learned my lesson. No matter how appalling the message, my face betrayed no response.

"All those who die in the camp must vanish without a trace." There it was, as plain as day, in bald, official jargon, as though they were talking about disposing of spoiled food. There should be no visible signs of torture on the bodies. When a prisoner was killed, or died in some other way, it had to be kept absolutely secret. Any evidence, proof, or documentation was to be immediately destroyed. Taking photos or video recordings of the corpses was strictly forbidden. Family members were supposed to be fobbed off with vague excuses as to the manner of death; and in certain cases, they explained, it was advisable simply never to mention they had died at all.

During my time at the camp, I didn't see them kill anybody, but I did know many people who disappeared. I saw people sprawled on the ground, close to death. The likelihood that human beings died at that camp is extremely high.

Very few employees — only those with the appropriate level of clearance — were told about the deaths and what caused them. Apart from them, no one was allowed to know a thing.

It made sense to me that all this was kept from the prisoners. They could never be allowed to know that they might die at the camp — it might make them harder to control, or cause a mass panic. But why were they telling me? I looked up, bewildered.

The officer held out a pen and paper. "Sign this!" he ordered. By doing so, I confirmed receipt of the document and accepted responsibility for its contents. If things went pear-shaped later on, they had my signature on a piece of paper they could use to hang me out to dry. I wasn't the one who was going to implement these orders — I was just an easily sacrificed pawn.

In each of the camps, one person was required to draw up a daily report that was sent to Ürümqi. The city was the site of a secret central hub known as the "Integrated Joint Operations Platform", which gathered information on camps across the country. This included all the data on the prisoners, including DNA, passports, and ID numbers. The office also received instructions from Beijing, which it passed on to various other regions and camps.

Once I had signed that directive about dealing with deaths, the officials would almost certainly have sent it to Ürümqi.

Showering

After a while, the prisoners' clothes would stick to their bodies. They stank of sweat and dirt, but they were only allowed to wash once every month or two. As an employee, meanwhile, I was allowed to shower once a week or once a fortnight.

Two guards escorted me to the door with their automatic weapons. They would either wait there or come inside with me. The washroom was basic, with each shower separated from the main room by a curtain. I was always alone. No other women were present. Nobody was allowed to linger too close to me, and the water ran for no more than two minutes. I wondered whether the prisoners were allowed hot water, too. Probably not.

I didn't notice until later that the whole shower room was under CCTV surveillance. Once, when I was mopping the floor in the control room, where footage from all the cameras was playing on various screens, I saw two Chinese employees ogling naked girls and women. They were laughing loudly and cracking dirty jokes. "Take a look at that!" they guffawed.

As I moved back and forth with my mop, I watched as they zoomed in on particular body parts, focusing on their breasts and genitals. A few of the girls had clearly realised they were being filmed, because some of them only partially undressed and hurriedly washed their hair.

The next time I was taken for a shower, I did my best to cover myself up. Cautiously raising my head, I examined the ceiling more closely, and noticed the camera lenses. They were so tiny it was easy to overlook them.

A list of the twenty-six most dangerous countries in the world

The next day in "class", I was instructed to smear the USA — public enemy number one, as far as China is concerned. The Party had put together a list of twenty-one countries, sorted according to which ones were the most hostile to the People's Republic of China.

No. 1: USA. No. 2: Japan. Nos. 3 and 4: Germany and Kazakhstan, although I can't remember which order those last two were in. Anyone with contacts in these countries was considered an enemy of the state.

The Party had made no secret of this list. They had used it as explicit justification for arrests. I told the prisoners in glowing terms how "sacred and good" the Communist Party was, ending with how "bad" some of the European nations, and especially the USA, were.

Any hardships experienced in China were the result of US policies directed against the Chinese people and designed to foment divisions, I explained, repeating what I had been told by the prison administration. Even if the Chinese tortured Muslims, the USA was ultimately to blame, because they were the ones who led people of other faiths to think incorrectly and act badly. This was the communist mindset.

According to Beijing, Western-style democracy was a failed model descending into crisis and chaos.

Secret codes: first straw shoes, then leather shoes

Many nights, I received secret coded messages:

1. Deal with the "straw shoes"'first and then the "leather shoes".

"Straw shoes" meant ordinary people, such as shepherds, farmers, and fishermen. By "leather shoes" they meant government workers — for instance, those in administration, schools, and security agencies.

"Dealing with the "straw shoes" meant that indigenous groups had to be made Chinese first. Anyone who resisted or refused to play along would "have their shoes removed" by force. That was the hidden meaning of this message.

I'm not 100 per cent sure why they used these secret codes. The Party follows its own logic. Maybe they didn't want everybody to be able to grasp the meaning straightaway? The messengers would deliver their communiqués to a member of staff, who would then pass them on, creating a long chain of people with access to the information. Because I was well educated and more able to interpret metaphors than most of the couriers, they evidently decided to communicate with me like this.

2. Categorise all households into three groups: 1. Main households; 2. Ordinary households; 3. Reliable households.

They were trying to establish levels of threat. "Reliable house-holds" were Chinese, and were left unmolested by the government. The other two households referred to Muslim minorities — those who, according to Beijing, required brainwashing. By "ordinary households" they meant families with maybe only one or two suspicious individuals. In a "main household", on the other hand, everybody ended up in chains.

After I had absorbed the content of the message, a staff member took out his lighter, and the document went up in flames.

The black room

During "class", I noticed a number of prisoners groaning and scratching themselves until they bled. I couldn't tell if they were genuinely ill or had gone mad. As my mouth opened and closed — I was barely even listening to myself talk about our self-sacrificing patriarch Xi Jinping, who "passes on the warmth of love with his hands" — several of the "students" collapsed unconscious and fell off their plastic chairs.

In threatening situations, human beings have a kind of switch in our brains that functions like a fuse in an electrical circuit. As soon as the level of anguish we're experiencing exceeds the capacity of our senses, we simply switch off: to stop us going out of our minds with fear, we lose consciousness in extremis.

When this happened, the guards would summon their colleagues outside, who rushed in, grabbed the unconscious person by both arms, and dragged them away like a doll, their feet trailing across the floor. But they didn't just take the unconscious, the sick, and the mad. Suddenly, the door would spring open, and heavily armed men would thunder into the room. For no reason at all. Sometimes it was simply because a prisoner hadn't understood one of the guard's orders, issued in Chinese.

These people were among the unluckiest in the camp. I could see in their eyes how they felt — that raging storm of pain and suffering. Hearing their screams and cries for help in the corridors afterwards made our blood freeze in our veins, and brought us to the verge of panic. They were drawn-out, constant, virtually unbearable. There was no more sorrowful sound.

I saw with my own eyes the various instruments of torture in the "black room". The chains on the wall. Many inmates, bound at the wrists and ankles, they strapped into chairs that had nails sticking out of the seats. Many of the people they tortured never came back out of that room — others stumbled out, covered in blood.

Occasionally, the guards took me into the cells so I could translate for them. I saw prisoners sprawled on the floor, so dreadfully injured after being tortured that they were unable to stand.

How do I know so much about the various implements in the black room? I was tortured there myself.

Conspiracy: my encounter with an elderly shepherd

One night in January 2018, a large group of new prisoners arrived. Among them was a Kazakh grandmother with a short grey braid, a simple shepherd from the mountains. You could tell that she had been snatched unexpectedly. The police hadn't even given her time to put on shoes. It was winter and very cold, yet she stood there in her socks. She was eighty-four years old.

Desperate for help, the old lady was casting around in all directions. When she saw my round face among the implacable Chinese guards along the wall, she rushed over with her arms outstretched, threw them around me, and begged, "Please, you're a Kazakh, you must help me! Please save me! I'm innocent, I haven't done anything! Please save me!"

It came out of nowhere. At that moment, I didn't know what to do.

I stood there in shock. She cried, trembling with cold and fear. Perhaps I put my arms around her for a few seconds. I don't really remember what I did — it all happened so fast. But my reaction was definitely perceived as a violation of the contract I'd signed.

The next moment, the guards had torn the old lady off me and dragged me away. Into the black room: the only place on our floor where there were no cameras, so that there would be no evidence of the monstrous things that went on inside.

I was suspected of conspiracy.

Where evil lives

The space, roughly twenty metres square, looked a bit like a darkroom. A messy black strip about thirty centimetres wide had been painted on the wall just above the floor, as though someone had smeared it with mud. In the middle was a table three or four metres long, crammed with all kinds of tools and torture devices. Tasers and police cudgels in various shapes and sizes: thick, thin, long, and short. Iron rods used to fix the hands and feet in agonising positions behind a person's back, designed to inflict the maximum possible pain.

The walls, too, were hung with weapons and implements that looked like they were from the Middle Ages. Implements used to pull out fingernails and toenails, and a long stick — a bit like a spear — that had been sharpened like a dagger at one end. They used it for jabbing into a person's flesh.

Along one side of the room was a row of chairs designed for different purposes. Electric chairs and metal chairs with bars and straps to stop the victim moving; iron chairs with holes in the back so that the arms could be twisted back above the shoulder joint. My gaze wandered across the walls and floor. Rough cement. Grey and dirty, revolting and confusing — as though evil itself was squatting in that room, feeding on our pain. I was certain I would die before dawn.

Two men were standing in front of me. One wore a black facemask and lace-up boots. It was clear from his accent that he was Han Chinese, and he was in charge of the interrogation. The first sentence he bellowed at me, repeating it over and over, was: "What have you done wrong?" They expected me to confess my guilt and make up a crime, even though I hadn't done anything. His Chinese colleague wore a policeman's uniform and no mask. He held a taser in his hand.

I was terrified they would strap me into the "tiger chair" with the nails or cut me open with a scalpel, but they had chosen the electric chair. They placed a close-fitting metal rod over my body so that I could barely move.

"What did the old shepherd say to you? Why did she act like that? Do you know her?"

"She begged me to save her," I replied truthfully. On the one hand, I wanted to save myself, but on the other I wanted to help the old woman, so I didn't tell them she had also said she was innocent. None of the Chinese spoke Kazakh, so if I had translated that part for these torturers, they would have punished her even more harshly. People in that camp admitted guilt — they didn't dispute it.

Suddenly, my whole body was shaking and twitching as though it was no longer my own. At the same time, blows started raining down. My head hanging, I saw the lace-up boots in front of my face. Slowly, very slowly, I raised my chin. "You're a conspirator! You're lying," the masked man roared. Then they hit me on the shoulder, on the head, the hands, until I collapsed again.

The longer it took me to answer or to confess my guilt, the more they upped the current. I had to tell them what they wanted to hear. "Yes, I know that woman from before. She asked me to make a phone call for her to let her relatives know that she left the door of her hut open …" Every sentence was a huge effort.

My torturers had no humanity, no sympathy or emotion. They were like rabid dogs on a chain. Vicious and wild. Those men didn't see us as people — we were more like test animals or lab rats. I kept losing consciousness because of the electric shocks.

It was obvious how much satisfaction they took in the suffering of others. They laughed while they were doing it. The more they heard me whimpering with pain, the more clearly I saw the pleasure on the face of the unmasked man, and the more avidly they tortured me.

You must not show your pain. I heard the voice of the mysterious healer in the taxi echo through my head, mingled with that of my father. It came from far, far away.

Even when everything felt numb, when the blood was throbbing in my ears and the world dwindled into a greyish-black fog, I forced my heavy tongue to slur through the same words: "I know that woman from before …" Each time, I tried to lift my head and let out as few moans of pain as possible. After a while they lost interest, and I was spared further punishment.

Three hours later, I was flat on the floor of my cell. Instantly, everything turned deep black. It was like night had mantled me in a black shroud. Yet, suddenly, there was a banging at the door. "Get up!" Every movement was like a knife through my body, but somehow I had to get to my feet and do my job. Otherwise I'd give them another reason to torture me. And that would have meant death.

Endurance

That night in the black room changed me. It left me a bundle of nerves. I felt like an alien: disconnected, different. My footsteps were heavy, as though the ground was trying to swallow me up; I barely had the strength to lift my feet. The pain was past bearing. Yet I continued teaching. There was a din in my head, as though a pneumatic drill was boring through it.

The first time a member of staff in the classroom confronted the old shepherd with her crime — "You're a spy, you made an international call on your phone" — she bitterly denied it. So they dragged that eighty-four-year-old woman into the black room and pulled out her fingernails. Afterwards, when they asked her why she was there, she struggled to form the words in clumsy Chinese, "I called abroad on my phone." The woman had never even owned a mobile phone, let alone knew how to use one.

As an additional punishment for my unauthorised contact with the old woman, I went two days without food. No matter how little life was left in me, I never lost hope of escaping that godforsaken place. Never!

To keep myself going, at night I used to imagine going for a walk with my children in Kazakhstan. By now, I hadn't seen Ukilay or Ulagat for a year and a half. The separation weighed heavily on me, like someone was pressing a fist into my heart.

Sometimes I'd toss and turn at night, until my father's voice reached me. *Stay strong, my daughter.* "Yes," I replied, and lay still — only my lips were moving. "If everything goes well, father, in the future I will travel to other countries with my loved ones and experience precious moments of freedom."

Dying wasn't an option, because I wanted to see my children again at least once more. And I was determined to escape the camp somehow so I could tell the outside world about the heinous atrocities being perpetrated.

In a normal prison, you're detained on the basis of a court judgement. You do your time and then you're released. In the camp, however, you never knew whether you were getting out, even though you were innocent. This process of extra-judicial arrests and systematic internment is one of the greatest crimes against humanity committed in the modern era.

Month after month, what kept me alive was the hope that there would be an outcry in the free world as soon as the truth about the horrors in East Turkestan came to light. Liberal democracies would realise the danger they themselves were in. And I imagined other heads of state intervening in Beijing's inhumane policies and making the world a better place once more.

These were the thoughts that kept me going.

Preventing disease while cranking out sick people

Back on sentry duty one night, I saw a long queue of prisoners outside the medical area. "It's just a vaccination program!" the nurses assured them, so that people wouldn't hyperventilate or lash out. A doctor chimed in, "It's simply a preventative measure to stop you passing on infectious diseases." That was as precise as they got. Nurses and doctors reached down and gave the inmates an injection in the upper arm. Some of them resisted, screaming with fear — "I don't want any injections!" — but two medics held them down while the third gave them the jab. Afterwards, the prisoners who'd fought back were beaten by the guards in the black room.

If they were genuinely trying to stop the spread of disease, then why didn't they take much simpler and more efficient measures? Why didn't they disinfect the cells? Why did they jam so many people into a tiny space twenty-four hours a day, surrounded by urine and excrement?

And why were they being given this drug in their upper arms? Why not other body parts? As a doctor, I knew that jabs were often given that way to children to prevent illnesses. But this wasn't necessary with adults, since they didn't offer the same protection. So why were all the inmates being forced to have this "vaccination"?

There were so many sick people at that camp. The administration knew exactly the state of each prisoner's health, because they kept such meticulous medical records. Why did they have to be "vaccinated" again nearly every month? If they really wanted to help those who were unwell, why did they refuse them treatment and palliative care?

Why didn't they help the woman who had had brain surgery before her arrest and was now virtually driven mad by the pain? Why did they let a young diabetic woman spend the whole day on the bare floor of her cell, drifting in and out of consciousness? Because they refused to give her medication, by now she was suffering from the worst form of diabetes, and could no longer stand upright. I don't know what happened to her. When I left, she was still lying there.

Medical annihilation

After a while, they prescribed me medication, too. "It's good for you and helps ward off illness," the doctor told me. From then on, I had swallow a large tablet once a week, watched by the nurse they called Xiao Chen. What else could I do?

The first time I took it, I had terrible stomach problems and nausea. After the second one, too, I found myself constantly battling the urge to vomit. The young Chinese nurse adjusted her camouflage cap and eyed me sympathetically. She was in charge of handing out the medication. She had a slim figure, a long face, and a strong character.

The next time I was standing in front of her in the dinner queue, she hissed into my ear, "No more swallowing! Poisonous!" The next time I was in front of her and the camera, I only acted like I was taking the tablet. She confirmed on her sheet of paper that I had taken it, while I unobtrusively wiped my mouth and dropped it into the bin while I was tidying up.

The administration did its best to stop employees fraternising or developing personal relationships — they didn't want people working together too long and becoming friends — so they were constantly reassigning staff.

But the Chinese nurse who helped me had been on my floor since my arrival and had known me for weeks, because I often sorted out the medical files and lent her a hand. Realising that there were a few individuals among the Chinese staff who had the courage to allow themselves human emotions made my heart race with joy. Perhaps it was she, too, who had stopped me being "vaccinated" like the others?

But they didn't stop at giving us only one tablet and one vaccination: they prescribed numerous drugs. Some prisoners clamped their mouths shut out of fear, and others whimpered that they didn't want any medicine, but nobody was let off. The medics would forcibly open their prisoners' jaws and give them the drug.

After that, many of the women stopped having periods. Maybe they wanted to make us infertile, so we couldn't reproduce? After I'd observed this phenomenon, the nurse confirmed it, telling me, "You won't have any more children." Other ingredients turned the inmates into apathetic zombies as soon as they'd taken the drug. A person like that feels no longing, no longer thinks of their family or of a free, normal life. Then there were pharmaceuticals that permanently poisoned our bodies.

Once, as I was tidying up the medical bay and picking up rubbish, Xiao Chen was walking past me and asked brusquely, "Can I throw this piece of paper in?" Before she moved on, she gave me a tiny kick. I got the message, but I had to be careful before simply fishing it out, because there was a guard in the room.

As I took out the bag of rubbish, I subtly picked up the small rolled-up note and hid it in my shoe, smuggling it into my cell that night. Lying on my plastic mattress, I pulled the blanket over my head, which I often did because of the bright lights. My fingers trembling slightly, I unrolled the note and read it. "Don't take any medication or injections! Extremely dangerous!"

They weren't experimenting on us. They didn't just want to make us numb or permanently insane. They were trying to annihilate us. I put the note in my mouth, chewed, and swallowed.

Even worse for women

Every day, we heard piercing screams coming from the black room. Every day, we hardened a little more. Torture has broken many strong men, but in the camp it was women and girls who had it worst. When I was working as a sentry or a cleaner in the evenings, I often noticed the guards fetching the youngest and prettiest girls from the cells, most of them eighteen or nineteen years old.

How were those helpless creatures supposed to defend themselves? If they had screamed or cried, they would have been tormented in the black room afterwards. The high-ranking employees had free reign over our bodies. Authorities at the highest levels in Beijing had given them limitless power. They were allowed not only to brutalise the prisoners, but to kill them.

While I was cleaning their offices or drawing up my reports, I listened attentively as members of staff discussed the new guidelines around torture, repeatedly reassuring each other, "It's a good thing we've got it in black and white. Now no one can be punished for torture." Two of them asked again, "Are you absolutely sure?"

"Yeah, yeah, we're protected. Nothing's going to happen to us. We can do whatever we want to them."

When I heard conversations like that, I always tried to catch as much as possible so I understood exactly what was going on. These men were merciless and unafraid. Only people who aren't afraid of retribution are that cruel. No court would ever hold the murderers acting out their sadistic fantasises in the camps to account.

The guards didn't bring the girls they'd taken back to the classroom until the following day. They looked pale and scared. Some had abrasions and swollen, blinking red eyes. Despite their exhaustion, you could tell how aghast they were and what horrors they'd suffered.

One of these girls, who had only been brought back half an hour before the lesson began, seemed completely absent. Her arms hung limply by her sides. She was unable to sit on her plastic stool or pick up her pen, so she slipped sideways off the stool and lay motionless on the floor.

"Sit down!" the guard barked at her, but she simply could not. I was ordered to give her a warning and addressed her loudly by her number. "You, girl number ..., sit down." No reaction. She merely replied with a single sentence: "I'm not a girl anymore." Then the guards took her into the black room.

You never knew in the morning how the day would end. You never knew if you'd be the same person that night. How the day's torment might change you. What things would get tangled up like barbed wire in your head, lacerating your brain overnight.

The final test

At the end of January 2018, they unexpectedly summoned about one hundred prisoners into a large room I'd never been in before. Lots of employees were already inside, sitting in semi-circles in several rows of plastic chairs. I stood at the back. Like the other prisoners, I had no idea what the meeting was about.

A man in a black mask and lace-up leather boots stepped into the middle of the semi-circle and called one of the girls forward to confess her crime, surrounded by onlookers. She hadn't been there long: she was a little plump, and shaved bald like everyone else. She was maybe twenty or twenty-one years old.

As instructed, she made her confession in Chinese: "When I was in Year Nine, I texted a friend on my mobile phone to wish her a blessed holiday. It was a religious occasion and a crime. I will never do it again!" All our lives, it had been normal for us Muslims to send each other greetings on holidays. It's no different from Christians wishing each other "Happy Easter" or

"Merry Christmas". Party officials had found this years-old text while checking her phone.

"Lie down!" ordered one of the masked men. The onlookers craned their necks in surprise. What was going on? The plump girl stared at them wide-eyed, then obeyed the order uncertainly, while two other masked men closed in.

One of them tore off her trousers with a jerk, then unzipped his own. "No!" screamed the girl, horrified, and tried to jump up, fending off the man with her hands, but a moment later he forced her to the ground and pinned her down with his whole weight. Panicking frantically, she stared at the onlookers and screamed, "Help me! Please help me!" while the man above her started to pant and wheeze like an animal.

At first, no one in the audience moved a muscle. We were frozen solid. Like naked people in ice. My temples were throbbing; my mind raced. *Run, Sayragul, run away!* My eyes flitted desperately to and fro, scanning for help, for an escape route, but there was nothing but closed doors. And everywhere the guards, watching our faces like hunters on the prowl.

A few of the onlookers collapsed and cried out loud. Instantly, they were grabbed, still in their chains, and dragged away. Suddenly, I understood why we were there. It was a test! They wanted to see whether we had been "cured" of our "sick religious thinking" and brought into line with the Party. "Help me! Please help me!"

Nothing was worse than being a helpless bystander witnessing this deranged torture. It felt like having a limb amputated without anaesthetic. But anyone who revealed their true feelings had proven, from the camp administration's perspective, that they still harboured national or religious feelings towards their Kazakh compatriots. *Stay calm, Sayragul, stay calm …*

We were supposed to watch unmoved as the young woman's

head whipped back and forth, frantic with pain and fear. When the first man was finished and pulled his trousers back up, like a hyena having eaten its fill, the second masked man set upon the abused body on the floor.

Some of the male prisoners couldn't stand it anymore. Leaping up from their seats, they shouted at the top of their lungs, "Why are you torturing us like this? Don't you have hearts? Don't you have daughters of your own?" Immediately, the guards grabbed them and led them away, while the girl screamed until she was empty, hollowed out inside, while the third man forced himself between her bloodied thighs.

A drop of sweat beaded on my forehead. By now, the girl had stopped screaming; all we heard was her rattling breath. She was their prey. They could destroy her if they felt like it. Some people couldn't bear to watch anymore and lowered their heads. The armed guards led away more than a few of the inmates. All of them disappeared.

After that, I couldn't sleep. I found no rest. Every night, I pulled the blanket over my head and buried my face in the thin plastic pillow so that no one would see me breathing jerkily. I couldn't think clearly. As soon as my eyes closed, I started awake once more. And I found myself staring into that panicking face, hearing those screams. *Please, help me! Why won't you help me!* But no one could help her. No one.

Even after I was free, I couldn't bring myself to tell that story for months, because talking about it made me feel like it was happening all over again. As long as I live, I will never forget it. I simply cannot come to terms with it.

A month and a half later, something else unexpected happened.

CHAPTER SEVEN

Better to Die Escaping Than Die in the Camp

March 2018: released

At midnight, I stood like a statue in the row of other sentries along the wall, watching out of the corner of my eye as several officers walked purposefully across the hall and disappeared into the office where the police had taken me on my first night. After a while, a guard emerged and ordered me inside. What did they want with me? I was always expecting the worst.

An unfamiliar officer sat hunched over the desk. He barked at me, "Your work here is over! You are going home today and will continue your job as head teacher at the kindergarten. You will tell your employees that you have been on a retraining program in central China."

Going home? I didn't believe a single word that man said. Probably they were taking me to another camp. He stared at my motionless face, his eyes narrow. "You will never tell anyone outside about this camp. Don't forget about your contract." The document I had originally signed lay in plain view on his desk like a warning. He was pressing his finger so hard against it that the nail went white. "Understood?"

"Understood," I replied, adopting a military voice.

Then he waved me out of the door like an irritating fly. "Hand in your uniform, put your own clothes on, and pack your things!" They would never release a witness like me. *How is this going to end, Sayragul?* I wondered. I barely had time to change and get my phone back before they pulled a black hood over my head.

Just as we had done when I arrived in November of the

previous year, we passed through several checkpoints. Several doors opened, and for a few seconds I felt the warm spring air on my hands as they closed the car door and two police officers got onto the back seat beside me.

I had never seen the exterior of the building. To this day, I don't know exactly where it was, but there are maps and satellite images that prove the existence of several camps in this area. I assumed they were going to kill me at the next street corner. But before they did, they'd probably rape me first.

When they pulled the hood off my head, I could scarcely believe my eyes. It was the end of March, maybe four in the morning, and I was standing next to my house. "Tomorrow you will go to work, like always," the driver ordered me, following up with a threat. "Think of what's in your contract." I wasn't supposed to tell anyone what I had seen and heard.

As though in a trance, I walked into the apartment, sat down on a chair in the dark kitchen, and remained there until dawn. Unanswered questions were whirring around in my mind, making me dizzy. *What's going to happen now?* I was still incredibly tense, and couldn't shake the suspicion that something awful was about to happen.

When I saw myself in the mirror next morning — for the first time in months — I was shocked. A pale mask made of skin and bone stared back at me. My collarbones were poking out like a skeleton's. I quickly put on some make-up, lining my eyes black and applying red lipstick, and chose my best clothes.

My employees had to believe I'd just returned to the province from a big city, just like the Party had been pretending all along. I couldn't let anyone figure out where I'd really been, or I was a dead woman.

"How did you get so thin?"

"Oh, wonderful, you're back at last!" My colleagues hurried over and clustered around me, thrilled. The younger girls especially were over the moon. "Which city were you in? What was it like there? Was it interesting?" At the same time they eyed me, worried: my clothes were practically hanging off me. "How did you get so thin?"

I waved their concerns aside. "Oh, I didn't have much time to eat, there was so much to do …" I had lost more than ten kilograms.

For a moment, I had to brace myself against the wall, because my vision grew dim. But I did my best to hide my dizziness and weakness, brushing them off by saying I was exhausted after my long journey and had a lot of work waiting for me at the office. "Later we can sit down and have a quiet chat while I tell you all where I've been," I told them, explaining that I'd had enough for one day.

Next morning, too, I went to work, greeting everyone with a smile as before — but my head felt like it was packed in cotton wool. Along the way, I bumped into a Kazakh who had once held a senior position at the school. He shook his head sadly. "How do you manage to keep going? If I were you I'd have thrown myself off a three-storey building ages ago." Our kindergarten had three storeys. He probably guessed, like everyone else, that I'd been in a camp and was struggling.

That afternoon, a group of people from the education authority appeared in my office. One of them informed me that I was being removed from my post with immediate effect. "You will go home," they told me, "and await further instructions." The rest of the day, my head was pounding. Had someone denounced me? What were they playing at? I scrutinised my every word and action in my mind, over and over, beset by a nagging fear that someone had found a mistake I had missed.

They have nothing to accuse me of, I told myself, and settled down to wait resignedly. About 9.00 pm, two policemen barged into my apartment, put a hood over my head, and bundled me into a car. Shortly afterwards, I found myself back in a cell at the police station, staring at a locked, barred door and the uniformed guard behind it, who leaned against the wall in his chair for about an hour until a second man in uniform joined him.

They planted themselves in front of the bars. The newcomer asked the questions; the other kept his mouth shut. Probably, both were from the secret police. This time, I was sure they'd lock me up with the other prisoners in the camp.

"2018 is the year when we start to purge those with two faces," the man began. Meaning people like me. "You are one of the worst traitors! Despite all the trust we have placed in you, you are wearing a mask. On one side you show a good Chinese face, but on the other you've kept your evil Kazakh one."

What had I done wrong? What had I overlooked? I was flabbergasted. "To this day you still have not recalled your family from Kazakhstan or divorced your husband. This proves that you still feel great affection for our enemies abroad." I would never have let them force me into a divorce. And even if I had, they still wouldn't have left me alone.

For half an hour, I tried frenziedly to defend myself. "I've had no contact with my family. And I don't understand what you're accusing me of ..."

The officer's face twisted, as though he was looking at a cockroach. "How could you do such a vile thing to us? As a Party member and a head teacher in such a senior role?" He threw up his hands in a dramatic gesture. "You urgently need re-education.

It will take up to three years to restore order to your sick mind."

I was instructed to use the next few days to hand over my work at the kindergarten to my replacements and familiarise them with all the paperwork. "Get your affairs in order. Then await our instructions. You will be picked up."

A punch to the gut? No, I had ceased to feel anything. At least, nothing but instinctive resistance, wild defiance, and profound disgust for the Party and the government, who wanted to "heal" us by getting us out of the way. By now I knew. If I went into a camp, I wasn't getting out. I would die there.

Every night, I stumbled into the shower. Knees, feet, back — everything ached. Then there was the racing heart, the fear, the shortness of breath. Whenever the lights of passing police cars coloured the walls blue, I froze. It wasn't that I'd come back from the camp with a single, identifiable illness. I was simply broken. As the hot water rained down, something clicked. *This isn't a nightmare, Sayragul. This is reality.*

Better to die escaping than die in the camp

One night, I found myself moving from room to room like a sleepwalker. In the children's room, I opened the wardrobes, took out a few items of clothing, and pressed them to my face. A sharp, caustic sensation crept up my throat, and I began to cry. Loudly and helplessly. Slumping onto the bed, my fists clenched, I curled into a ball and clung to the children's clothes with both hands, sobbing.

It was the first time in so long I'd allowed myself to show my emotions. Everything I'd so painstakingly repressed over the past few months came pouring out. All those terrible images bubbling up like gas from a swamp. The prisoners' shackled feet, their tortured bodies, the girl's panicked, wide-open eyes. *Please help me!* I screamed and sobbed until I was numb.

By morning, my tears had run dry, and I had made a decision. I was fleeing to Kazakhstan. I knew, of course, that from this point on every step I took might mean instant transportation to a camp, but I preferred to die escaping than in there. I had to be quick. Quicker than the security agents in pursuit.

I saw on my phone that my mother, sisters, and brothers had tried to reach me several times over the past few months. Nobody in my family knew I was in a camp. Like the others, they'd assumed I was in another city, retraining. As much as I missed them, I couldn't call them back. I was desperate to keep them from getting into trouble because of me.

First, I tried to get my passport back. But I had no idea where they had taken all the documents they'd collected from teachers. I went to the police station the next day and asked, but they merely shrugged and said they didn't have a clue.

Then I remembered a close Chinese friend who might know. I called him straightaway. "Do you know how I can get my passport back?" He muttered in a panicked voice, "Don't talk to me about stuff like that! Otherwise they'll chop my head off first, then yours." Beep, beep, beep … he'd hung up. Fine. I'd have to do without the passport. I'd come up with some way to cross the border. The main thing was not to waste time, and to get away as soon as possible.

A neighbour ran up to me when she saw me pulling into my driveway after work. "I still haven't had any news about my children. I've been trying to get a visitor's permit for six months," she told me, wiping the tears from her eyes with her sleeve. Her sons had been incarcerated since 2016. She pressed a handkerchief to her face. "I just want to know if they're still alive." What was I supposed to say? I laid a comforting hand on her shoulder. "I'm sure they'll be released soon." But the truth was that we both knew better.

Scarcely had I closed the door behind me than my phone rang. It was a Kazakh friend who worked with the police. "I need you to lend me some money. About 30 yuan. Can you?" I was taken aback by his unexpected request and the small sum. "I really need the money." His tone of voice brooked no opposition. "I'm on my way to another city right now, but we can meet briefly."

I waited for him on the outskirts of the city, as agreed. When the young man arrived, he was behind the wheel of a police car, with two Chinese colleagues who spoke not a word of Kazakh chatting on the back seat. Leaning casually out of the window on his elbow, he beckoned me over and took the envelope of money. As he did so, he whispered, "In the next few days seventy people will be arrested and taken to a camp. You're third on the list." He had simply wanted to warn me.

Undeterred, I spent the day at the main office of the kindergarten, handing over my role to my new colleagues, smiling at passers-by, ignoring their shocked glances, and sorting out my paperwork quickly and neatly, falling into my old habits, as though I hadn't been staring just a few days earlier into the deepest recesses of the human soul.

Outwardly, I kept up appearances. I continued to function. If I'd suddenly stopped showing up for work, it would have looked suspicious. In reality, I was using every spare minute to prepare for my escape. I knew they were watching my every step.

In order to be allowed into the Free Trade Zone at the Kazakh border, you needed a permit. Desperate, I called my old Chinese friend, the one who'd previously hung up on me. "Please help me! I need a permit for the Free Trade Zone." This time, he gave me the phone number of a Uighur before cutting the conversation short.

That night, I called the stranger's number. He reacted very nervously to my request. "Who told you I could help? It's more than my life's worth!"

I gave him my friend's name and hastily promised, "I'll pay you whatever you want if you can get me the permit." I had to call him a couple more times before he finally agreed.

"Give me 40,000 yuan," he demanded. "Call me when you're at the border."

"Okay, but how …?" I was going to ask for more details, but the line was already dead.

I'm not sure now whether it was on the third or fourth day after this that I returned home after a full day's work and made dinner that night. I laid the table and put some Chinese music on the radio, turning it up so loudly that it could easily be heard by the guards outside my house. I had already opened the windows extra wide. Outwardly, I looked like a woman doing normal, after-work activities. Then I pulled on my jacket, shoved some money and my ID in my inner pocket, and went over to the window.

It was 4 April 2018, just before midnight.

Escape

Followed by the blaring music, I put my feet on the windowsill and jumped down into the garden. Under cover of darkness, I hurried across the neighbour's plot onto the next street, where I impatiently tried to hail a passing taxi. But nobody stopped.

With every passing car, more and more sweat broke out on my forehead. I spun around, my nerves increasingly frayed. Were they already on my heels? Finally, a private car stopped. There was a Chinese man at the wheel. "Where do you want to go?" he asked. "I'm sick, and I need to go to the hospital in Ghulja," I said, offering him a large sum of money to drop me off. From there it wasn't far to the border.

Lots of drivers knew that patients from Aksu often had to set off very early in the morning in order to reach the clinic in time for blood samples at 9.00 am, so he wasn't surprised to see a Kazakh woman with no luggage waiting alone by the roadside. I didn't even have a handbag. The journey took roughly five to six hours.

Every time we reached a police checkpoint, my breathing faltered. Was my escape going to end here? Was it all over? Each time, the driver leaned out and told them where we were going, and that everything was in order with his vehicle. I didn't have a passport, of course, but I did hand over my ID card. Fortunately, in the middle of the night the police were too tired to check closely, and quickly waved us on.

I didn't want the driver asking questions, so I leant back my head and pretended to be asleep the whole time. It felt like someone was kneeling on my chest, their weight growing heavier and heavier. I was running through every conceivable worst-case scenario in my head. My Uighur contact had told me to notify him as soon as I reached the border. But what if he didn't answer the phone? And what if the car behind us was from the secret police — what if they'd geo-located my phone?

I felt like throwing the thing out the window, but I needed it to get in touch with my contact. The security services in East Turkestan bundled together all the information from apps and other sources — such as data from surveillance cameras or government bodies — into an "integration platform", and monitored them continuously. Probably, I reassured myself, they wouldn't be expecting me to make a hasty escape attempt. They were confident I was too paralysed by fear after the way I'd been treated, frozen like a mouse before a snake about to sink its teeth into the little animal's flesh.

The driver dropped me off outside the hospital. As soon as his car disappeared, I took the next private taxi to the border city of Khorgos. The other four passengers were Uighurs and Dungan. We didn't ask each other any questions; each of us was absorbed in our own thoughts. Another two hours. Again, we passed through all the checkpoints. By the time we got to the border, I was drenched in sweat.

The last time I'd been in this vast complex of buildings, I'd said goodbye to Uali and my children. This was one of the major hubs along the east–west trading route known as the New Silk Road, where workers loaded countless Chinese containers onto railroad cars. If they wanted to transport goods to Europe, there was no getting around Kazakhstan.

Hordes of people from all areas were pouring through the gates into the Free Trade Zone between China and Kazakhstan, eager to buy and sell. Pressing my phone to my ear and turning my face to the wall, I called the Uighur and murmured, "I'm here." "Good. Transfer me 40,000 yuan now."

What should I do? Trusting a complete stranger was the only chance I had. I used my bankcard to transfer him the amount at the nearest ATM. Of course, the authorities in Aksu kept a close watch on all payments and withdrawals, but even they couldn't spend every single second checking every single bank account. By the time they noticed, I would be long gone. I hoped.

"I did what you wanted," I told him. "Okay, now take your ID …" He instructed me to write a Chinese character for "must" on it. Then I was supposed to take my ID to a specific desk. Only that — not to say or do anything else. *Stay calm, Sayragul, stay calm …* I must have been white as chalk. Still, I kept a smile plastered to my face.

The official looked me over and flipped open my ID, stared

at the character and then again at me. I felt so weak. My temples were throbbing. Would he betray me? Call the police? Maybe I'd be back in the black room within the hour? Without a word, he handed me back the permit.

Success! Thanks to God's help, I was still alive. For a moment, I allowed myself to be carried forward limply by the crowd between the rows of shops, as though I were one of them. If I wanted to get anywhere in Kazakhstan, I'd have to convert my yuan into tenge. *What will I do if they short-change me?* I wondered, scanning for a face that looked trustworthy.

I spotted a man with a white beard standing to one side. "Could you change my money?" I asked him, adding, "I hope you don't cheat me — I have a family and children."

He replied, "I'm a decent guy. I have a family and children myself." So I put my last 5,000 yuan into his hand, and he gave me back 90,000 tenge. That was half of what it was actually worth, but I was satisfied, because I believed him.

But where was the stand for the taxi shuttles to the border? "I need to get to Kazakhstan. Are you going there, too?" I asked a couple of people who were wheezing past me, heavily loaded with goods.

"If you want, you can come with us," they offered.

Once I was sure where I was going, I took the batteries and SIM card out of my phone, and threw them into the nearest bin. Then I climbed into the next available taxi with the others.

It took roughly ten minutes to get to the border. From there, we all went our separate ways. I watched enviously as people simply showed their passports at the checkpoint and crossed into Kazakhstan.

But what was I supposed to do now?

The barrier

So far, I'd been putting off that question, hoping a solution would pop into my head. But now I was standing at the border with nothing but a giant question mark, faced with armed guards and a barrier. For ten minutes I padded up and down like a wild animal in a cage. How on earth was I supposed to cross?

At the passport checkpoint, I noticed an elderly Kazakh standing on tiptoes, negotiating with the officer through the high guardhouse window. He was surrounded by bags. I turned around. No one was behind me. The officer looked exasperated, shooting constant glances at the clock on the wall: he was obviously keen to be rid of the old man as quickly as possible. Evidently, he was nearing the end of his shift.

The moment he turned his back — to fetch some documents or stamp something — I hurriedly ducked down, made myself as small as possible, and slipped past underneath the window, behind the old man. Ahead of me were a couple of doors. Was a police officer about to burst out and arrest me? But there was no one. I ran and ran.

Suddenly, a voice shouted, "Taxi, taxi, taxi!" As soon as I heard this, I felt for the first time in twenty-four hours that I could breathe. *Thank God! I'm still alive! I'm in Kazakhstan!* I drew several deep breaths, in and out. Until now, my brain had been switched off. I'd not even registered what I'd been doing all this time.

When I gradually came to my senses, I saw I was standing at a taxi rank where several cars were waiting for passengers heading further into Kazakhstan. "I'm going to Baidebek," I told a driver, because that was where Uali's relatives lived. It was a village on the way to Almaty. The driver explained that I would have to travel via the city of Zharkent.

At the next stop, I climbed into another taxi, and took a note out of my jacket pocket and unfolded it gingerly. On it was my husband's telephone number, which I'd carried with me every single second in Aksu. "Please may I use your phone?" I asked the taxi driver in a broken voice.

As though in a daze, I dialled the number and heard Uali pick up at the other end.

"Hello?"

"It's Sayragul, I'm in Kazakhstan," I replied as matter-of-factly, as though I were a secretary casually filing papers. In fact, I was so tense I could feel my stomach puckering. I knew I might fall into the next trap at any moment, so I was doing everything I could to hide my nerves from the driver. For Uali, of course, it was a huge surprise.

"What? How did you get your passport so quickly?"

We hadn't spoken for nearly two years. I replied as succinctly as possible. "I'm coming home in a taxi now." He laughed, and told me to get out at the apple bazaar in Baidebek. He would pick me up there.

5 April 2018: reunion

I got out at the bazaar. Although dusk was falling and the traders were gradually shutting up shop, it was still a hive of activity. I peered around cautiously. In a little place like this, everyone knew everybody else. A stranger like me would stick out like a sore thumb.

It was a known fact that Kazakhstan was teeming with Chinese spies. Nursultan Nazarbayev, the "Leader of the Nation", held ultimate sway over the fate of the country. An autocrat, Nazarbayev routinely locked up his opponents or liquidated them, and ruled according to the principle of economy first, then politics. Kazakhstan and China maintained strong trade relations, thanks mainly to the New Silk Road, China's global infrastructure and investment project. Kazakhstan was in significant debt to China.

This uneven power dynamic meant that Beijing was able to go into Kazakhstan and kidnap Muslims from East Turkestan at will. I simply did not understand why their relationship was so close, especially as the Chinese government had put Kazakhstan on their list of twenty-six countries considered dangerous enemies of the state.

Terrified that someone was going to find me out, I tried to act as unconcerned as possible, as though I came by every day. I was breathing shallowly, tense as an arrow drawn back in the bow, every time a passer-by brushed the sleeve of my jacket. Who was that? Were they spies? When Uali made a beeline for me, his eyes glowing, and hugged me, I shrugged off his arms coolly and said soberly, like a distant acquaintance, "Let's not talk here. Let's go home first ..." I saw joy and anxiety flit across his eyes — he could tell at once that something wasn't right.

We walked home without a word. It took fifteen minutes. I looked neither left nor right; we had to be fast. At any moment, someone might leap out of a dark corner and drag me away. When we turned onto their street, Ukilay and Ulagat were already outside, waiting by a large iron door. They dashed towards me, arguing and shoving one another. "I want to be the first to hug Mama!" "No, me!"

And then the lot of us were through the iron door, behind the protective walls of the house, howling and laughing at the same time. My eyes widened in astonishment as I held my children at arm's length to look at them. "You've both grown so much!" I marvelled. Then I pulled them close again and didn't let them go. The last time I'd seen them, both of them had been tiny, with round cheeks. Now thirteen-year-old Ukilay and nine-year-old Ulagat were growing up fast. All the suffering I'd endured over the past couple of years, every day and every hour — I'd borne all of it so that I could one day hold my children in my arms once more.

We didn't sleep a wink that night. The four of us nestled close together, hugging and kissing and talking until the sun rose. The children wouldn't budge from my side. "You've got to go to school," I admonished them at dawn, but they were both petrified I would be gone again when they came home. "Please let us take the day off and stay with you," they urged me.

"No, people would notice. You've got to go to class, same as every day," I insisted. "Don't let anyone find out your mother has arrived." Once they'd packed their satchels and set off, I wandered through the house and among the apple trees in the garden, maybe one hundred metres long, as though in a dream. Directly behind it were the peaks of the Trans-Ili Alatau. Yet I could not savour their beauty.

For a couple of days, I tried to stay hidden. Ultimately, however, it was only a matter of time before they found me.

Nerves

For the first few days, I anxiously avoided thinking about the past. I didn't want to remember. It felt like pressing an old wound that might burst open again and make me relive the pain a second time. Even though I was living with my family in this gorgeous house, I still felt like a prisoner in the camp. I had to come back to myself first, to collect myself. I had to understand who and where I was, and analyse my new situation. I just couldn't get my head around the fact that I had actually escaped.

During the interrogations, my tormentors had repeatedly drummed into my head that the government was able to bring escapees back to Xinjiang from Kazakhstan at any time. China's reach was long, its influence powerful. *We can do anything we want to Kazakhs like you.* Their threats felt like a noose tightening around my neck.

I waited until we were alone before telling Uali that I had crossed the border into Kazakhstan illegally. He went quiet and thoughtful, put his hands behind his back, and paced back and forth, muttering softly, "What will we do if they come looking for you?"

It was very difficult, almost impossible, to put into words or even think about all the dreadful things I had been agonising over for so long. It wasn't until the fourth day that I could bring myself to tell my husband that I had spent hours alone in the apartment of a single Chinese man as part of the "friendship" campaign in Aksu. Although it's not like I could have hidden it anyway. Everyone in Kazakhstan knew that in East Turkestan the locals had to stay overnight with Chinese people.

I described my experiences to Uali. If I hadn't, he would secretly have wondered why I wasn't telling him about it. He might even have jumped to some ugly conclusions. Everyone in Kazakhstan was worried about daughters, cousins, or granddaughters who lived on the other side of the border. Because we held ourselves to such high moral standards, I didn't think about my own suffering, only of the guilt I felt about those visits.

The next moment, I withdrew, staring rigidly into space. I couldn't break out of it, although I could tell how uncomfortable my aloofness was making Uali. "Just talk!" he pleaded, reaching for my cold hand. At that, summoning all my strength, I turned my eyes to him and opened my lips. "I was in a camp!" At last it was out! It was liberating — like one of those poisonous tablets I'd spat out in the medical area.

Since 2017, rumours had abounded in Kazakhstan about their compatriots being suppressed, tortured, and killed in China, but hearing about it from his own wife left Uali dumbstruck. Hesitantly, I went into more detail about how they were mistreating people. My breath was jerky, and although I held back a lot and only roughly outlined what had happened, Uali was visibly shocked. "That can't be true," he stammered. "How could a modern state like China be so brutal and so primitive?" It was impossible to talk about my experiences without crying. When Uali heard that children and old people were also being abused, he burst into tears as well.

But we had no time to console each other: even in our own home, I was on the run. Visitors and work friends were constantly ringing the doorbell, popping in and out. I'd managed to hide my presence for a week, but in the long run it was difficult to maintain the illusion in a one-storey house with four large rooms. The next person might notice my jacket, or catch a glimpse of my shadow as I flitted away, and report me to the authorities. Our whole family was trapped in a psychological cage. What were we supposed to do next? The immense pressure of continually having to weigh up our options, never knowing whether our next move might send me to the gallows — it was sending us all into a tailspin.

Chinese secret-service agents might show up at any moment and spirit me away. Ulagat and Ukilay swiftly erased all trace of my presence when other people were around. They flinched just as hard as I did whenever the doorbell rang. Whenever we were together, they clung to my arms. "No, nobody is ever going to take you away from us again!" they told me. "We'll protect you. As long as we're with you, you don't need to be afraid!" Still, they were always afraid that agents would show up when they were at school. "What will we do then?" mused my nine-year-old son, distraught.

There were so many unanswered questions gathering above us like baleful stormclouds. Uali ran his hand through his dark hair, which was growing greyer by the day. "What's the best authority to approach about you? Who should we trust? Where can we find help?"

I told him clearly, "It's better for all of you if I leave here."

Who to trust?

Finally, we plucked up the courage to tell Uali's brother, who immediately offered me a place to stay. Luckily, it was only an hour's drive away, so my family could visit me every other day.

"You've got to call Serikzhan Bilash," my brother-in-law urged me. He was the most important port of call for ethnic Kazakhs with Chinese citizenship. If we couldn't trust the leader of an organisation like Atajurt, then who could we trust? Every day, Bilash recorded interviews with victims, documenting their statements and posting them online as proof of systematic human-rights abuses in East Turkestan. A human-rights activist originally from Xinjiang himself, Bilash was a frequent guest on television and displayed his number at the end of every broadcast. Anyone who needed information on the camps — or could provide any — was urged to call him. When you're as afraid as we were, however, it's difficult to trust anybody.

So we dithered and delayed until, suddenly, a thought flashed white-hot into my mind: *I've heard of this man before too!* News of his organisation had been censored by the Chinese, marked with a red cross: anyone who got in touch with him was threatened with death.

Not long after that, we dialled the number of Bilash's Astana office several times and tried to reach him via letter and WhatsApp, but he was so inundated with questions and new cases that he didn't reply.

Even in my new apartment, I stayed hidden in a single room. I didn't dare set foot outside. I felt like I had reached a dead end. It was hard to let anyone get too close. I wanted to keep myself at arm's length, because everything hurt. Every part of my body was screaming.

I hadn't even been there a week before I fell seriously ill. One day, out of nowhere, I couldn't move: I couldn't even get out of bed in the morning. My back, my stomach, my guts … searing pain. Nothing was working anymore. Uali and his brother rushed me to a private hospital, where you didn't have to give all your details. They really only cared whether or not you paid. It seemed the safest option for a wanted woman like me.

For a month, doctors and nurses tended to my body with medication and physiotherapy. In the meantime, Uali tried in vain to get help; we were still in limbo. After a while, I managed to sit up when the children came to visit. "We're taking you back home with us," my husband said when I'd recovered somewhat. The doctors were reluctant to let me go, and insisted I come back in for a check-up after a month.

I was discharged from hospital on Saturday 19 May 2018. On Monday 21 May, they came for me. I was lying in bed in the morning. I was weak, pumped full of painkillers, and unable to put up much resistance. I heard voices at the door. "The Chinese are looking for your wife. They want her back," two strange men told my husband, shoving him aside like an inanimate object. "We've got to take her in." With trembling fingers, I put on my blouse and jeans.

My husband and daughter were aghast. Ulagat shouted, "Mama! Leave my mama alone!" The men were from the national security services but wore plain clothes: jeans, shirts, and leather jackets. They were around thirty years old. One had darker skin and was medium height, while the other was a bit stockier.

"Where are you taking her?" Uali demanded. "What is my wife being accused of? Is there any evidence against her? Show me the warrant that says you can take her."

The answer was brief and harsh. "No."

"Please let me take my medication," I asked as I put on my jacket and followed them, my feet sluggish.

"You won't need it," one of them told me. "If you confess, we'll bring you back tonight anyway."

But those men lied.

The Kazakh secret police

An unmarked car was parked outside our house, and I was instructed to get in. Looking out of the window, I saw Uali and the two distraught children by the iron door. We drove for a long time. Along the way, the man sitting beside me made a call. "We've got her!" he said.

Flustered, I struggled to find the words. "What do you want with me?"

He replied, "Just tell the truth and explain everything in as much detail as possible, then nothing will happen to you and you'll go home tonight."

I believed them, because they weren't yelling at me. They seemed calm and normal. Besides, my foggy brain reasoned, they were Kazakhs like me, and they would definitely have let me bring my medication if I were staying long. "Fine," I sighed. "Then I'll do that."

After about two hours, the driver stopped outside a small farm with a hay barn. Two or three men were chatting on a terrace in the garden, one of them wearing a military uniform. They followed us into a small interrogation room. I was made to sit at a wooden table, opposite the two men who had brought me, before they were joined by a third man, a giant roughly fifty years old, with a paunch so large it looked like he'd stuffed a sack of flour underneath his shirt. The others kept a beady eye on me, prowling back and forth around the room.

All the men in the room were clean-shaven, dark-haired, and tall. They seemed experienced and practised. It was clear they all belonged to the same intelligence unit. They knew each other by name, and understood exactly which job was whose. None of them introduced himself.

My throat clenched with fear. "Who are you?"

They looked me up and down contemptuously, sinister grins on their faces. "You're not the one asking the questions here!"

The trio in front of me only cared about one thing. "How did you manage to get over the border? Who helped you?" But they didn't believe my answer. A throbbing vein appeared in the fat man's forehead, and he slammed his fist into the table, but I tried to sit upright and stick to my story: the truth. "I ducked down under the checkpoint and ran across …"

"That can't be true! Tell us the names of who helped you!"

"Only God helped me."

"Have you lost your mind? Who's behind this?" I could tell from their grim faces that they'd already made up their minds.

I kept trying to tell them about what was happening in China. "There are lots of camps in Xinjiang where our fellow Kazakhs are being tortured — your relatives, brothers, and sisters. We've got to do something about it, together! Let's write to the president and ask him for help, so we can make everyone aware of these atrocities!"

244 THE CHIEF WITNESS

But the men weren't remotely interested. "Don't tell us this stuff. We don't care, we don't want to talk about that. You should be trying to save your own skin first." There was only one question that mattered to them: "How did you get over the border?"

After a while, they started to threaten me. "You're lying! And if you don't tell us the truth, we'll send you straight back to China." The fat one, the dark-skinned one, and the pale one kept edging closer. Like predators readying themselves to pounce. One of them hit me so hard it knocked me to the ground. I wanted so badly to be swallowed up by it — to simply dissolve. Instinctively, I curled my arms around my head to protect it, hiding my face behind my black hair, but they tore my hands away.

I was terrified, gasping for air like a drowning swimmer. Those men were brutal. They showed no mercy. They used every means at their disposal to force the truth out of me. They beat and kicked me. I'm not sure now whether the others stayed in the room or if they'd already left. I only know that they destroyed me to my very core. That they smashed my dignity to pieces, like a carelessly shattered glass. But whose honour was really being lost? The innocent person, or the tormentors who ordered and carried out those atrocities?

Afterwards they locked me up behind a large iron door. It wasn't a room; it was more like a large hall, but without a roof. The rain was falling inside. Cold and empty. Cut off from the outside. It was so dreadfully cold. The world seemed such a terribly lonely place. Lying on the bare concrete floor, I drifted in and out of consciousness.

All that was remained of me was a husk. There was nothing else left.

Powerless

I hated myself and my own helplessness. I was so appalled, so profoundly disappointed, so angry and desperate. To be so mistreated and degraded by my own countrymen — it had shocked me to my core. I hadn't seen it coming. I was nearly choking on my own bitterness. When they brought me food in the evenings, I turned my head away. For three days, I ate and drank almost nothing. There wasn't even a bucket for a toilet, but I didn't need to go anyway.

"Come out for interrogation!" On the third day, they brought me back into that room. I tried to stand up, vainly at first, but then I got arduously and waveringly to my feet. My cheeks were burning. Everything was so blurry and unclear. One of them said, "You're being deported to China in two hours."

As if that wasn't enough, the second added, "And your husband will go to prison for helping you. He broke the law. After all, he hid you and didn't immediately inform the authorities of your arrival." Yet not even that seemed to be enough for them. "And we're sending your two children to an orphanage."

At that moment, I lost consciousness and fell off my chair. When I came to, I was somewhere else. My eyes took a minute to adjust. Beside me stood a young man. Slowly, I realised that I was on a stretcher in an old and primitively equipped ambulance.

The next time I opened my eyes, I was in bed in a small room, possibly part of a medical clinic. The young man was still beside me. After a while he spoke: "So, you're awake again?" Then he glanced at his watch. "You were out for nearly twenty-five minutes."

I tried to get up and leave at once, but I couldn't. I could hear my own blood rushing in my head. *I've got to get out of here!* All my alarm bells were ringing, but I couldn't even move my little finger. My whole body was paralysed, as though I was lying underneath an invisible pile of stones. After what felt like an eternity, I managed to shift my arms and legs. It was late afternoon when the dark-skinned thirty-year-old who had previously interrogated me appeared.

I watched uneasily, my gaze flitting around the room, as he took out his phone and showed me a picture. "Do you know this person?"

My chest rose and fell. "Yes, I know him. That's my husband's brother. Where did you get that picture? Why are you showing me? What is this about?"

"You don't need to know that. In two hours you'll be back in China," he replied, and then he was gone. They had everything ready to deport me. I spent those two hours inwardly preparing myself for the camp. *It's all over soon, Sayragul, all over soon.* There would be no grave for me. I would simply disappear, maybe in some crematorium somewhere.

To my boundless astonishment, a couple of police officers dropped me off shortly afterwards at an office in Zharkent. It was 23 May 2018. A judge asked me a few questions in his office, then announced, "A court will decide whether you will be sent back to China or not." Why was it so foggy in the room? My eyes were dimming. Half his face disappeared. Where was that voice coming from? Where was I? "First, your case must be investigated. You must be patient. It will take some time." Throughout the conversation, my vision kept going black, and I passed out several times.

Then they took me into custody and locked me in a cell.

Captive

I still had no idea what had happened in the meantime. After they took me, Uali and his brother had moved heaven and earth to find me, but I had vanished, seemingly without a trace. Neither the police nor any other officials knew where I was. Frantic, my husband and my brother-in-law hurried to Serikzhan Bilash's Atajurt offices and banged on the door. "Listen to us! It's an emergency!"

Moments later, Bilash took both men to a large bus station to shoot a short video in which Uali's brother begged the whole population for help: "An innocent Kazakh woman, Sayragul Sauytbay, has been tortured in a Chinese prison camp … She fled from East Turkestan to Kazakhstan, and in the early hours of the morning two days ago she was abducted from her home by Kazakh middle-men … her life is in terrible danger! Please help us to find Sayragul!" The recording was uploaded online, and within a few hours my case was famous nationwide.

My friends took up the search once more. Pictures of me popped up all over the internet, and people were discussing me on the street. "Where is this woman? Her relatives are searching for her desperately." Many Kazakhs were especially outraged, because they, too, were in despair over countless missing relatives in Chinese camps. From their perspective, a Kazakh had finally managed to escape, and now her very own government was trying to silence her and give her back into the hands of her captors.

The indignation quickly reached the highest levels of government, pressuring officials to act. Hushing it up was no longer an option, nor could they simply give me to the Chinese without an outcry on their hands. It was because of this video that the secret-service agent had brought the picture of Uali's brother to the hospital and sent me to court instead of to China.

Meanwhile, in my cell in Zharkent, I felt like my head was being held underwater. I kept scrabbling up and gasping for air. I lost consciousness repeatedly. It was a depressing, leaden period. There was a camera in the corner, but I doubt anyone paid much attention to the footage. In the morning, there was warm water to drink. At midday and evenings, they gave me a meal. Slowly, very slowly, I came back to life. Did Uali know where I was? How were the children doing? *If they send me back to China,* I thought, *I'm dead.*

While I was drifting in and out on my camp bed, press conferences were taking place outside. Within a short period of time, several organisations had become involved to provide support. A well-known lawyer had even approached Uali and offered to take my case. At the end of May, the lawyer — Abzal Husman — brought me clothes, something to eat, and, above all, the courage to keep going.

Unfortunately, as it turned out, he was working for the other side.

3 June 2018: detention in Taldykorgan, a bird, and a ghost

After ten days, I was transferred to the state prison in Taldykorgan, where I shared a cell with two Russian murderers and a Kazakh fraudster. From the third woman I learned that one had stabbed a thief and the other had killed her violent husband. The Russian women shoved and kicked me when the guards weren't looking. I was an easy victim. I was stuck in an intermediate world, far away and yet present. Not living and not dead.

The horrors of the past had a direct impact on my body and mind. Although I was given regular medication and injections by a doctor at the new facility, I kept losing consciousness. Maybe

I was too overwhelmed by all the emotions that kept rushing in out of nowhere. Not knowing how to deal with it was profoundly unsettling.

I could scarcely keep any food down, and missed my children so painfully that it felt like someone had ripped out my heart and held it pounding in front of me. Then I saw a small bird land on the barred window. Cautiously, I placed a crumb of bread in front of it. It picked up the crumb in its beak and flew away. I was pleased, because I knew the bird would use it to feed its brood in a nest somewhere nearby, but the tears ran down my face because I was missing my own children so deeply.

Once, when I was alone in my cell, another Russian woman abruptly appeared. She wore a long, flowing white garment and was wondrously beautiful, with curly blonde hair down to her knees. "Who are you?" I asked her nervously. But she did not reply.

What did this eerie woman want from me? Panicking, I backed up against the wall and called for help. At that she scolded me, "Turn the light on!" and disappeared. From then on, she made an appearance every day. Sometimes she rummaged through my bag of clothes on the floor. At night, I saw her clearly; during the day, she was like a shadow. Little by little, we became friends.

Occasionally, she'd stand behind me, her breath warm on my neck. "Do you see that woman, too?" I once asked the guard who opened the door each morning, bewildered. A superstitious man, he replied, "It's the ghost of a woman who was locked up here once. She was innocent, and hanged herself in her cell." Sometimes her warm, pale hands wiped the tears from my face. The light was so garish, the din so loud, my lips so dry. I asked the Kazakh woman in my cell for confirmation, too. "Do you see her as well?"

"That woman gives you hope that you will be released soon," she was convinced.

To this day, I can picture that Russian woman's face clearly in my mind's eye. It's remarkable what magical powers the brain can call upon to protect our psyches.

My physical health, however, was deteriorating day by day. On 22 June, I was alone with the two Russians in the cell, because the Kazakh was in court. As I was getting out of the top bunk, they dragged me off and started beating me. My head hit the concrete floor, and everything went dark. Suddenly, all the important nerves to my brain were rerouted, searching for a last resort: escape or resistance? Both were impossible. I lay there motionless. "She's dying!" I heard someone shout. A doctor and paramedics were fighting for my life, and asked the prison administration to transfer me to a clinic immediately. I didn't regain consciousness for thirty-four minutes.

I was woken by an intense pain in my left arm. Where was I? Images whirled through my head like a carousel. I saw men beating me with their fists, heard women screaming in pain, and felt my face twitch … it took a while before I regained control of my confused thoughts. I tried to move my hand, but as I did so, I realised it was handcuffed and covered in blood. The other was attached to a cannula. "You nearly died," an armed guard informed me. Lifting my head a fraction, I realised I was not alone.

Waking up

The doctor had diagnosed me with severe concussion, dangerously high blood pressure, and an abnormal heartbeat. I was so weak, I could barely sit up. Three police officers, two armed with machine guns, kept me under a twenty-four-hour watch. They had locked the door from the inside. What were they so scared of? That

I'd run away, in my condition? That their hulking next-door neighbour, Beijing, would be furious with them if I did? They only unbolted the door to let medical personnel inside. It was summertime — humid, hot, sticky. There was barely enough air for the four of us in that tiny room.

My husband and children weren't allowed in, but Uali waited for a moment when the door opened and two guards went to the toilet. He bolted into the room with a plate of food, and then ran back out. "Get out of here!" they yelled. They put the food he'd brought too far away from my bed for me to reach it. I felt like a dog on a leash. Anger pulsed in my veins. I was shackled like a hardened criminal, soaking wet, unable to move, eat, or sleep.

Once my condition had stabilised, a few days later, they took me back to the prison. All the aid packages sent by my supporters sped up my recovery. They were chock full of delicious-smelling food, toothbrushes, soap, and good wishes. I kept seeing the name of one particular aid organisation, Atajurt. "Serikzhan Bilash has dedicated his entire life to protecting fellow Kazakhs who have suffered under Chinese rule. That's the kind of guy he is," gushed my Kazakh cellmate. Knowing I had the support of all these people filled me with hope. And that hope gave me fresh strength.

Compared to the Chinese camp, prison in Kazakhstan was practically a luxury hotel. You were given three square meals a day. You were even allowed ten minutes in the courtyard. Tilting back my head, I gazed up at the sky through the bars above. I also had access to the library, where I found books exploring legal issues. The content was in Kazakh, but not in the usual Arabic letters.

I had to teach myself to read the Cyrillic alphabet in short order, but by doing so I was able to find out more about how my case might be treated. The fact that my husband and children were Kazakh citizens and that I was ethnically Kazakh militated against my deportation to China. When I read that, I was more hopeful still.

I spent more than a month in that prison. Two days before the trial began, I found myself back in the Zharkent facility where I'd previously been in custody. *They're planning to deport me straight across the border into China,* I thought uneasily when I first realised this, but in my next breath I was simmering with excitement about the trial. Maybe, at long last, this would be my chance to be heard! Unless, of course, it was the end of the road.

CHAPTER EIGHT

Kazakhstan: Beijing's interference in neighbouring countries

9 July 2018: the first day of the trial

Ever since I was a child, my father had encouraged me to be strong and proud. I tried to have faith in this inner strength and not let myself be broken by unforeseen events. It helped me to stand before the court in Zharkent on 9 July 2018, the first day of the trial, which was eagerly awaited by people across Kazakhstan.

There were perhaps twenty seats in the small courtroom, but more than one hundred people were crammed in there, including human-rights activists and foreign journalists. Many interested onlookers had to stand outside the door. I was the first chief witness in the world who had the courage to publicly give evidence about the crimes committed in Chinese camps. The only teacher who had got to know this highly secretive system from the inside. And the only Kazakh public-sector worker who had emerged from the world's biggest surveillance state alive, despite what she knew.

All the visitors rose as the court staff walked in and took their seats. The judge was a Kazakh woman; the prosecutor, a Uighur. I followed behind them in handcuffs. When I entered the packed room, I flinched at the confusion, the uproar, and the journalists yelling, "Can we have an interview?" For a moment, I was terrified. Then, however, I realised that all these people were supportive and wished me well. *Maybe I won't be sent back to China after all?* I thought. Inside, I tried to keep my chin up. *You've got to fight, Sayragul, fight!*

The guards walked me through the room and into a glass box, where I sat down. The room was still in a tumult. The trial hadn't yet begun: the judge and the other participants were still sorting through their documents. In those five minutes, my children elbowed their way through the crowd and ran up to me. Ulagat stood behind the glass wall and called to me. "Mama! I missed you so much. Please, give me just one kiss."

My son's face was so full of hope, it was like a stab to the heart. I tried to do as he asked, but his head didn't fit through the narrow gap in the glass. So he begged, "Mama, at least take my hand so you can kiss it." And he pushed his hand through the gap. As I bent down to kiss his little fingers, a photographer snapped a shot of the moment, which later did the rounds in the international media and became famous.

"Order!" shouted the bailiffs, and everybody had to sit down. "The trial is beginning!"

The judicial officers took my details and positioned two interpreters by my side, a Chinese-speaker and a Russian-speaker. The latter was often used as an official language in Kazakh courtrooms. Since I spoke no Russian, they assumed that, as a former resident of China's north-west province, I would want to communicate in Chinese. Both interpreters were supposed to take turns translating into Russian.

But my advocates had boosted my confidence. All of a sudden, I forgot to be afraid, and rage lent my voice strength: "I have come to Kazakhstan because I consider this country my home. And in my homeland I only wish to speak in my mother tongue, not Chinese. Otherwise I will refuse to testify." And thus the trial ground to a halt after only a few minutes.

There followed a tense pause. Everyone was surprised, and there was a loud debate. "How can we solve this problem?" "She's a Kazakh! Of course she wants to speak Kazakh!"

"Do you really want another interpreter?" the judge enquired.

I stuck to my guns. The court staff continued to argue, but after a while they reached a unanimous consensus: "We are in Kazakhstan. This trial is extremely important to our country and its inhabitants, so it can only be conducted in Kazakh." Even the prosecutor turned out to be as kind and friendly towards me as if she were my own lawyer, and allowed my family to visit me in the afternoon.

After half an hour, the judge adjourned the trial to a later date.

A family visit in my cell

Lots of people had gathered on the street outside. Some had travelled from distant cities and countries especially to see me. I was so grateful, so touched, and utterly bewildered. Witnessing the concern of all these strangers restored a little of my faith in justice and humanity.

Shortly afterwards, the guards led me into the visiting room at the prison, where Uali and the children were already sitting at a table, craning their necks to look out for me. It was the first time we'd seen each other since my kidnapping nearly two months earlier. We had ten minutes to hug and talk. The thought of being separated again so soon when every second was precious felt awful.

"What have you been doing all this time?" Ukilay asked.

"Was everything alright? Have you been eating well?" Ulagat added.

Uali put his hand to his throat. "Have they hit you or abused you?" His eyes glistened.

I replied, "Everything's fine, I was just locked in a room." It was impossible to talk in that situation. I was only barely holding everything together internally, dealing with a wound that might never heal. And I wanted my children to be calm. I didn't want them afraid. That way, I felt better, too.

Meanwhile a queue was building up outside the prison gates. People had brought me gifts, but the police turned them away. "Only relatives are allowed to drop off packages for Sayragul Sauytbay." At this, all those strangers started claiming, "I'm a brother! I'm a cousin! I'm a sister!" so they could drop off their presents. A police officer winked at me in my cell. "Lots of relatives, eh?"

"No," I defended myself, red in the face. I lowered my gaze, still afraid of making a mistake that might cost me my life. "I really didn't ask anyone to do anything …"

Later, another official told me, "Your patrons come from all walks of life. Rich and poor, young and old."

Since 2016, people in Kazakhstan had been fretting every day over how their relatives in East Turkestan were getting on, wondering why they'd suddenly fallen out of touch and what was happening to them in the "vocational training camps". But their questions fell on deaf ears, breaking against the silent wall encircling the border around East Turkestan. All of them were intent on finally getting answers.

There were people out on the streets, angrily demanding, "Why are you locking up one of our own? She's innocent! Set Sayragul Sauytbay free immediately! She must be given asylum in her home country!"

But the government was writhing like a worm that had been cut to pieces, each segment squirming in a different direction. What should they do? On one side were their own people; on the other side was the neighbouring giant, raising a menacing leather boot …

13 July 2018: the second day of the trial

The second court date was set for four days later. On the way to court, the police officers in the car seemed pleased, and pointed through the windows. "Look, you don't need to worry about your freedom! The whole city is behind you!" Every square, every garden, and every corner was jam-packed with people. They waved at me from the roadside, wearing white T-shirts with blue lettering — *Freedom for Sayragul Sauytbay!* — in three languages: Kazakh, Russian and English.

Atajurt had managed to organise mass protests that were unprecedented in Kazakhstan, which were making it impossible to deport me. But Kazakhstan is a country with an autocratic government, so it takes a lot of courage to pour out onto the streets and make your voice heard. It's not like the West. Demonstrations, loudspeakers, and posters are not welcome. "We want the truth!" someone shouted. Hundreds of peaceful demonstrators were calling for the government to take pity on its own populace. If the Kazakh government had given in to Beijing, they would have lost face and might even have been confronted with a rebellion on the home front, so they grudgingly let it happen.

This time, before getting out of the car, I asked the officer beside me, "Could we hide the handcuffs from my children?" With a friendly smile, he held my hand behind my back so that the cuffs were nearly hidden underneath his sleeve. The throng of people in the courtroom was even bigger than the first time, and security had to clear a path for us through the corridor. "Stay strong!" the onlookers called out to me. "You'll be free soon!"

The court had acceded to all my wishes. A Russian interpreter had been declared superfluous, and the whole trial was to be conducted in Kazakh. That meant we could communicate easily. I understood the judge, the judge understood me, and the audience understood everything. This way, everyone could follow my political show trial.

The main charge against me was that I had illegally crossed the border. So I had to justify why I had broken the law. This was my chance. Straightening my back, I fixed my gaze directly ahead. "The whole population in Xinjiang is under tremendous pressure. There are penal camps there that the Chinese refer to outwardly as 'vocational training centres'. In reality, however, the people there are treated worse than in any prison. There is a genocide underway in China, directed against us Kazakhs and other Muslims. I know this because I was a teacher in one such camp. It's a fascist system there. The indigenous population is tyrannised …"

I did my best to explain the situation in the north-west province and in the camps as objectively as possible in just ten minutes. "Because of my decision to inform the world about what's going on, my life is now in great danger. That's why I had to escape." I added that the authorities had confiscated our passports, which was why I couldn't leave legally.

Some of the people in the audience reacted to my statement with shock; others leapt up with their fists clenched, full of loathing for the Communist Party and the Chinese government. "We can't let this go on any longer! Free our people from the concentration camps!" they demanded.

I watched with bated breath, but for the first time in my life I saw people making a ruckus yet not being immediately detained and tortured. The judge was quite understanding, and allowed them to continue loudly expressing their outrage. "We're selling our country to Beijing!" and "The only thanks we get is being oppressed and robbed of our freedom!"

The trial adjourned in the late afternoon. I wasn't allowed to see my family again until 23 July, during which time I was beset by constant uncertainty. Would I be sent to China the next day? Sentenced to life in a Kazakh prison? Or maybe I'd soon be a free woman?

23 July: my final days in court

During the final phase of the trial, something happened that had seemed unthinkable: even more people had squeezed in. The international press, as well as representatives from the political world and various large organisations, had congregated in the courtroom.

The judge read out the names of the countless foreign organisations that had passionately campaigned for my release. The United Nations, Amnesty International, ambassadors from countries such as the USA, Italy, and Germany, the European Union, the Society for Threatened Peoples ... all these important institutions had been in direct contact with President Nazarbayev himself, and it was having an effect. In a situation like mine, international aid was crucial to survival. Their support gave me hope for a better future. For the first time, I dared to think, *No matter how powerful China is, maybe the free countries are more powerful still ...*

Every time someone asked me a question in court, I used it as an opportunity to describe the conditions in the camps. This time, it had an even bigger impact, because the media broadcast my message across the globe.

Until then, Beijing had stubbornly disputed the existence of those camps. It had duped the world with images of laughing students, who, according to their propaganda, were "in schools where they are provided with free meals and language lessons".

All the relevant documents and evidence were presented that afternoon. By this point, they had even granted me a temporary card that identified me as an asylum-seeker. The state lawyer who was supposed to be prosecuting me selected the least serious paragraphs from the criminal code, and recommended in her closing arguments that I receive the minimum sentence.

A week later, when the judge announced the verdict on the fourth day of the trial, a loud cheer rang out: "Freedom for Sayragul!" I was allowed to leave the prison, and was merely under house arrest. Everyone leapt up, surrounded me, and congratulated me. There were microphones thrust towards me from every angle.

I'm free, I thought, stunned. And for the first time in many years, I was filled with immense pride.

The party is cut short

What with the crush of people in the corridor, it was almost impossible to put one foot in front of the other, so I let the crowd carry me towards the exit. I kept standing on tiptoes, scanning for my husband and children, but I saw nothing but flying hats and outstretched arms. Ahead of me were ten or fifteen steps that led straight down to the next crowd.

There were lots of women with flowers, as well as children and old people with gifts, waiting for me downstairs. A few had tears running down their faces. Others had brought Kazakh instruments and were playing music. Several well-known poets and writers shook my hand. I kept having to dry my eyes. Wealthy businesspeople had reserved whole restaurants, slaughtered lambs, and donated food for all the visitors. What was I supposed to say? Air, light, and laughter, all at once. What a triumph! It was an incredibly happy moment.

Outside the courthouse, I addressed the crowd: "When I came to Kazakhstan, I felt like I was alone. Now I'm confident that's not true. I have found my people, my nation, my homeland!"

According to the court's ruling, I was supposed to spend six months under surveillance and house arrest. If I wanted to go anywhere, I had to get a permit from the local authorities first. I was used to much worse, so it really wasn't a big issue for me.

"Long live Kazakhstan!" the crowd was chanting around me. In my heart, I felt like bright rays of sunlight were breaking through the eternal twilight, filling the world with light as I took my first steps into freedom. I got into the police car against the backdrop of singing and cheers, and they took me back to prison so I could pick up my things. I didn't see my loved ones until later that afternoon, in one of the restaurants where my release was being celebrated.

The children were beside themselves with joy. Ulagat said merrily, "You know, Mama, I prayed to God all along that you would be set free and come back home to us." And Ukilay threw her arms around my neck. "See, God has granted our wish," she said, and nearly suffocated me with kisses. My husband put his arm around my shoulder, and, bursting with gratitude, I felt my body fill with warmth. It had been a long road.

Afterwards, we got into the car and set off for Almaty, roughly three hours away. The longer we were on the road, the longer became the convoy of supporters behind us. "The whole of Kazakhstan seems to have been following your trial," marvelled Uali. I merely nodded mutely — I was so moved. People had gathered in the streets to cheer us on. We couldn't even get through in some places.

Hundreds of them were waiting for me to get out and greet them, talk to them. They launched into the national anthem. I saw nothing but cheerful faces and hands passing me food and gifts. Everybody wanted a photo with me. There were even people waving at us along the motorway. *Maybe this is just a dream?* I thought. I glanced back uncertainly at my children, but they were with me. They were close.

In Almaty, a generous restaurant proprietor had served a lavish feast for around two hundred people, including a few local celebrities and my family. So many strangers, and everyone hugging me and giving free rein to their feelings of gratitude. The Kazakh flag fluttered on enormous flat-screen TVs, and our folk music played. It wasn't until morning, when the birds were twittering in the trees, that things calmed down and we were able to lie down and rest at our host's home.

The next day, the truth about life in the camps appeared in the *New York Times* and the *Washington Post*, and in reports on the BBC and other important media. After a couple of hours' sleep, we were back on our feet once more. The landline and my mobile phone were both ringing off the hook. I gave brief interviews to one journalist after another. "In my home country I experienced what it means to live under hardship and restrictions. And I can tell you: freedom is an overwhelming joy!"

Dog-tired but happy, we wanted to set off for Uali's home village. "One more interview with a Canadian reporter," my host asked me, beckoning me to the telephone. The interpreter next to me was translating when I suddenly noticed that everyone around me was looking concerned. I'm not sure what I told the reporter after that. We had received news that pulled the rug out from under my feet.

Under house arrest: from one house to another

"Your youngest sister has been arrested back home today," I heard my host say, as he stood in front of me with his eyes lowered. Although it was hot outside, I froze. Then he cleared his throat and added, "They also picked up your mother yesterday, immediately after the verdict was announced." In China, this was a common form of retribution when refugees dared to go public with their stories. My whole body was trembling, as though I had a fever.

I sank helplessly onto the sofa. It felt as though someone had sucker-punched me from behind. Suddenly, I saw the men in the black masks and the crying girl in the camp. *Save me!* But it was my relatives' faces I was picturing. My frail mother, seventy years old. My sister, twenty-six, a teacher like me. She was in the middle of preparing for her wedding. She had been so looking forward to finally getting married.

To this day, I'm not sure whether my sister and mother ended up in a camp. Some people claimed they spent a month in a prison. Others said two months. How they were treated there, I can only guess.

The exhilarating sensation of being free didn't last long. In a country like Kazakhstan, where China's power was increasing, corruption, cover-ups, and greed were flourishing more than ever, killing off the last healthy cells in our society like a cancerous tumour.

Barely three days after the celebration in Almaty, we arrived home in Baidebek, worn out, where the next shock awaited us. Strangers had been in our house. All the drawers had been pulled out; papers and clothing were scattered all over the floor. Even the children's rooms looked like they'd been hit by a whirlwind.

Ukilay and Ulagat started crying amid all the mess. Nothing had been stolen, but everything was ruined.

"I wonder if it was the Chinese secret police?" mused Uali. We were terrified that we weren't safe anymore even in the refuge of our own home. Ukilay and Ulagat grabbed my arm vehemently and tried to drag me away. "Mama, Mama, let's go! The Chinese are trying to kidnap you again!"

Uali had already sold the house anyway, because he urgently needed the money to pay for my stay in the private clinic, the search for me, the lawyer's fee, and all sorts of other expenses. All the money was gone. The new owners had kindly offered to let us stay until we had found a cheaper place to live. But at that moment, we all knew we couldn't stay there a minute longer. It felt like the intruders were still in the house. We were disgusted. What had they touched?

We hurriedly grabbed our documents and left, not even taking food or clothing. We had gone through so many mind-boggling things that the idea the secret police might have poisoned our belongings no longer seemed so strange. First, we rented a small flat on the outskirts of Almaty. Luckily, we were supported financially by several organisations such as Atajurt until we could get back on our feet.

From that moment on, there was not a single minute of our lives not lived in fear.

Fugitives in our own land

The court's ruling took effect within two weeks. We were forced to move to the small town of Esik, because from that point on we were registered in that district. I had a temporary right of asylum for six months, after which I would have to extend it every three months if the government did not grant me permanent residence. It might be refused at any time, which would mean going back to China. It would mean death.

Our family was relentlessly harassed by Kazakhs who were hired by the secret police, all of them on Beijing's payroll. Who else would have been interested in constantly grinding us down psychologically? We had just moved into a bungalow when strangers tried to force open our windows in the middle of the night. That happened several times. Every time, the blood froze in my veins. We were so afraid of being attacked that we all slept in the same room, with the children in the middle.

Eventually, some of these informers turned up at Ukilay's and Ulagat's school, trying to winkle information out of other parents. "Keep an eye on them for us and eavesdrop on their children. What are their routines? Where do they go, and when? Who do they visit?" They were actually brazen enough to approach our children directly: "Tell us, are you expecting any more journalists? Who are you in touch with?" Uali and I were perpetually checking our surroundings and trying to keep everything within our eyeline. Were we sure all the doors and windows were locked?

Again, it was ordinary Kazakhs who came to our rescue. The writer Habbas Habsh, roughly eighty years old, promised me, "As soon as you're free, Sayragul, I'll throw a massive party for you!" He kept that promise, even though he himself was seriously ill, and had a lamb slaughtered for us on a mountain by the hot springs of Almali.

Lots of intellectuals, artists, and famous celebrities attended to congratulate me on my newfound freedom and to support my asylum application. As we said goodbye, Habbas Habsh gave me and Uali one of his books of Kazakh stories, with a personal dedication. We took the book home with us: it's one of our most precious treasures.

On 3 October 2018, the court rejected my first application for asylum in Taldykorgan. I had to go through the process by myself: my family had to wait outside. But what had happened to my lawyer? Abzal Husman was a no-show.

A small band of helpers came together to improve my chances of being granted permission to stay. "Next time they're discussing your asylum application, we may have good news for you," Serikzhan Bilash said. He was quite a hefty man, roughly around my age, I think, very well educated and eloquent, with a tremendous knowledge of politics. With his credibility and expertise, he had long been a point of contact for international organisations and journalists.

It was also Serikzhan Bilash who filled me in on the true extent of the detention camps in East Turkestan. It was much worse than I had feared. This was the largest system of gulags known to our era. Everyone agreed that only external intervention offered any hope of bringing the nightmare to an end.

After one such meeting with my supporters, I was intercepted on the street by two Kazakhs from the secret police. "If you don't keep your mouth shut from now on and you keep blabbing to journalists about the situation in China, you will disappear forever once your six months are up," they told me.

I wanted nothing more than to be granted asylum in Kazakhstan and to devote myself to motherhood. But now I wasn't sure if that was even possible. I was torn. On the one hand, I wanted to solidify my status as a Kazakh; on the other, it was becoming increasingly clear to me how important it was to give the media an even more detailed picture of the dire situation in my homeland. So far, I had kept a low profile. I didn't want to reveal everything without the necessary security and back-up.

Meanwhile my lawyer, Abzal Husman, was making demands similar to those of the secret-service agents, insisting that I immediately and completely withdraw from the public eye. Nobody understood this strategy. "Is it just about doing what China wishes?" we wondered in the evenings, when it was just us. Their plan was transparent: the Kazakh government wanted to secretly deport me as soon as all the attention and notoriety had died down.

All day long, I met with journalists, mostly clandestinely in cars somewhere away from home, to give very broad-brush reports on our current living situation. After that, I would sit at the kitchen table until late in the evening, filling out applications for aid from various international organisations.

On behalf of my incarcerated mother and sister, I wrote one petition after another to the United Nations and important political institutions. "Please help them! Both of them are innocent and have nothing to do with my actions! They didn't even know I was in a camp or that I fled to Kazakhstan."

Ultimately, political pressure led to their release. Yet I still don't know how they're doing. It's difficult to get hold of reliable information. My parents' house has been under CCTV surveillance, inside and out, ever since. The authorities keep a record of all their movements, whether they're in the bathroom or the kitchen. Nobody wants to visit them anymore. Friends, acquaintances, and even my sister's fiancé have all turned their backs. They're terrified of being dragged into the gaping maw of the camps as well.

This is why I still blame myself. It's my fault that my sister can't get married and start a family. It's my fault my ageing mother was thrown behind bars to suffer privation and hunger. It's my fault that my relatives, friends, and everyone else I know is in mortal danger. Sometimes I get messages from East Turkestan via circuitous routes, but it's impossible for me to speak to my friends, brothers, or sisters, since their houses, too, are under around-the-clock surveillance.

Followed

Our situation became increasingly threatening. Whenever we left the house, we were followed by strangers. The same cars were always parked near our apartment, usually with a different driver behind the wheel.

My second application for asylum was rejected in Astana on 26 December 2018, although they didn't actually notify me. I kept asking about the ruling to no avail, until I was finally informed on 6 January 2019. Again, my lawyer was nowhere to be found. Still, Uali and I refused to let it get us down. Over the previous few months, so many people had boosted our spirits. There were hundreds of video clips online in which Kazakh children and grandmothers, families and businesspeople, intellectuals and workers appealed to the government: "Sayragul Sauytbay is an innocent woman who suffered terribly in a Chinese internment camp. She is one of us. Please give this woman asylum and protection in Kazakhstan."

Everyone who believed, as we did, that something good might come of this — no matter how slim the chances — made every effort to achieve that goal. This hope spurred us on. We reached our breaking points, and went beyond them. My husband and I were casting around for ways to lead a halfway normal life once more. We considered opening a business together. "We could keep animals, and pay back something to our supporters with the profits," I suggested. "And open another shop," added Uali. We had already bought a cow. Some of the milk, we drank ourselves; the rest, we sold at the market.

But the minute we left the house, milk cans in hand, there were people on our heels. A couple of times, I whirled around furiously and marched straight up to them. "Why are you following us?" They didn't say a word, just stared at me contemptuously.

Sometimes Uali and I would dart around the corner and take the long way round, but they stuck to us like chewing gum. Occasionally, we'd breathe a sigh of relief — "We've shaken them off!" — but then they'd appear at the next corner, ready to pick up their pursuit.

All the while, Beijing's propaganda machine was churning out false information about my family so that people in Kazakhstan and the rest of the world would stop giving us help. It was a routine tactic used by the CCP to silence opponents. They smeared us online and on social media, calling us criminals, liars, and traitors. My sister, my brother, and other people we knew were forced to slander us in a video.

For days, I was laid up in bed with a fever. Uali, worried, took me to a private clinic in Esik in January 2019, where a doctor examined me and gave me an injection. When we returned later that afternoon, we found our two children in a state of utter panic. Mute with horror, trembling with shock — incapable of tears, their stifled cries for help were still in their throats.

"What's wrong?" we asked, aghast. Still feverish, I ran over to Ulagat, who was clasping his neck and gasping in pain.

He was so upset he almost forgot to breathe. "There was a big man in the apartment!" Ukilay started sobbing. "I didn't have time to lock him out. He ran through the door behind us and just shoved us out of the way! He wanted to know where you were and what you were doing."

"Then what?" Uali was trying to calm the children down. But, like me, he was struggling to maintain his composure.

"He kept asking the same questions. *What people come here?*" our daughter continued, chalk-white and beaded with cold sweat, "and then Ulagat tried to call the police!" We had stuck the phone number of the nearest police station onto the wall in case of emergencies. But the guy had ripped the phone out of his hand

and had bellowed, "What are you doing? Who are you calling?" He grabbed the boy by the throat with one of his massive paws and lifted him into the air. As our son was choking, he bawled down at our daughter, who was screaming for help, "Next you'll be kidnapped by the Chinese and murdered!" The way he had treated our children was brutal. He'd scared them half to death.

Yet because I was under house arrest, we had no choice but to stay in Esik. After this incident, my husband and I took turns keeping watch, day and night. While one of us slept, the other stood guard. We had no weapons to defend our lives with, except for a large wooden stick.

We didn't let the children out of our sight for even a minute. Every day, we took them to school and picked them up again. Ukilay and Ulagat lived in constant fear; at night, it loomed before them like a vast wave, and just before it swallowed all of us, they woke up whimpering and crying. After that, we couldn't sleep anymore, either. The four of us just stood there, waiting for the sunrise.

Even now, nothing has changed for me. I wake at midnight and stay alert throughout the night. Sweaty with fear.

Uali and I had hoped to earn some money, but that was impossible. My husband rubbed his furrowed brow. "What if I leave, and that's exactly the moment they break into the house? What if something happens to you or the kids?" Our nerves were in tatters.

After my third application was denied, I appealed, but no one informed me that my case would be heard on 11 February 2019 before the court in Taldykorgan. My lawyer, the person representing me, was not available. After all that had happened, I decided not to stay silent, but to publicise our situation even more aggressively in the media.

On our own, we were lost.

Subterranean camps

As I'm telling you all this, I'm wondering how I can bear to make myself remember it. Every time I have a conversation with a journalist about the camps, it's like I'm bringing the past back to life, and it's just as unendurable as it was at the time. It feels like I'm back in the same situation. My heart pounds, and my sweat-drenched shirt clings to my skin. The images in my head spin and whirl until I'm too exhausted to go on.

Usually, when reporters ask me about those days, I jump up and send them away, because I can't stand it for another second: "Please leave!" Then, dead tired, I crawl into bed and stay there for a day or two; only then, with effort, am I able to get up again. It's bad enough hearing about what happened to other inmates. My chest tightens, and I feel like I'm reduced to nothing but my beating heart.

Like the story of a police officer in a camp near Hulija, the town centre in Ili, who tore a page out of a Koran and wiped his backside with it, threw it on the floor, trampled it with his feet, and finally urinated on it. After doing this in front of the inmates, he forced them to imitate his behaviour, shouting, "This is our God! This is our Allah! This is our Holy Koran!"

Countless other statements from survivors testify to prisoners being deliberately infected with tuberculosis and hepatitis in the camps, and pregnant women being forced to have an abortion. These reports have been verified by human-rights organisations.

Most recently, stories have been circulating about subterranean camps. International human-rights organisations have been using satellite images to gather information about the number of camps, and on this basis they estimate that between 1.2 and 1.8 million people are in concentration camps in East Turkestan.

In reality, there are numerous hidden and underground concentration camps that cannot be seen by satellite. The Bingtuan — the Production and Construction Corps in East Turkestan — run several underground camps that are not so easily discovered.

I heard about two underground camps from a friend who visited his parents in Guliden last year. He moved to Kazakhstan from East Turkestan a couple of years earlier, and is now a Kazakh citizen. When he went to see his parents in Tougztarau, a county in the Ili Kazakh Autonomous Prefecture, he heard from his family and other witnesses about a subterranean camp there in Guliden. Apparently, 14,000 were detained there. My friend drove to Sumen, Qapqal County Number 6, to find out from a policeman friend where exactly his own relatives were incarcerated. The policeman explained that his relatives were being held in an underwater prison in Sumen, and gave him additional, horrifying, inside information. Many other people were also being held in this underwater camp.

The guards there kept the prisoners in chains attached to the ceiling. They hung side by side in water that reached up to their mouths, their hands shackled above their heads. Any attempt to stretch out their legs and alleviate the pain soon became unbearable, because they would swallow water and be unable to breathe. Any urine or faeces they passed was left swimming in the same water. They were only allowed to get out of the water three times a day, for meals. They would be kept there for weeks at a time. I don't know how long a person can bear such a thing. I don't know if there were many survivors. I only heard that there are several such underwater prisons.

When my friend returned to Kazakhstan, he told me about both camps. His brother was unjustly imprisoned there last year. I passed on the addresses and all the information I had to the relevant international organisations.

Based on reliable witness testimony from numerous prisoners kept in subterranean camps, I and other activists estimate that the true number of detainees held in East Turkestan is close to 3 million.

When I hear these stories, I feel like I'm a prisoner again myself. I feel like an invalid.

Threats: "You're not changing your lawyer!"

"I'm going to change my lawyer," I announced in February 2019 in a video I posted online. I needed to make a public statement so I had legal proof that this man no longer represented me and no longer had the right to speak on my behalf.

Not long afterwards, around 6.00 pm, our front door burst open and four officers barged into our apartment. The children ran screaming into another room and hid. "Sit down!" the intruders ordered harshly. Uali and I sat next to each other on a stool, stiff as boards, while the uniformed officers made themselves comfortable on the sofa and bellowed orders at me.

"You're not changing your lawyer!"

"But I have the right to a different one," I insisted in my soft voice.

They mocked me. "Rights, someone like you?" What was I even thinking?

My husband and I were sick with fear. "You're going to make a new video on your phone right now, publicly announcing that you have changed your mind and you want to keep your lawyer!" I hesitated, aware that if I agreed, it would mean the end of the road for me. They stayed for several hours, trying to intimidate us.

During that time, we weren't allowed to stand up, drink anything, or look for our trembling children. "If you don't do what we say, your family will suffer a terrible fate. Then you'll really be sorry." Around midnight, they got what they wanted. I was so worried about Ukilay and Ulagat and so hopeless that I gave in.

Next morning, several policemen took me to the station, where I had a surprise meeting with my lawyer, Abzal Husman, and a senior official who had flown in specially from the capital. The second man did not give me his name, or his exact position. His message was brief, his threat the same as that of the other government thugs: "You're going to keep your mouth shut and keep working with your lawyer. Woe betide you and your family if you don't." What choice did I have? They were practically holding a knife to my loved ones' throats. All I could do was agree.

My husband and I were profoundly frustrated. That afternoon, I was sitting in an armchair, eyes wide open, when Uali called, "Sayragul, I need to talk to you!" I didn't respond. I was asleep. With my eyes open. Three days later, the judge in Taldykorgan was due to rule on my appeal. The night before, we sat in the living room, nervously joggling our feet, until at last we summoned up the courage to engage a new lawyer despite all the threats. Minutes later, Aiman Umarova received my desperate video message. "Please take my case, otherwise I'm done for. Beijing is demanding my deportation …"

We wanted to disappear immediately afterwards, but police officers were watching our front door in a car outside.

Victims of politicians kowtowing to Beijing

What should we do? In the middle of the night, we called a friend: "Please come and pick us up! We can't stay here a minute longer!"

When he showed up in his car a little later, the police officers outside our house chased him off. "Get out of here!" they yelled. "What are you doing?"

He made up an excuse. "I'm just here to buy and pick up coal." Then he parked his car in a side street and used his phone to tell us he'd arrived. We waited until the officers fell asleep in their car, then Uali, the children, and I climbed over the wall around our house, ran down the street and leapt, panting, into the car. Once we were safely in my friend's village, my new lawyer uploaded my most recent video, entitled *I want to change my lawyer!*

The following morning, on 11 February 2019, I bumped into my former lawyer, Abzal Husman, outside the courthouse in Taldykorgan. Our heads swimming with indignation, my husband and I told him in no uncertain terms that we didn't want to work with him anymore. He hadn't seen that coming.

My new lawyer, Aiman Umarova, was exceptionally brave, and took my case even though it was politically fraught. I know that she, too, was threatened and followed. Once, when we were waiting at a café for some journalists from CNN, we noticed that someone was tailing us, but we ignored them.

But as soon as one of the journalists asked me the first question, this guy — dressed in trousers and a jacket — planted himself in front of us, feet apart, and started filming us on his phone. "Please stop that! You're disturbing us. Go away," the reporter complained, irritated by his rudeness, but he simply stayed put and kept filming.

Further investigation revealed that he worked at the local police station, although at the café he was in plain clothes. In another attempt to scare off my lawyer, someone killed her dog in her garden and left the dead animal on her doorstep. Its mouth was full of soil. Later, they did the same to her cat.

Ultimately, the court ruled against me. Around the same time, Serikzhan Bilash was apprehended in mid-March for "inciting ethnic hatred" and placed under house arrest. He was prohibited from continuing his work as a human-rights activist until further notice. My extraordinarily courageous lawyer, who took on his case, too, was smeared as an "enemy of the nation".

Nonetheless, she continued to address the media, calling the case a "political trial" that was profoundly influenced by the immense power China wielded in Kazakhstan. "The government does not want people speaking openly about the situation in these Chinese camps. I say this very clearly, with tremendous fear and at personal risk." Meanwhile, despite the ban, Serikzhan Bilash — another extraordinarily brave person — continued publishing witness testimony from the camps.

By this point, it was impossible for the government to secretly deport me to China. The whole world would have found out about it. That's why they eventually let me move to the West. They were simply getting rid of a fly in the ointment: from then on, the relationship between Kazakhstan and China would no longer be tarnished by a chief witness.

It is some consolation to know that my case has helped pave the way for other refugees who followed in my footsteps from East Turkestan. Since Nazarbayev handed over power to his loyal acolyte Kassym-Jomart Tokayev in June 2019, and now that Beijing has come to be viewed more critically on the world stage, the Kazakh government has become a little more generous in dealing with asylum applications from my old homeland.

Our family were victims of politicians who kowtowed to Beijing, politicians who grovelled in the dust even as the Chinese government subjugated their own people. Kazakhstan is in a tricky political predicament, because it owes China roughly twelve billion dollars for projects related to the Belt and Road Initiative.

All told, we had been permitted to live as a family in Kazakhstan, the land of our mother tongue, for a little over under fourteen months, from 5 April 2018 to 3 June 2019.

CHAPTER NINE

Viral: warning the world

3 June 2019: arriving in a new world

Less than three days before we left, we found out where we were going. "Sweden has accepted us!" cried Uali. When we heard the news, my husband put both hands on my shoulders and said to me, "God has given you your third life." I gazed at him uncertainly, feeling my stomach twist. Saying goodbye to Kazakhstan would be painful, but I was excited about our future in a foreign country.

"First you managed to flee China," explained Uali, raising a finger for each point. "Second, you survived torture and detention in Kazakhstan. And third, an indignant outcry rang out throughout Kazakhstan only a few hours before you were due to be sent to your death in China."

"Where is Sweden?" my daughter enquired. She and her brother sat down at the computer and checked online to see how people lived in Scandinavia. Curious, we had already looked up various countries in the West, including Canada, America, and Germany.

Ukilay read aloud: "Sweden deeply values human rights. They even award the Nobel Peace Prize to famous human-rights activists."

Ulagat gasped, shouting into our astonished faces, "Look, there are loads of islands and lakes, big pine forests, and glaciers. The largest cities are all on the coast ..."

"At last we're going to be left in peace. We won't have to be afraid!" cheered my daughter.

On the one hand, we were glad we were finally going to be

able to live in peace; but on the other, we were sad. Tears would roll down my children's cheeks in the evening. "Why can't we stay here?" wailed my son. They had settled in well at school, and we had plenty of friends and relatives nearby.

Kazakhstan is an autocratic state, of course, but compared to China life there felt like freedom — despite the persecution and psychological terrorism. We were allowed to move around unobstructed, speak to people, and look up information online. Kazakhstan was where we experienced our worst panic attacks, but also the most wonderful moments of our lives.

When our children realised how upset they were making us, they both tried to swallow the lump in their throats and put on a brave face. "The main thing is that we're away from the danger of the Chinese," said Ukilay, chewing her lip.

"Yes, we'll be better protected in Sweden," Ulagat agreed, giving me a squeeze.

My husband's shoulders were hunched, his head lowered, as though he were listening. "If we stay here, things will get even worse," he mused, looking me in the eye. "They will kill you."

I clasped my hands, raised my head, and said, "Okay, then we'll start a new life. A third life."

We packed the essentials. There wasn't much. Our children's outstanding report cards, important documents, papers, photos from parties in Kazakhstan and our life in East Turkestan. Most of the space was taken up by books given to us by Kazakh writers, personalised with handwritten dedications. Finally, we rolled up one large and a couple of small Kazakhstani flags, and tucked them between the few clothes we were taking.

For safety's sake, we told only our closest relatives and friends about our departure, a small group who came to see us off at the airport. They asked me to record another short video message for the people of Kazakhstan, which they would release later. But I cried the whole time and could barely get a word out. Until the very last second, I'd been clinging to the hope that we might be granted asylum in Kazakhstan after all, because so many thousands of people there had given me such whole-hearted support. But, sadly, that wish never came true.

It was night-time when we flew from Almaty to Astana. I gazed down at the city through the window. Nobody was on the streets. Everyone was asleep. I found the sight deeply touching. All those good people who had done so much for us, with no idea that I was flying away above their roofs forever.

In my mind's eye, I kept replaying their video clips, which they'd continued sending to the government right to the very end. *Please give Sayragul Sauytbay and her family asylum in her homeland of Kazakhstan.* I turned my face aside so that no one would see me cry, and tried to comfort myself. *The fact that we're flying above the clouds right now is a gift from God.*

At the airport in Frankfurt, I asked my friends on the phone not to publish my last video message after all. "If the people watch that, they'll be sad to see me in such a sorry state," I explained. I wanted to send them my thanks in Sweden, composed and without any tears. At every airport there were people waiting for us, holding signs with our names, until finally someone picked us up in Stockholm and drove us to Trelleborg via Malmö. "Where are they sending us?" we whispered softly to one another.

We really didn't want to attract any attention by making demands. Until now, we'd given little thought to what our life in Sweden might be like. Uali and I were picturing a cheap hotel room, or shabby, cramped accommodation with hundreds of other refugees. What exactly lay in store for us? The uncertainty made us faintly uneasy, but our expectations were modest. What mattered was that we were safe.

Where are we staying?

As we pulled up in a small side street outside a two-storey terraced house, Uali leant forward and asked the driver doubtfully, "So where are we staying?"

"We are here," he replied.

Our eyes widened. "But that's a hotel, isn't it?" I gasped.

The driver said, "No, that's your apartment. From now on, it belongs to you." He called an interpreter on his phone, who translated his words for us.

Utterly perplexed, we followed two other Swedish people into the house. "Ooooh!" Our jaws dropped. Everything was clean; everything was new. There were two children's rooms, a living room, and a bedroom. The furniture smelled like it had just been unpacked, and in the kitchen we found food for a couple of days. Everything was ready for us. Finally, a Swedish man pressed the key into my husband's hand, and they both wished us goodnight.

Just to make sure, Uali turned the key in the lock three times and the children pulled the curtains before we all ran back through the four rooms several times, excited and happy.

"This country is even more beautiful than we thought," decided my son, as we ran our hands over the furniture carefully and warily, as though they might burst like soap bubbles at any moment.

Ukilay laughed, her eyes twinkling. "How can a country do something so nice for strangers like us?"

From the very first moment, everyone in Sweden was incredibly helpful. We felt accepted straightaway. It was a wonderful feeling. Unfortunately, it didn't last long.

We spent the first night huddled together in a single large bed in our new home.

On top of the world one minute ...

The next morning at 8.30, we received a visit from two social workers. After they had helped us to fill out all the necessary forms, they showed us to the city centre, roughly one kilometre away. Hand in hand with the children, we walked from the post office to the bank, and from the supermarket to the most important local-authority offices.

As the four of us were walking back that afternoon and were within sight of our apartment, Uali stopped short and took a deep breath. "The sea must be around here somewhere."

I frowned. "How do you know that?"

"I can smell it."

How could a person from the area around Ürümqi, a city further from the ocean than any other on earth, recognise the smell of the sea? We made a beeline across a large street, and then we saw it, directly behind our row of houses — the waters of the Baltic. Not far away was the ferry port, and beside it the main station.

It was summer, June, the most beautiful time of year. As though drawn by a magnet, we went down to the beach, the children running ahead. Families were splashing around in the sea with their young children. Ukilay and Ulagat hurled themselves into the water, still wearing their shirts and trousers, and tried to swim, even though they'd never done it before in their lives.

"Come back!" I cried out anxiously, "you can't swim, it's dangerous!" But the children didn't want to come back. Ulagat called out, "Look, Mama, the children are swimming like this," and he imitated them with his thin arms. They were both struggling to stay afloat, coughing and swallowing salt water, yet they immediately started learning to swim.

Someone came to help us every day. Since in Kazakhstan we'd been constantly moving out of fear and a lack of money, it was relaxing to finally be able to settle down in one home. The inhabitants of this small town weren't snobby; they didn't treat us like second-class citizens. They were friendly. They treated us like equals. It felt wonderful to be a completely normal person. My daughter tossed her braid merrily over her shoulder. "We can finally stop wondering where we're going next week."

Uali agreed. "This is paradise!"

Although our neighbours didn't know us, they came up to us on the street and greeted us in a friendly manner. "When did you arrive? Do you come from Syria or Uzbekistan?" Evidently, many refugees here came from those places.

"No, we come from Kazakhstan," we replied, to their amazement.

In the next couple of days, Ulagat found a large supermarket nearby on the internet. "Come on, Mama, we'll go together." He was already dragging me behind him. Among the shelves of food, I was approached by an old Swedish gentleman about sixty years old. "Welcome, Sayragul Sauytbay," he said.

I didn't understand a word except for my name, but my son spoke Russian and a few fragments of English, so he was able to partially translate. The Swede had spent years living in Central Asia, and still followed the news there online. In Kazakhstan, I was a famous person, so he recognised me from pictures. He congratulated me several times, and seemed very pleased that we had found asylum in Sweden. "Welcome to your new homeland!"

This was my next wonderful experience in Sweden. After a few days, however, our euphoria transformed into the exact opposite. We sank into the doldrums.

... Down in the dumps the next

It was the summer holiday. Life was tough. No friends, no school, no job. Our children had been excellent students, with a close relationship with their teachers. Now, however, they spent hours swiping through pictures in their WhatsApp groups and reading messages from their former classmates. After a couple of days, Ulagat and Ukilay came to the dinner table with their eyes rubbed red. They were deeply lonely.

There were no Kazakhs, Uighurs, or Muslims from East Turkestan anywhere in the vicinity. My husband, who had once been so active and cheerful, who usually wore his heart on his sleeve, who had liked to invite friends and relatives around, morning, noon, and night, suddenly fell silent. We'd always had guests at our table. But suddenly the house was so silent. All we heard was our children crying.

We had all changed profoundly. The slightest thing brought tears to our eyes. My husband was hit especially hard. Usually, I was the one who withdrew into myself with my troubles, closed and inaccessible. Uali was the exact opposite. At least, until now.

For a few days, he'd been carrying around Habbas Habsh's book, which we had been given at the party on the mountain. During this period, the ageing writer was the only person my husband felt understood him fully. He kept reading the same book of Kazakh stories, over and over, starting from the beginning. Poems like, *The beautiful moon is invisible / The stars, too, have vanished* ... My husband, such a lovely, open person, suddenly stopped wanting to talk to anybody.

One morning, Uali locked himself into the bedroom with the book. After a few hours, the children and I — first one after another, and then together — tried to coax him out. We rattled the handle, but he only yelled, "Leave me in peace!"

We were very worried. "What's wrong with Papa?" sobbed Ukilay. By the time the sun set, Uali was still alone in the room. He'd never done anything like this before.

Late that night, I stood outside the closed door, my head leaning against the frame, and started talking to him. "How are we supposed to go on if you're acting like this? Please come out." I'd known plenty of people in East Turkestan who were eaten away by their sorrow, as though it were a disease. Many of them had started drinking to numb the pain. "If you keep on like this, you'll never get out of this hole!" I continued, putting my mouth very close to the edge of the door. Silence, the only answer. I spoke more loudly. "Yes, I know you have no friends here right now. But you can at least tell me what's bothering you, so you can get it off your chest." It was night by the time Uali opened the door.

This period, between 3 and 17 June, when our first language course began, was very difficult. Materially speaking, we were fine, but we felt incredibly alone and tormented by homesickness. The children still talked only of their friends in Kazakhstan, whom they missed terribly. "Everything is nice here, but we can't communicate," they complained. "How are we going to cope?" Without language, without relationships. We saw utter helplessness in their wide, childish eyes.

Occasionally, I sent Ukilay and Ulagat out to play so I could talk to Uali in the living room, undisturbed. "We've been through much worse than this. We've got to persevere. This, too, will pass." My husband dropped his head wearily into his hands. "You mustn't bottle everything up and let it destroy you," I continued, pulling him closer to me. "We've got to stick together. That's the only way we'll get through this."

Telephone calls were expensive, because we didn't have our

internet connection set up properly, but I still tried to put Uali in touch with our relatives in Kazakhstan every day. I was constantly doing my best to pique his curiosity and convince him to visit neighbouring towns, walk down to the beach, or head down to the local-authority offices to deal with paperwork.

One day around noon, there was a knock on our door. When I answered, there was a little blond boy outside, presumably a neighbour's child. Not sure what to do, I called to my daughter, "Come and ask him what he wants. You can speak a bit of English, at least. Give it a try."

The boy explained, "I saw you've got a boy living in your apartment. Tell him to come out to play." I'd been expecting a complaint or something nasty, so I laughed with relief.

I shooed Ulagat out with my hands. "Go with him. Even if you don't understand what he's saying, play with him. Maybe you'll meet some other boys out there." So my son went. After a while, however, he came back crying. "What's wrong?" I asked him.

He pressed his wet face into my belly as I hugged him with both arms. "I tried to talk to them," he sobbed, "but nobody understood me. What am I supposed to do now?"

After a few days, the children started getting used to their unfamiliar situation. Eventually, I bought them swimsuits, and they started going down to the beach and teaching themselves to swim.

Drawing Kazakh flags in Sweden

Roughly two months before the start of school, the language course for new arrivals began. I felt queasy as I dropped off my son and daughter. Would they be treated with contempt because they were Muslims from East Turkestan? But the two teachers accepted Ukilay and Ulagat as warmly as though they were their own. I was so touched to see the smiles now permanently glued to their faces.

Ulagat and Ukilay were learning alongside refugee children from Sudan, Iraq, Syria, Afghanistan, and other crisis-afflicted regions. Drawings of flags from seventeen different countries hung on the wall. That night, all the new children were told to draw a flag from their home country and bring it the next day so they could add them to the wall.

"We're in a foreign country, but our teachers are actually interested in where we come from," marvelled my son and daughter in baffled pleasure.

I raised my eyebrows doubtfully. Was their interest and openness genuine? No hidden accusations, no criticism?

My son confirmed it with a vehement nod: "The teacher even said, 'You should keep your fatherland in mind, because that's where your roots are.'"

"Those women are like our aunts," added Ukilay, smitten, and put her hand over her heart.

Straight after we were finished eating, they both sat down and started drawing in coloured pencil. As they moved the pencils across the paper, they started sniffling, because they were so overwhelmed by happy memories of their homeland. Their tears rained down onto the paper, and the colours ran. Radiant turquoise, representing the sky above the broad Kazakh steppes, mingled with the golden yellow of the sun and the steppe eagle underneath, its wings spread wide.

They had to keep starting from scratch. The colours and symbols on our flag represent peace and unity, hope, and the free flight of thought. They were drawing and crying until midnight. Once the children were in bed, I sat down on the sofa and let the tears stream down my face.

Next morning, the teachers pinned up the flags so that every child could be proud of their country. From that day on, things took a turn for the better. The children learned much faster than anticipated, and soon made friends. The four of us spent the evening learning vocabulary, doing our homework at the kitchen table. We even got a competition going. "Who's going to finish first?" I teased the kids.

"You'll see," I said, turning to their father next to me and nudging him gently with my elbow. "In the end, everything will be even better than before."

Uali raised his head and looked at me, sadly but hopefully. "Will it really be like before? With new friends? Will we be able to earn our own money?"

"Yeah, of course. Maybe we can even work as teachers," I replied cheerfully.

A beaming smile spread across his whole face, and he took me in his arms. "You're right. Why should we be sad? We only have reasons to be happy!"

For us, this was the beginning of a great adventure. Uali and I met lots of interesting people from many different countries, learning about their culture and way of life. To our enormous pleasure, we were honoured with a visit from a Kazakh who had been living in Denmark for decades — our first guest. In the middle of June, our next guest arrived. This time, it was a Swede from America who had made the trip especially so he could drive us around his beautiful country. Before he left, he gave us a flatscreen TV. "As a Swede, I'm very proud that my country has taken you in," he told us as we said goodbye. What an experience! I will never forget that exceptional man.

In August, I was invited to Stockholm by the Swedish foreign ministry, where I gave a statement about the situation in the Chinese camps. It was a challenge that did my family good. My lawyer from Kazakhstan also visited us twice. And so, gradually, we began to get settled. The Swedish school system is much better than in Kazakhstan. The children will have a future here. There are lots of doors open to them.

And the journalists and invitations from foreign political organisations keep coming. In March 2020, I was among twelve women given the International Women of Courage Award by American Secretary of State Mike Pompeo in Washington, in part for what was described as our "exceptional courage and leadership in advocating for human rights ... often at great personal risk". But I don't think I did anything special: all I did was report on what I experienced.

I won't stop telling the truth

To my surprise, as I wandered down German shopping streets during breaks in interviews for the original edition of this book, I saw loads of "1 Euro" shops crammed with cheap Chinese goods. These colourful little items look harmless. But the thoughts and the policies behind them — those are a big deal.

Beijing is stealthily gaining a foothold in many parts of the world, overwhelming the market with cheap products and offering generous loans. The long-term goal of the government is to gain monopolies and establish a new world order. Once they've done so, the CCP — and only the CCP — will dictate the rules. Then we will all be ruled by tyrants.

The government and the Party have been reaching their kraken-like tentacles into universities across the globe for a long time now, increasing their influence over the elites and opinion-makers in economics and politics, trying to divide Europeans, ensnaring right-wing Eastern European countries such as Poland

and Hungary with vast sums of money, persecuting free thinkers aboard, putting pressure on media outlets and universities, advocating to build and control mobile-phone networks, and importing Chinese censorship.

In free countries, this has led to incidents such as the world-class footballer Mesut Özil being barred from the field for daring to criticise the use of camps in China; such as Daimler, a major corporation, issuing a grovelling apology to Beijing for posting a harmless quote from the Dalai Lama, and then, as instructed, deleting it; and such as Lufthansa behaving like a naughty toddler because it referred to Taiwan as a separate country. So long as companies and citizens in the free world continue to value financial interests above human rights, we will be selling our souls to the devil.

Germany, along with twenty-two other nations, has condemned the human-rights abuses in Chinese camps. Yet not a single Muslim country has expressed solidarity with their brothers and sisters in the faith living in north-west China. Immediately after this condemnation, Beijing was offered support by thirty-seven other countries, including Russia, Syria, and Myanmar, whose own rulers trample the freedoms of their citizens underfoot and serve their own interests above all others.

China has bought their loyalty with financial deals and investments, forcing them into dependency; but the citizens of these countries don't live the flourishing, prosperous lives that Beijing promised. In fact, these states are in mountains of debt, and have sold off whole networks of streets, their farmland, their ports, power stations, pipelines, airports, and railway lines to Beijing, piece by piece. When those in power have hawked everything in their home country, what's left, in the end, for their own people?

In contrast to this irresponsible policy, the twenty-three Western countries give me hope. Although economic interests are vitally important to them as well, they have the foresight to prioritise human rights. For instance, China is Germany's most important trading partner, and that gives hope to all the people on Earth who live in misery and suffering, just like those who fight for freedom and justice, and against despotism. At some point, perhaps, we will be more successful than the rest! Then there will be a better future for all the peoples of the world.

Even if Beijing continues to brand me a liar and a traitor, spreading violence and disinformation, using my family as hostages and doing everything in their power to silence me, I will never stop bearing witness. I am deeply grateful to these twenty-three countries for enabling me to live in peace with my family in Sweden. And for giving me the freedom to speak the truth.

At my trial in Kazakhstan, two representatives from the Chinese consulate asked to meet with me alone. They intended, of course, to frighten me — to shut my mouth for good. But I shouted out in the middle of the courtroom, at the centre of public attention, "There are two Chinese here trying to silence me, but I won't stop telling the truth!"

Behind me are forty-three lost years. Ever since I was a child, I have lived under the control of the Communist Party. When the Party said, "Jump," we said, "How high?" I should have come to Europe twenty years ago. I would have learned many languages and had many jobs, visited many countries, and got to know many people. But even now, it's not too late for me. I want to use the time I've been given to make up for what I've lost and fight for freedom by peaceful means — because freedom cannot be taken for granted.

The mass internments in East Turkestan are proof that the government in Beijing has no qualms about brutally destroying those who stand in their way. After reading this book, no one can claim that they didn't know.

A virus of the mind

The interviews for this book were still continuing in the middle of December 2019, when the number of people infected with coronavirus rose alarmingly in Wuhan, a city of eleven million. The governor of the province, Hubei, had no mandate to act independently, so he reported on the situation to the national centre for disease control in Beijing. But nobody did anything to stem the virus.

Instead, the CCP did its best to stop all testing, and destroyed samples confirmed by laboratory analysis; Chinese reporters and individuals who warned of the rapidly spreading virus were arrested. The governor of Hubei province was removed from his post. Another twenty days passed, in which the virus ran rampant through the sprawling city.

Epidemiologists estimate that the initial transmission of the virus took place in October. When the inhabitants of Wuhan learned that the city was going to be under lockdown from 23 January, approximately five million people left. Those with money and a passport flew to countries across the world; others fled to Xinjiang or travelled within China.

At a single stroke, the CCP unleashed a tragedy that has ultimately affected the entire world. Millions of innocent people have suffered because of the virus, paying a bitter price for Beijing's obscurantist policies. If Beijing had taken active measures at the start of the outbreak to prevent the spread of the virus and notified the World Health Organization in good time, humanity would have been spared the subsequent devastation.

But by falsifying medical files, hushing up cases, and cooking the statistics, they made it impossible for other countries to learn from their example and better protect their own populations.

As I write this, the Chinese government is using a tried-and-tested strategy, presenting itself as a humanitarian "soft" power. By adroitly twisting the facts, it is trying to make the world believe its response to the virus has been exemplary, distracting everyone from its own systemic failures, and encouraging us to forget where and how the virus originated. In exchange for "generous" humanitarian aid — including financial support and the donation of masks — it will be able to demand fealty from even more countries in the future. Through targeted disinformation campaigns, Beijing — like other autocratic states — has also used this crisis to sow confusion and undermine Europeans' faith in the unity of the EU.

The brave individuals who reported on the catastrophic situation in Wuhan before they were silenced have been swiftly forgotten. Forgotten, too, is the fact that earlier pathogens like the first severe acute respiratory syndrome–related coronavirus (which caused the SARS outbreak) and strains of the influenza A virus (which caused avian flu) also originated in China. According to experts, this fact is closely connected to the prevalence of wet markets and relentless environmental destruction. A virology lab near one such market in Wuhan, where research was being conducted into coronaviruses, has also come under discussion. The *Washington Post* highlighted flaws in its security protocols in 2018. A virus of this kind cannot be combated by theorising — only with global cooperation and open exchange. Yet Beijing's latest fairytale is that the virus comes from a military laboratory in the USA. China, they claim, has defeated the virus thanks to its superior resources, and is now magnanimously helping out the rest of the world.

Even more frightening than the coronavirus itself is the fascist Chinese "virus of the mind" that has developed in the laboratory of East Turkestan and spread to all corners of the globe. Those infected do not realise that freedom, peace, and human rights are under threat all across the world. And that Beijing wants to use the much-propagandised "Chinese model" to prove the superiority of dictatorship over democracy. A virus capable of afflicting people right across the planet makes it doubly clear how supremely important it is to understand the world as a whole.

After a while, the coronavirus will gradually recede. The situation will normalise. But China's virus of the mind will never stop attacking the free world. I hope that people around the globe come to understand that the CCP and the government in Beijing threaten not just the Chinese but every citizen on Earth. This virus is far more dangerous that COVID-19.

It is hell.

Afterword

by Alexandra Cavelius

It didn't take long for our work to have an impact. Since *The Chief Witness* has been published, Sayragul Sauytbay's telephone in Sweden has barely stopped ringing. The numbers on the display are, as usual, mostly from China. Again, the callers threaten her with the most terrible thing you can say to a mother: "Think of your children …"

I worry constantly about the life of this extraordinarily brave human-rights activist, who is still fighting for peace, justice, and freedom for Uighurs, Kazakhs, and other Muslim ethnic minorities in her homeland. As I came to write my first book about fourteen years ago — *Dragon Fighter* — about the internationally famous Uighur Rebiya Kadeer, nominated several times for the Nobel Peace Prize, I received some shocking news shortly before she came to see me in Germany: she had been the victim of an assassination attempt, which she nearly did not survive. The FBI traced the attack to the Chinese embassy. Clearly, these were not empty threats.

Nevertheless, soon afterwards, in 2006, we were able to begin the interviews. Kadeer arrived still bearing the marks of her attack. She was delicate, yet incredibly combative and lively, with a neck brace and a bruised forehead. Suddenly, however, our translator began to look increasingly anxious. He tried to throw me off

track, and withheld key documents. It wasn't until the publisher
threatened him with legal action that he admitted Beijing had
put him under pressure.

This mistake — choosing the wrong translator for
the interviews — was not one I wanted to make with the
internationally famous Kazakh whistleblower Sayragul Sauytbay
in 2019. This time, I chose an interpreter based not on academic
background but because he was considered trustworthy by a
human-rights organisation.

Yet this man, too, changed after we started recording our
conversations. He translated certain things incorrectly and
deliberately suppressed key information about the camps that
Sayragul Sauytbay had dictated to him onto a notepad specifically
for me. His behaviour ultimately forced me to re-examine all of
the other information with the help of other interpreters. This
was not only stressful, but took time and money, which could
have meant the end for a small independent publisher such as
Europa Verlag.

After initially trying to sabotage our work on the book, that
translator attempted to prevent it being printed, and finally
spread malicious rumours about his fellow Kazakh online. What
made him do it, we'll never know. We do know, however, that
the CCP often punishes family members still living in China, or
prevails on them to switch sides by dangling huge sums of money
in front of them. The sad fact is that this man had stood next to
Sayragul Sauytbay only a few months earlier in Brussels, where
she had been invited by the EU in recognition of her courage and
commitment to human rights.

There were several hurdles to overcome before I could turn
our conversations into a book. I saw how strong and powerful
Sayragul Sauytbay is at press conferences, and how immediately
afterwards — away from the public eye — she struggles with

the after-effects of the camp. She is plagued by trauma-induced stress that manifests itself with various symptoms, including a racing heart as well as constant nausea, because her gut health has been ruined.

I watched as she leaned back in the taxi, exhausted, one hand clapped to her spasming heart, her eyes closed, groaning, at the mercy of those images from the past. "What are you doing to my country people at this very minute? I know. You're throwing the girls you've raped into their cells, discarding them like trash. You don't even let them cry …" I gaped in wonder as she pulled herself together so she could comfort others and work tirelessly late into the night in the fight against oppression in East Turkestan.

This woman puts her life on the line at every public appearance. Every interview she gives brings her hideous memories back to life. Yet she endures all this so that she can publicise the torture of innocent children, women, old people, and men in her homeland. So that their unspeakable suffering will one day end. And so that the world can no longer avert its gaze, feigning ignorance.

While Sayragul Sauytbay and I were on a press tour for our book in June 2020, sitting on a train from Berlin to Munich, she spent the trip researching Beijing's policies on her phone, scouring the internet. The first things she showed me on the website of the human-rights organisation Atajurt were pictures of a Buddhist house of prayer in Tibet, above which was hung a propaganda poster in Chinese script: "Without the Communist Party there is also no Tathagata Buddha." Sayragul looked up thoughtfully. "In East Turkestan the CCP preaches to people: your lives and everything you own have been given to you by the CCP. Without the CCP, there is no God."

In the next post, she tapped her finger on a photo from Brazil — another propaganda poster. "Even the Brazilians are mad about China!" She then played me a film featuring two crying

African children who had been forced by Party officials in their own country to learn Chinese and sing loudly, "We all have one family, and it's called China." There was obvious distress on their young faces, but they opened their mouths wide to sing. "And we have many brothers and sisters, and the landscape there is beautiful ..." Sayragul knew this song — "Great China" — from East Turkestan. Her Kazakh and Uighur schoolchildren had been made to sing it, too.

All of a sudden, Sayragul's eye was caught by a video from the nineteenth Party congress in Beijing, where high-ranking Party officials were giving speeches before a large audience.

"Who is the person speaking?" I asked.

"That's the education minister, Chen Baosheng."

"What is he saying?"

"He says that by 2049, the Chinese educational system will be accepted worldwide as the primary system of education."

Startled, I raised my eyebrows and probed further. "How exactly does he phrase it?"

"By that point, the global education system will be led and governed by the CCP. China will decide what kind of educational system the world has."

"What?"

"The whole world will obey the CCP and only use the materials provided to them by the Party."

I could barely stay in my seat. "Go on ..."

"The Chinese system will be introduced in every school worldwide. All students will be given Chinese materials and speak Chinese."

Here I couldn't help blurting out, "They're not even making a secret of their plans for global dominance. This speech by Chen Baosheng is another key piece of evidence to support the Three-Step Plan!"

While doing some internet research of my own, I came across a photo of Chen Baosheng visiting the Munich-based Hanns Seidel Foundation, an organisation affiliated to the Christian Social Union, a German conservative political party. A few days later, on 27 June 2020, it was reported in the German media that a well-connected Federal Intelligence Service spy who had been working in a senior role at the foundation had defected to Chinese intelligence. Part of his job was to "squeeze" (to use intelligence-agency jargon) information out of speakers during the World Uighur Congress. This spy had previously tried several times without success to invite and question me. Rumour has it in security circles that this case is typical of the way the Chinese intelligence service likes to strategise. "In addition to attacks in the virtual world, they relentlessly recruit human sources in all areas of public life," reported the television studio at ARD in Berlin. The case, they added, was serious.

When I told Sayragul Sauytbay in July 2020 that a major political organisation had cancelled a planned event with us in Berlin, vaguely postponing it until next year, for a moment she was deeply saddened. But because of the new security law introduced in Hong Kong, the organisers feared that their colleagues in China might suffer reprisals because they were publicising our book.

One week later, I read that the foreign ministry had deleted the flag of Taiwan from its website and replaced it with a blank space. The headline in the *Münchner Merkur* read: "Foreign Ministry Raises the White Flag: Flag Vanishes from Homepage — Shame on You." Not long after that, my eye was caught by a headline in the *Frankfurter Allgemeine Zeitung*: "When Criticising China, Federal Government Recommends Self-Censorship." In future, Germans were supposed to be especially careful when criticising China, the foreign ministry warned.

The new security law allowed the CCP to arrest anyone who criticised Beijing's policies — including freethinkers who lived abroad and were merely travelling in China. Having co-authored this book, *The Chief Witness*, I could expect life imprisonment, or perhaps even the death penalty. The charge in such cases is usually separatism or terrorism.

Am I afraid for my own life? I often get that question from journalists. No, I reply, but it's certainly made me think. The simple fact that this is a frequent and obvious question indicates how pernicious the CCP's influence already is in Germany. I have not been intimidated by the actions they have taken against me personally. Frequent calls from Chinese numbers during my work on the book. An automated voice telling me "goodbye", or strangers breathing quietly into my ear. When I wrote my first book, on Rebiya Kadeer, I'd been sent photographs of knives on a table, and Kalashnikovs propped against a wall, as well as quotations from the Koran wishing death on infidels like me. It was supposed to look like Muslims had sent me these messages, but a police investigation revealed that the images originated from Beijing.

In July 2020, *Die Welt* published an article on "How Beijing Is Expanding Its Power", and *Der Spiegel* followed up with "China Massively and Publicly Expands Military Presence in Africa". If you put together all these reports and all the individual pieces of the puzzle, it reveals exactly what the Party officials have in mind for the world, and how long Beijing's reach is, even in democracies such as Germany.

Yet, despite the overwhelming evidence, many politicians, journalists, and decision-makers across the globe still don't believe what they're seeing and hearing with their own eyes and ears. They turn a blind eye as the CCP implacably widens the scope of its power. For the rest of us, this means censorship, propaganda, corruption, lies, racism, torture, camps, and fascism. In footage secretly recorded for a Westdeutscher Rundfunk documentary, the Chinese head of a department for internal security in Xinjiang puts the dire situation of Muslims in the region in a nutshell: "Their human rights aren't being violated, because they have no rights." With every passing minute the world keeps silent about these atrocities, more innocent people die.

Before I become overwhelmed by a suffocating feeling of hopelessness, I often go outside and get some fresh air by the river near my home. A black swan lives in the area, and it regularly comes gliding past along the bank. In China, this extremely rare animal is believed to be an omen of something unexpected shattering carefully made plans. If old truths suddenly no longer apply, this can have a catastrophic impact on the existing system. The black swan represents the advent of a new age.

This rare natural phenomenon reflects how incalculable political consequences can sometimes be. The black swan, like Sayragul, is exceptional. Strictly speaking, she shouldn't exist. If the CCP had got its way, she would have died long ago in one of their countless concentration camps. Yet her voice is bringing to light more and more facts about the atrocities committed in East Turkestan by the Chinese government. Suddenly, there are conflicts erupting with Hong Kong, Great Britain, the USA, India ... but what if life is less amenable, less vulnerable to surveillance than the CCP thinks? What if, ultimately, its own people rise up against oppression, debt, and increasing poverty? Then Xi Jinping's plans will be derailed. The dictatorship will be at an end.

Back home, I texted Sayragul an emoji of a flexing bicep via WhatsApp. It's the symbol we use to convey courage and strength when we're facing yet another hurdle to overcome. Underneath it, I wrote, "As long as we live in freedom, we will never stop spreading the truth! We will never be disrupted! Not by anybody!"

Straightaway, Sayragul answered: 👍 👍 👍 👍 👍 👍

Photograph credits